FROM STONE TO FLESH

From Stone to Flesh

A SHORT HISTORY OF THE BUDDHA

Donald S. Lopez Jr.

The University of Chicago Press   Chicago and London

DONALD S. LOPEZ JR. is the Arthur E. Link Distin-
guished University Professor of Buddhist and Tibetan
Studies in the Department of Asian Languages and Cul-
tures at the University of Michigan. He is the author,
editor, or translator of a number of books, including
Prisoners of Shangri-La, *The Madman's Middle Way*,
Critical Terms for the Study of Buddhism, *Introduction
to the History of Indian Buddhism*, *In the Forest of Faded
Wisdom*, and *Buddhism and Science*, all published by the
University of Chicago Press.

The University of Chicago Press, Chicago 60637
The University of Chicago Press, Ltd., London
© 2013 by The University of Chicago
All rights reserved. Published 2013.
Printed in the United States of America

22 21 20 19 18 17 16 15 14 13   1 2 3 4 5

ISBN-13: 978-0-226-49320-6 (cloth)
ISBN-13: 978-0-226-49321-3 (e-book)

Library of Congress Cataloging-in-Publication Data

Lopez, Donald S., 1952–
    From stone to flesh : a short history of the Buddha /
Donald S. Lopez Jr.
        pages ; cm. — (Buddhism and modernity)
    ISBN 978-0-226-49320-6 (hardcover : alkaline
paper) — ISBN 978-0-226-49321-3 (e-book) 1. Gautama
Buddha. 2. Gautama Buddha—Christian interpre-
tations. 3. Gautama Buddha—Cult—Europe—
History. 4. Buddhism—Study and teaching—
Europe—History. I. Title. II. Series: Buddhism
and modernity.
BQ894.L67 2013
294.3′63—dc23

                                        2012030881

♾ This paper meets the requirements of
ANSI/NISO Z39.48-1992 (Permanence of Paper).

This Account of the Life of *Fo* is not in every Respect conformable to that which we have already given you of *Xaca* in the Article on *Tunquin*. But how is it possible for any one perfectly to reconcile the Contradictions of so many various Idolaters, who have fashioned their various Traditions according to their own particular Fancies, more authentic or imperfect, in Proportion to the Distance they were from their Original?

BERNARD PICART, 1733

CONTENTS

PREFACE

Everyone likes Buddhism. Its teachings are profound yet accessible. It is a religion that does not have complicated rituals to perform or dogmas to believe. In fact, it might not be a religion at all. It might be more accurate to call it a philosophy, or just a way of life. The credit for creating Buddhism goes to the Buddha, certainly the least threatening of the founders of the world religions. He never turned rivers of water into rivers of blood or caused a hail of toads; he never ordered the execution of his enemies; he never overturned the tables of moneylenders. He simply sat under trees and talked to whoever happened to be passing by. He is never depicted carrying stone tablets, or wielding a sword, or hanging on a cross. Instead, he just sits on the ground with his legs crossed, his hands folded in his lap, his eyes directed down.

But this view of the Buddha as a benign and benevolent Oriental sage, so familiar to us today, is rather recent, originating only a little more than 150 years ago. Yet Western knowledge of the Buddha reaches back to Saint Clement of Alexandria in the third century CE, who wrote, "Some of the Indians obey the precepts of Boutta; whom, on account of his extraordinary sanctity, they have raised to divine honors." Over most of this long history, Europeans, whether they were diplomats, merchants, physicians, or missionaries, did not particularly like the Buddha. Many regarded him as an idol; some thought he was the most dangerous idol of the pagan world.

This is a book about the Buddha before he was the Buddha. How was he portrayed before he became the pacific and positive figure so familiar and beloved today? And what happened a century and a half ago to make him that man? How did he turn from a stone idol into a man of flesh and blood? These are the questions that I will try to answer in the pages that follow. Although the narrative I provide will be my own, many of the words will come from figures of a forgotten past, expressed in the quaint language beloved by antiquarians.

Introduction

Long ago, there lived a man named Sumedha. Troubled by the fact that humans are subject to sickness and death, he retired to the mountains to practice meditation. He soon developed yogic powers, including the ability to fly. One day, as he was flying through the air, he looked down and saw a large crowd gathered around a teacher. Sumedha landed nearby and asked someone in the crowd who this man might be. He was informed that this was the Buddha named Dīpaṃkara. When Sumedha heard the word *Buddha*, he was overcome with joy. Then, as Dīpaṃkara approached, he noticed a mud puddle in the teacher's path. So he loosened his long, matted locks and lay facedown in the mud, spreading his hair over the puddle to protect the Buddha's feet. As he lay waiting for the Buddha to step on his hair, Sumedha reflected that he had the capacity to practice the teachings of Dīpaṃkara and be liberated from rebirth in that very lifetime. But then he thought to himself:

> But why thus in an unknown guise
> Should I the Doctrine's fruit secure?
> Omniscience first will I achieve,
> And be a Buddha in this world.
>
> Or why should I, a valorous man,
> The ocean seek to cross alone?
> Omniscience first will I achieve,
> And men and gods convey across.[1]

Dīpaṃkara stopped before Sumedha's prone form and announced that many eons hence, this austere yogin with matted locks would become a Buddha. And eventually he did: many lifetimes later, he became the Buddha that we know, the Buddha who lived in India twenty-five hundred years ago. But it took Sumedha millions of lifetimes and billions of years to become the Buddha. From the moment he vowed to become a Buddha to the moment that he did so encompassed a period of "four incalculable eons and one hundred thousand eons." According to some calculations, one incalculable eon is 10^{140} years. There were four of those. An eon is 4,320 million years. There were a hundred thousand of those.

Thus, a history of the Buddha would recount not years or centuries but eons. Accordingly, traditional biographies begin with the story of Sumedha, then proceed to the story of many of his subsequent births—sometimes as an animal, sometimes as a god, sometimes as a human. This book is more modest; it describes the Western encounter with the Buddha, beginning in antiquity a mere two thousand years ago and ending in the nineteenth century. This is a life of the Buddha that begins long after his death. This is a short history of the Buddha.

Before the nineteenth century, there was a Buddha who was revered in Asia and a Buddha who was reviled in the West. Today there is a single Buddha, beloved by both worlds. But the story is more complicated and more interesting than that. Each of the Buddhist traditions of Asia—China, Korea, Japan, Sri Lanka, Burma, Thailand, Tibet—had its own traditions about the Buddha: its own pronunciation of his name; its own way of depicting him in painting and sculpture; its own version of his story, a story that sometimes included a visit by the Buddha to its land.

It is important to realize that throughout much of the history of Buddhism, few Buddhists could read Buddhist texts; they knew the life of the Buddha through the stories that they heard from monks and the paintings and statues that they saw in temples. With very few exceptions, the European travelers who encountered the Buddha in Asia could not read Buddhist texts either; nor could they easily understand the many languages that they heard. For them, the Buddha was just another idol worshipped by pagans in foreign lands, an idol known by various garbled versions of his local name (see appendix 1 for almost three hundred European versions), his story told as various garbled versions of his local biography, with unseemly elements often added.

When Europeans came upon images of the Buddha in their journeys across Asia, they had little reason to assume that the idol they saw in Japan represented the same god, demon, or man as the idol they saw in Sri Lanka. Long into the eighteenth century, Europeans were unsure of the Buddha's race, the Buddha's place of birth, and the Buddha's gender. The German botanist Peter Simon Pallas (1741–1811), remarking on the statues of the Buddha he saw in the Kalmyk region of Russia, wrote, "It is remarkable that almost all their idols, except the *Dalai-Lama* and some other priestly-looking images, are represented as women, with the flaps of their ears long and pierced, having Indian ornaments, and their feet turned underneath themselves, or else in a sitting posture; yet I saw some standing images with many arms and faces."[2]

And so for centuries, there was a great discrepancy between the Buddha of Asia and the Buddha of Europe. They did not seem to be the same person, and in important ways they were not. In this book, I explain how and why they differed so much by exploring a wide range of European sources from such lands as Portugal, Britain, Italy, the Netherlands, and France, and a wide range of Buddhist sources from such lands as India, Sri Lanka, Thailand, China, and Tibet.

After centuries of seeing the Buddha as an idol, something remarkable occurred in the nineteenth century. European scholars began to gain the ability to read Buddhist texts in their original languages, and with a certain degree of accuracy. From this process a new Buddha was born, the Buddha that we know today. The old idol was a composite, created from shards of information and misinformation gathered by various Europeans over the centuries. The new Buddha, however, emerged fully formed from the brow of a single scholar, who never set foot in Asia. And not only did this new Buddha displace the old idol of Europe; in important ways he displaced the Buddha of Asia. The Buddha that we know was not born in India in the fifth century BCE. He was born in Paris in 1844. It is this short history that I tell here.

Histories of the European encounter with Buddhism typically begin with Saint Jerome and Clement of Alexandria, make a brief mention of Marco Polo, and then move quickly ahead to the nineteenth century. For example, in J. W. de Jong's *Brief History of Buddhist Studies in Europe and America*, published in 1974, the first chapter is entitled "The Early Period: 300 B. C.–1877." There he wrote, "A religion like Buddhism which is based upon principles which are very different from the guiding principles of Christianity cannot be understood without a thorough study of its scriptures."³

This short history of the Buddha is about the long period before a thorough study of Buddhist scriptures was possible. It is devoted to those whose knowledge was based on what they observed, to those who could not read the classical Buddhist languages of Sanskrit, Pāli, Chinese, and Tibetan. Over several centuries, knowledge of the Buddha progressed by fits and starts. Chance encounters, historical accidents, and cases of mistaken identity were shaped by ideological manipulation and sometimes sheer folly, creating an image of the Buddha that we would not recognize today.

This book ends where other histories of the European encounter with Buddhism generally begin—with what the Jesuit scholar Cardinal Henri de Lubac called the scientific discovery of Buddhism. At the end of this short history, a new Buddha will emerge, one who had not existed before, one born in Europe, different from the Buddha of Asia. He would eventually become the Buddha of the world. This Buddha was the child of perhaps the greatest nineteenth-century scientist of Buddhism, Eugène Burnouf.

This book is about the European encounter with the Buddha, not with Buddhism, which would be a different and much larger project. But it is also devoted to Buddhist views of the Buddha. It is in four parts, which follow a rough chronology. Chapter 1, "The Idol," examines the writings of the early European travelers to Asia, including Marco Polo himself, who likely learned about the Buddha in Kublai Khan's pleasure dome in Xanadu. For them, the Buddha was yet another of the myriad idols they encountered in Asia. For them, the question was, What is it? Is it divine or human, demonic or benign?

The second chapter, "The Myth," focuses especially on the intrepid Roman Catholic missionaries to Asia, including such famous figures as Matteo Ricci. Their contact with Buddhist communities was more sustained than those of other travelers, and their stakes were different. The Buddha remained an idol to them, but in order for them to convert the heathen to the true faith, these missionaries needed to learn some of the stories about these idols known by many names. For them, the central question was, Who is it?

The third chapter is entitled "The Man." By the end of the seventeenth century, it was generally assumed that these idols encountered across Asia represented a single figure, and that he had originally been a historical figure. Although missionaries continued to play their part, the main characters now were soldiers and officials, many of them British, of the newly established European colonies in Asia. For them, the central question was, Where did he come from? For many, the answer was Egypt.

Chapter 4 is entitled "The Text." By the beginning of the nineteenth century, scholars in Europe, already trained in the classical languages of Greek and Latin, began to learn the classical languages of Asia, especially Sanskrit and Chinese. It was only in this period that Europeans began to read Buddhist texts (with some degree of accuracy) in the original languages, no longer needing to rely on Buddhists, or recent converts from Buddhism, to explain things to them. For these scholars, the Buddha was a historical figure of Indian origin. With his name and place of birth now established, the task was to learn something more substantial about his identity. Here, the main characters are scholars and philologists, and their question was, Who was he?

Throughout these pages, I offer detailed accounts of various visions of the Buddha from the Buddhist cultures of Asia, traditional views of the enlightened master, in order to provide both a context for and a contrast with the European accounts, thereby allowing us to better understand not only what they got right and what they got wrong but how and why they did so.

This book is meant to end in 1844, with the publication in Paris of *Introduction à l'histoire du Buddhisme indien* (*Introduction to the History of Indian Buddhism*) by Eugène Burnouf. Burnouf is one of the leading protagonists of our tale. Whether or not he is its hero is a question left to the reader. In the brief conclusion, I describe the portrait of the Buddha in the aftermath of Burnouf. But the book essentially stops in 1844 because the place of the Buddha after that time in the Western imagination, both scholarly and popular, is familiar to us, both well known and well studied.[4] And although much progress has been made in the study of Buddhism over the last century and a half, the view of the Buddha that emerged in Europe 150 years ago has remained essentially unchanged, remaining fresh in our imagination, while the Buddha that came before is lost to a certain amnesia. It is a loss that should be lamented.

Many of the figures quoted in these pages are also long forgotten. And perhaps they should be. Why, then, write a book about people who were so often wrong when we know better now? It is easy enough to respond to such a question by noting that in the formation of knowledge, right and wrong are relative terms. Yet although such a statement is in its own way true, there remain standards of accuracy in research by which judgments can be made. By those standards, derived after more than a century of sustained research on the life of the Buddha by philologists, historians, epigraphers, and archaeologists, much of what is presented here from the period before 1844 is simply mistaken—although a number of other things are presciently correct. However, the authors of past centuries had their own standards to which they adhered with their own remarkable, and often admirable, fidelity. What emerges from reading their words centuries later is not only the ability to identify what they got right and what they got wrong, but also an understanding of what they saw and thus an intimation of how they saw it; how the single figure that we know today, almost casually, as the Buddha was so many figures for them. I seek to describe those Buddhas, and their evolution, ending in the Buddha that we know today.

From Stone to Flesh is told in part in the words of others, often through generous passages from their writings, selected to support but also shape the narrative, speaking directly to the reader. Thus, in many ways this book is a work of ventriloquism—an attempt to rescue the heavily accented voices of the distant past and to hear them somehow as our own.

CHAPTER ONE. The Idol

And I tell you they say that on this mountain is the sepulchre of Adam our first parent; at least that is what the Saracens say. But the Idolaters say that it is the sepulchre of SAGAMONI BORCAN, *before whose time there were no idols. They hold him to have been the best of men, a great saint in fact, according to their fashion, and the first in whose name idols were made.*

MARCO POLO

The transformation of the Buddha—from unknown foreign god, to dangerous idol, to venerable founder of a world religion—spans fifteen hundred years. Accounts of the European encounter with Buddhism inevitably begin with Clement of Alexandria, and so shall we. In the third century CE, Saint Clement, describing gymnosophists, or "naked philosophers," wrote, "Among the Indians are some who follow the precepts of Boutta, whom for his exceptional sanctity, they have honored as a god." Elsewhere, presumably describing a stupa, or reliquary, he mentions that the holy men of India "honor a kind of pyramid under which they believe the bones of some god are resting."[1] In 393, Saint Jerome condemned the heresies of Jovinian, a monk who came to reject asceticism. Jovinian claimed that married women and widows, once baptized, were of equal merit to virgins; he also denied the perpetual virginity of Mary. This led Jerome into a long discourse on virginity, where he wrote, "To come to the Gymnosophists of India, the opinion is authoritatively handed down that Budda, the founder of their religion, had his birth through the side of a virgin. And we need not wonder at this in the case of Barbarians when cultured Greece supposed that Minerva at her birth sprang from the head of Jove, and Father Bacchus from his thigh."[2] The ninth-century Benedictine monk Ratramnus also made mention of the supposed virgin birth of "Bubdam."

Those Christians who mentioned the Buddha during the first millennium of the Common Era likely knew his name in connection with yet another of the myriad heresies attacked by the fathers of the church. One of these heretics was Mani (Manes in Latin), the third-century Assyrian prophet regarded as the founder of Manichaeism. According to a fifth-century Manichaean text, his father was a Christian, but Mani set out to find the true Christ. He is said to have traveled to India, although that reference is probably to regions of Afghanistan, where he may have encountered Buddhist monks. He returned home to declare himself the Seal of the Prophets, in a lineage that included Noah, Abraham, Zoroaster, the Buddha, and Jesus. Mani famously set forth a strict dualist philosophy, with good and evil, light and darkness, spirit and matter locked in eternal struggle. Over the next four centuries, his teachings spread widely, into Europe in the West and China in the East. They were declared a heresy by the Christians (Augustine of Hippo had converted from Manichaeism), and his followers were persecuted in Europe and North Africa in the fourth century. Here, the Buddha seems to have been condemned through guilt by association.

Also in the fourth century, Saint Cyril of Jerusalem provided an unflattering biography of Mani, explaining that Scythianus, a Saracen (by which he likely meant a pagan from Arabia) who was neither Jew nor Christian, traveled to Alexandria and imitated the life of Aristotle. He intended to go to Judea, but God smote him with a deadly disease. Terebinthus, his disciple, spread the errors of his teacher in Judea, but was driven out. He then set out for Persia, but fearing that word of his defeat in Judea may have reached there, he changed his name to Budas. While in Persia, Terebinthus lived with a widow until God cast him from the rooftop while he was performing a ritual. The widow inherited his money, which she used to buy a slave boy named Cubricus. When she died, the slave boy changed his name to Manes.

By the fifth century, the story had been expanded to include reference to the doctrine of reincarnation. Hence, we read in the *Historia Ecclesiastica* of Socrates of Constantinople:

•

A Saracen named Scythian married a captive from the Upper Thebes. On her account he dwelt in Egypt, and having versed himself in the learning of the Egyptians, he subtly introduced the theory of Empedocles and Pythagoras among the doctrines of the Christian faith. Asserting that there were two natures, a good and an evil one, he termed, as Empedocles had done, the latter Discord, and the former Friendship. Of this Scythian, Buddas, who had been previously called Terebinthus, became a disciple; and he having proceeded to Babylon, which the Persians inhabit, made many extravagant statements respecting himself, declaring that he was born of a virgin, and brought up in the mountains. The same man afterwards composed four books . . . but pretending to perform some mystic rites, he was hurled down a precipice by a spirit, and so perished. A certain woman at whose house he had lodged buried him, and taking possession of his property, bought a boy about seven years old whose name was Cubricus: this lad she enfranchised, and having given him a liberal education, she soon after died, leaving him all that belonged to Terebinthus, including the books he had written on the principles inculcated by Scythian. Cubricus, the freedman, taking these things with him and having withdrawn into the regions of Persia, changed his name, calling himself Manes; and disseminated the books of Buddas or Terebinthus among his deluded followers as his own. Now the contents of these treatises apparently agree with Christianity in expression, but are pagan in sentiment: for Manichæus being an atheist, incited his disciples to acknowledge a plurality of gods, and taught them to worship the sun. He also introduced the doctrine of Fate, denying human free-will; and affirmed a transmutation of bodies, clearly following the opinions of Empedocles, Pythagoras, and the Egyptians.[3]

•

As we shall see, the association of the Buddha with the Pythagorean theory of reincarnation (more commonly called metempsychosis) would be a commonplace in European descriptions, extending more than a thousand years into the nineteenth century. So, too, would the apparently preposterous claim that the teachings of the Buddha—and, according to some, the Buddha himself—came from Egypt.

In 1956, archaeologists excavating a ninth-century Viking house on Helgö Island in Sweden unearthed an Indian statue of the Buddha. The statue dates from the sixth century. No one is quite sure how it found its way to the Vikings. It is doubtful that they knew who the Buddha was; only in the thirteenth century did more detailed accounts of his life, sometimes rather garbled versions, begin to appear. One of the first and most detailed of these comes from Marco Polo. Before turning to his account, it will be useful to survey briefly what the Buddhist texts themselves say about the events of the Buddha's life.

The Life of the Buddha

The Buddhist sutras—the discourses attributed to the Buddha—contain surprisingly little that might be regarded as autobiographical, despite the fact that the Buddha is said to have achieved enlightenment at the age of thirty-five and died at the age of eighty, teaching the dharma (doctrine) during the intervening decades. In what is regarded as perhaps the earliest account of the Buddha's quest for enlightenment, a Pāli text called *The Noble Search* (*Ariyapariyesanā*), the Buddha's description of his departure from home is remarkably spare: "Later, while still young, a black-haired young man endowed with the blessing of youth, in the prime of life, though my mother and father wished otherwise and wept with tearful faces, I shaved off my hair and beard, put on the yellow robe, and went forth from the home life into homelessness."[4]

What might be termed biographies of the Buddha did not begin to appear until some four centuries after his death. The earliest versions seem to have been included as chapters in the *vinaya*, the section of the canon dealing with the monastic code, eventually expanding into freestanding works. These early biographies are often more concerned with the lives of previous buddhas than with the life of Śākyamuni Buddha, the buddha of our age, and almost always include an account of how, eons ago, a yogin vowed in the presence of the former buddha Dīpaṃkara to attain buddhahood in the distant future. That bodhisattva, after perfecting himself over the course of millions of lifetimes, eventually became Śākyamuni. In the portrayal of his lifetime, there are often detailed descriptions of his "descent" from the heaven of Tuṣita, or the Joyous, into his mother's womb. However, in these early biographies the description of his life on earth rarely extends to his final days, and sometimes ends with the conversion of two particularly famous disciples—Śāriputra and Maudgalyāyana— said to have occurred in the first years after his enlightenment. A separate work, the *Great Discourse on the Final Nirvana* (*Mahāparinibbāna Sutta*), describes Śākyamuni's final days, his death, his funeral, and the distribution of his relics.

The work regarded by scholars as the oldest biography, the *Mahāvastu*, is considered to have elements dating from the second century BCE, though it did not reach its present form until the fourth century CE. Tellingly, it contains two separate stories of the future buddha's decision to leave his worldly life as a prince and go out in search of liberation from suffering and death. In the first we find, among the Buddha's descriptions of his pampered youth, "I was delicately, most delicately brought up, O monks. And while I was being thus delicately brought up, my Śākyan father provided me with the means of enjoying the five varieties of sensual pleasures, namely dance, song, music, orchestra and women, that I might divert, enjoy and amuse myself."[5] Yet the prince simply concludes one day that life in the home is too full of hindrances, while the homeless life is blameless and pure. Thus, "against the wishes of my sobbing and weeping parents, I left my sumptuous home and the universal kingship that was in my hands."[6] In the same text, however, just two chapters later, the story of the renunciation is told again, and in much greater detail, with many of the elements that would become famous in the West, such as the future buddha's four chariot rides outside the city. The most famous of the Indian biographies of the Buddha, translated into English several times, is the *Acts of the Buddha* (*Buddhacarita*) by Aśvaghoṣa, a work usually dated to the second century CE. From the time of this text, the story of the Buddha's youth and his departure from the palace remain relatively consistent throughout the tradition. What follows is the story in brief.

An extraordinary child is born to King Śuddhodana and Queen Māyā. Ten lunar months after the queen dreams that a white elephant has entered her womb, an infant emerges from her right side and takes seven steps, with a lotus flower blooming under his foot with each step. His father calls on the royal astrologers to foretell the child's destiny. All but one agree that he will become either a great monarch or a great saint. The sole dissenter declares that the prince's destiny is certain: he will become a great saint. Determined that his son not enter the religious life but instead succeed him on the throne, the king builds a palace where the prince will be protected from the troubles of the world. He is surrounded by beauty and the beautiful; no one who is sick, old, or ugly is permitted into his presence. The prince excels at all the arts and sciences, partakes of the pleasures of his harem, and eventually marries a beautiful maiden.

Finally, at the age of twenty-nine, he becomes curious about the world outside the palace walls. His father is eventually persuaded to allow him to venture out in his chariot, but only after taking the precaution of carpeting the road with flowers, stationing musicians in the trees, and removing all unsightly persons from the route. But somehow the prince notices an old man, the first such person he has ever seen. Learning from his charioteer that this is not the only old man in the world, and that old age awaits all, he becomes dejected and returns to the palace. On subsequent excursions, he sees a sick man, a dead man, and a meditating mendicant. He thus learns of old age, sickness, and death, and of those who seek to escape them.

The prince returns to the palace and asks his father to grant him permission to renounce the world. The king replies that a man should go to the ascetic grove only after having enjoyed his youth. The prince agrees to remain in the world if his father will grant him four boons: that he will never die, that he will never become sick, that he will never grow old, and that he will never lose his fortune. When his father explains that this is impossible, the prince resolves to leave. And so he escapes that night, leaving his wife and infant son behind, exchanging his royal raiment for his charioteer's clothes, cutting off his long locks, and going off alone in search of the state beyond birth and death. Six years later, sitting in meditation under a tree, he finds that state, called nirvana.

"The First in Whose Name Idols Were Made"

Perhaps the first European to tell this story was Marco Polo, the intrepid Venetian traveler who spent 1271–95 in Asia, where, among many places, he visited Shangdu, the summer capital of Kublai Khan, emperor of China and patron of Buddhism. (Shangdu is the Xanadu of Coleridge's poem, "In Xanadu did Kubla Khan / A stately pleasure dome decree.") Here is Polo's account of the prince:

.

He was the son, as their story goes, of a great and wealthy king. And he was of such an holy temper that he would never listen to any worldly talk, nor would he consent to be king. And when the father saw that his son would not be king, nor yet take any part in affairs, he took it sorely to heart. And first he tried to tempt him with great promises, offering to crown him king, and to surrender all authority into his hands. The son, however, would [have] none of his offers; so the father was in great trouble, and all the more that he had no other son but him, to whom he might bequeath the kingdom at his own death. So, after taking thought on the matter, the King caused a great palace to be built, and placed his son therein, and caused him to be waited on there by a number of maidens, the most beautiful that could anywhere be found. And he ordered them to divert themselves with the prince, night and day, and to sing and dance before him, so as to draw his heart towards worldly enjoyments. But 'twas all of no avail, for none of those maidens could ever tempt the king's son to any wantonness, and he only abode the firmer in his chastity, leading a most holy life, after their manner thereof. And I assure that he was so staid a youth that he had never gone out of the palace, and thus he had never seen a dead man, nor any one who was not hale and sound; for the father never allowed any man that was aged or infirm to come into his presence. It came to pass however one day that the young gentleman took a ride, and by the roadside he beheld a dead man. The sight dismayed him greatly, as he never had seen such a sight before. Incontinently he demanded of those who were with him what thing that was? and then they told him it was a dead man. "How, then," quoth the king's son, "do all men die?" "Yea, forsooth," said they. Whereupon the young gentleman never said a word, but rode on right pensively. And after he had ridden a good way he fell in with a very aged man who could no longer walk, and had not a tooth in his head, having lost all because of his great age. And when the king's son beheld this old man he asked what that might mean, and wherefore the man could not walk? Those who were with him replied that it was through old age the man could no longer walk, and had lost all his teeth. And so when the king's son had thus learned about the dead man and about

the aged man, he turned back to the palace and said to himself that he
would abide no longer in this evil world, but would go in search of Him
Who dieth not, and Who had created him.[7]

•

This is a relatively accurate rendering of the story of the Buddha's
renunciation of the world—what the nineteenth-century American
translator Henry Clarke Warren would call "The Great Retirement"—
when accuracy is measured by the degree of conformity to traditional Buddhist sources. Polo mentions only two of the "four sights,"
a dead man and an old man; he omits the sick man and the mendicant.
Apart from this, the only substantial irregularity is the last line, and
even there, "Him Who dieth not" is an understandable deviation by
a Christian writer; indeed, nirvana is often called the deathless state
in Buddhist works.

Marco Polo's biography of the Buddha occurs in his account of the
island of Sri Lanka or Ceylon, where his ship stopped on his return voyage to Venice, possibly in 1292. Specifically, the story is found in Polo's
description of a mountain on the island known to Europeans as Adam's
Peak. Muslim geographers identified the island of Sri Lanka as the place
where Adam and Eve lived after their expulsion from Eden (which in
Islam is located in paradise). When Adam left the garden, he set foot on
the mountain, leaving a giant footprint. The Muslim scholar and dervish
Alī al-Rūmī, a resident of Bosnia also known as Alī Dede al-Bosnawī, explains: "The first place where Adam descended was the mountain called
Rāhūn on an Indian island, in the kingdom of Serendip in the place
called Dujnā, upon which is his footprint (peace be upon him). On the
footprint is a luminosity that dazzles the eyes, which none can endure
to see. The length of his footprint in the rock is seventy spans, and on the
mountain there is a light like dazzling lightning. There is no doubt that
it rains there every day and washes his footprint."[8]

But among the Sri Lankans, the mountain is known as Sri Pada,
"Glorious Foot," and they believe the footprint is that of the Buddha,
who flew through the air from India and descended to Lanka in order
to teach the dharma. The Sinhalese count this event as his third visit
to the island.

In 1659, a young Englishman named Robert Knox (1641–1720) was
among a crew of sailors taken prisoner by Rājasiṃha II, the king of

Sri Lanka, after their ship lost its mast in a storm. Knox spent more than nineteen years living on the island, escaping eventually to a Dutch settlement there. On his long voyage home, he drafted a volume entitled *An Historical Relation of the Island Ceylon in the East-Indies; Together, With an Account of the Detaining in Captivity the Author and divers other Englishmen now Living there, and of the Author's Miraculous Escape*. Published in 1681, it was widely read, and served as one of Daniel Defoe's inspirations for *Robinson Crusoe*. In it, Knox presents a somewhat garbled description of the Buddha's footprint on the peak: "There is another great God, whom they call *Buddou*, unto whom the Salvation of Souls belongs. Him they believe once to have come upon the Earth. And when he was here, that he did usually sit under a large shady Tree, called *Bogahah*. Which trees ever since are accounted Holy, and under which with great Solemnities they do to this day celebrate the Ceremonies of his Worship. He departed from the Earth from the top of the highest Mountain on the Island, called *Pico Adam*: where there is an Impression like a foot, which, they say, is his."[9]

And so the Buddhists and the Muslims disagreed about the source of the footprint. This would not be the last time that they would clash over the nature of a place.

Marco Polo introduces his account of the life of the Buddha with this statement, from which the epigraph for this chapter is drawn:

•

Furthermore you must know that in the Island of Seilan [Ceylon] there is an exceeding high mountain; it rises right up so steep and precipitous that no one could ascend it, were it not that they have taken and fixed to it several great and massive iron chains, so disposed that by help of these men are able to mount to the top. And I tell you they say that on this mountain is the sepulchre of Adam our first parent; at least that is what the Saracens say. But the Idolaters say that it is the sepulchre of SAGAMONI BORCAN, before whose time there were no idols. They hold him to have been the best of men, a great saint in fact, according to their fashion, and the first in whose name idols were made.[10]

•

In reporting the Muslims' opinion on the footprints, Polo calls them "Saracens," a common European term for "Muslims" since the

time of the Crusades; according to a fanciful medieval Christian etymology, they were descendants of Hagar, the slave of Abraham and
Sarah, but claimed descent from Sarah—hence, Saracens. And Polo
refers to the prince not as Siddhārtha, or as the Buddha or Gautama
Buddha (or some version of the same), as he would have been known
to the Buddhists of Sri Lanka, but rather as "Sagamoni Borcan," a
name he would have learned at the court of the great khan, for this
is the Mongolian name for the Buddha. Sagamoni is Śākyamuni, the
"sage of the Śākya clan," one of the standard epithets of the Buddha,
especially in the Mahāyāna, the form of Buddhism that developed in
India some four centuries after the Buddha's death, and which would
become dominant in China, Japan, Korea, Tibet, and Mongolia. *Borcan*
is Mongolian for "Buddha." We will have occasion to return to Polo's
use of this term later. For our present purposes, the more important
matter is how he refers to Buddhists. He calls them idolaters.

It seems strange that Marco Polo would describe the Buddha as
"the first in whose name idols were made." Is he claiming that idols
of the Buddha preceded those said to have been made by Eber, great-
grandson of Noah's son Shem, or by Serug, great-grandfather of
Abraham, and that idols of the Buddha existed before the idols of the
Egyptians and before the Golden Calf? Did he know the story of King
Asa from the Bible, retold by Herman Melville in chapter 95 of *Moby
Dick*?—"Such an idol as that found in the secret groves of Queen
Maachah in Judea; and for worshipping which, King Asa, her son, did
depose her, and destroyed the idol, and burnt it for an abomination at
the brook Kedron, as darkly set forth in the 15th chapter of the First
Book of Kings."

Rather than referring to biblical history, however, Polo is likely
alluding to a story he would have heard in China. It is said that Emperor Ming of the Han dynasty, who reigned from 58 CE to 75 CE, had
a dream in which he saw a golden being flying in front of his palace, emitting rays of light from the top of its head. The next day, the
emperor asked his ministers who this spirit might be. One of them
replied that he had heard about a sage in India called Buddha, who
had attained the Way (*dao*) and could fly. The emperor dispatched a
delegation in search of this sage. Arriving finally in the Tarim basin
in Central Asia, the party acquired a copy of a work called the *Scrip-*

ture in Forty-Two Sections, and presented it to the emperor; ironically, it would be the first Buddhist text to be translated, or to be attempted to be translated, into a European language, by Joseph de Guignes in 1759.[11] A fifth-century source reports that during its journey, the delegation also acquired the famous Udāyana image of the Buddha— according to legend the first image of the Buddha ever made, one for which the Buddha himself had posed.[12] This statue is said, then, to be the prototype for all future Buddha images, hence Polo's reference to "the first in whose name idols were made."

Several centuries after Marco Polo, a French Jesuit missionary to China, Louis le Comte (1655–1728), offered a somewhat less laudatory version of the story, referring to the Buddha by his Chinese name, Fo (during the Tang dynasty, the character today pronounced as *fo* was pronounced *budh*). After describing what we would call Confucianism, he turns to Buddhism:

•

The second Sect which is prevalent in China, and is more dangerous and more universally spread than the former, adore an Idol which they call *Fo* or *Foë* as the only god of the World. This Idol was brought from the *Indies* two and thirty years after the Death of JESUS CHRIST. This Poyson began at Court, but spread its infection thro' all the Provinces, and corrupted every Town: so that this great body of Men already spoiled by Magick and Impiety, was immediately infected with Idolatry, and became a monstrous receptacle for all sorts of Errors. Fables, Superstitions, Transmigration of Souls, Idolatry and Atheism divided them, and got so strong a Mastery over them, that, even at this present, there is no so great impediment to the progress of Christianity as is this ridiculous and impious Doctrine. . . .

Thus the Devil making use of Mens Folly and Malice for their destruction, endeavours to erase out of the minds of some those excellent ideas of God which are so deeply ingraved there, and to imprint in the minds of others the Worship of false Gods under the shapes of a multitude of different Creatures, for they did not stop at the Worship of this Idol. The Ape, the Elephant, the Dragon have been worshipped in several places, under pretence perhaps that the God *Fo* had successively been transmigrated into these Creatures. *China* the most superstitious of all Nations, increased the Number of her Idols, and one may now see all sorts of them in the Temples, which serve to abuse the folly of this People.[13]

·

Here we see a pattern that will persist throughout our story. A Buddhist account—in this case, the story of how the teachings of the Buddha and his first image reached China—would be retold by a European, but with a sinister twist. Art historians speculate that the veneration of images was in fact introduced to China by Buddhism; an early Chinese term for Buddhism is *xiang jiao*, the religion of the statues. Yet in Father le Comte's account, he turns those images into idols. For centuries, Europeans would blame the Buddha for importing idolatry into China; as a result, what we call Buddhism would become for the Europeans the idolatrous religion par excellence in Asia. There were obviously myriad images, or idols, of Hindu gods in India; but Hinduism, limited largely to that country, although condemned, was not condemned in quite the same terms in the missionary literature. In the nineteenth century, only Buddhism and Christianity would be exalted as *Weltreligionen,* "world religions," because their teachings had spread around the globe. Other religions, including Hinduism and Judaism, were *Landesreligionen,* "local religions," tied to a particular land. But before Buddhism could be exalted, it was excoriated. Unlike Hinduism, Buddhism had a founder—and he could be blamed for spreading the pestilence of idolatry across Asia.

Marco Polo was not the first European to refer to the Buddha as an idol. King Het'um I of Armenia spent the years 1253 to 1255 at the court of the Mongol khan Möngke (1208–1259) at Karakorum, in an unsuccessful attempt to convert him to Christianity. In the description of his time there, we find the following:

·

There is also a country with many idolators who worship very large clay idols called Šakmonia; and they say [this is] a god three thousand and forty years old. And there are also another thirty-five *tumans* of years, one *tuman* being ten thousand, and then he will be deprived of his divinity by another god called Matrin, of whom they have made clay images of immense size, in a beautiful temple.

And the whole nation, including the women and the children are priests and are called *toyins*. They shave both the hair of the head and the beard; they wear yellow cloaks like Christians, but they wear them from the breast and not from the shoulders. And they are temperate in their food and in their marriages. They take a wife at twenty, and up to thirty approach her three times a week, and up to forty three times a month, and up to fifty, three times a year; and when they have passed fifty, they no longer go near her.

The learned king related many other things regarding the barbarous nations which we have omitted lest they might appear superfluous.[14]

•

Šakmonia is Śākyamuni and Matrin is Maitreya, the future buddha currently said to be residing in Tuṣita, the Joyous Heaven.

Thus Marco Polo, and the travelers who preceded and followed him, never identified the religion he encountered with the name Buddhism (or some rough Chinese or Mongol equivalent); according to the *Oxford English Dictionary*, the word does not appear in English until 1801. He did not describe its monks as "Buddhists." Instead, Polo referred to the monks he encountered at the court of the great khan and in his travels through Asia simply as idolaters, and the statues that they worshipped as idols, terms that would continue to name Buddhists and the Buddha across Asia for centuries to come.[15]

Before leaving Marco Polo, we might consider the remainder of his description of Sagamoni Borcan—rather less accurate, but no less interesting. After relating the prince's decision to leave the palace, he continues:

•

So what did he one night but take his departure from the palace privily, and betake himself to certain lofty and pathless mountains. And there he did abide, leading a life of great hardship and sanctity, and keeping great abstinence, just as if he had been a Christian. Indeed, and he had but been so, he would have been a great saint of Our Lord Jesus Christ, so good and pure was the life he led. And when he died they found his body and brought it to his father. And when the father saw dead before him that son whom he loved better than himself, he was near going distraught with sorrow. And he caused an image in the similitude of his son to be wrought in gold and precious stones, and caused all his people to adore it. And they all declared him to be a god; and so they still say.

They tell moreover that he hath died fourscore and four times. The first time he died as a man, and came to life again as an ox; and then he died as an ox and came to life again as a horse, and so on until he had died fourscore and four times; and every time he became some kind of animal. But when he died the eighty-fourth time they say he became a god. And they do hold him for the greatest of all their gods. And they tell that the aforesaid image of him was the first idol that the Idolaters ever had; and from that have originated all the other idols. And this befel in the Island of Seilan in India.[16]

•

The Buddha's father died long before he did, and so there is no Buddhist account of the father ordering that images be made of his dead son. But we do find here a rather garbled reference to the Buddha's previous lives as a bodhisattva. According to the tradition, he lived millions of such lives, not the eighty-four mentioned by Marco Polo, but some of those lives were spent as an animal. Among the famous *jātaka*, or "birth" stories are those that tell of the bodhisattva when he was reborn as a fish or a rabbit or a deer or a monkey.

Also worthy of note is Polo's generally positive assessment of Sagamoni Borcan and his life; there is none of the condemnation that would become so common in later centuries. Indeed, Polo suggests that had it not been for the historical accident that prevented him from hearing the Gospel, the Buddha would have become a Christian saint. In fact, he almost did.

Saint Bodhisattva

In 1446, an unnamed editor of Marco Polo's account added a comment to Polo's description of the Buddha's encounters with death and old age: "This is like the life of Saint Iosafat who was son of the king Avenir of those parts of Indie, and was converted to the Christian faith by the means of Barlam, according as is read in the life and legend of the holy fathers."[17] The editor's observation was correct, though it would

be more accurate to say not that the life of the Buddha is like the life
of Saint Josaphat, but that the life of Saint Josaphat is like the life of
the Buddha.

The statement made earlier that little was heard of the Buddha in
Europe between Clement of Alexandria and Marco Polo is not entirely
accurate. The story of the Buddha became a persistent presence in
Europe throughout the Middle Ages and the Renaissance, although
it was not identified as such. It would become one of the most popular stories in Christendom, with versions in Greek, Latin, Georgian,
French, Italian, Spanish, Portuguese, German, Polish, Romanian,
Yiddish, Norwegian, Icelandic, Swedish, Hebrew, and Tagalog. But
the protagonist was not called Prince Siddhārtha, the bodhisattva; he
was called Prince Josaphat.

Just as Marco Polo reported two contending views concerning the
footprints of Adam's Peak—with the Muslims seeing it as the sign of
"our first parent," Adam, and the idolaters seeing it as the sign of Sagamoni Borcan—so the story of Barlaam and Josaphat pits Christian
against idolater.[18] It tells of Barlaam, a Christian monk from Senaar
(that is, Serandip or Ceylon), and Josaphat, an Indian prince. In the
story, the Indian king Abenes (Avenir), an idolater and a persecutor
of Christians, possesses everything except a son. Finally, that son is
born:

•

Nowhere in that land, they said, had there ever been seen so charm-
ing and lovely a babe. Full of the keenest joy at the birth of the child,
the king called him Ioasaph [that is, Josaphat], and in his folly went in
person to the temples of his idols, for to do sacrifice and offer hymns
of praise to his still more foolish gods, unaware of the real giver of all
good things, to whom he should have offered the spiritual sacrifice. He
then, ascribing the cause of his son's birth to things lifeless and dumb,
sent out into all quarters to gather the people together to celebrate his
son's birth-day: and thou mightest have seen all the folk running together for fear of the king, and bringing their offerings ready for the
sacrifice, according to the store at each man's hand, and his favour toward his lord.[19]

•

The astrologers are summoned. They predict greatness for the child. But one dissents, saying that the prince will not attain the glory of the world but will be a great guide on the road to truth. Fearing that his son will become a Christian, the king has a city built in a remote place, where his son is protected from all that might be dispiriting; the words *death*, *disease*, and *eternity* are not to be uttered in his presence. The prince eventually asks his father's permission to take a ride outside the city. The king agrees, but only after stationing musicians in the trees and instructing the prince's escort to steer him away from anything unpleasant. But on the first of his excursions, he encounters a blind man carrying a lame man. On the second, he encounters a sick man, and is informed that sickness ends in death, from which there is no escape. Learning that life is transitory, he returns, dejected, to the city:

·

When our wise and sagacious young prince saw and heard all this, he sighed from the bottom of his heart. "Bitter is this life," cried he, "and fulfilled of all pain and anguish, if this be so. And how can a body be careless in the expectation of an unknown death, whose approach (ye say) is as uncertain as it is inexorable?" So he went away, restlessly turning over all these things in his mind, pondering without end, and ever calling up remembrances of death. Wherefore trouble and despondency were his companions, and his grief knew no ease; for he said to himself, "And is it true that death shall one day overtake me? And who is he that shall make mention of me after death, when time delivereth all things to forgetfulness? When dead, shall I dissolve into nothingness? Or is there life beyond, and another world?" Ever fretting over these and the like considerations, he waxed pale and wasted away, but in the presence of his father, whenever he chanced to come to him, he made as though he were cheerful and without trouble, unwilling that his cares should come to his father's knowledge. But he longed with an unrestrainable yearning, to meet with the man that might accomplish his heart's desire, and fill his ears with the sound of good tidings.[20]

·

Josaphat eventually meets the monk Barlaam, who has come to India from the land of Senaar. Barlaam instructs him with many

parables (some of which would become famous in European literature, such as the "Parable of Three Caskets," which appears in Shake-
speare's *The Merchant of Venice*), converting him to the true faith, and
then departs. Josaphat eventually converts his father, who destroys
all the idols in his kingdom, consigning them to fire. Upon his father's
death, Josaphat converts the entire kingdom and then abdicates,
becoming an anchorite and setting off into the desert in search of
Barlaam, finding Barlaam shortly before his old teacher dies. After
Josaphat's own death, the uncorrupted bodies of teacher and student
are transported back to India, where they are enshrined in Josaphat's
city, among many miracles.

The parallels to the life of the Buddha are clear. They were even
clear, at least to one traveler, in the sixteenth century. The Portuguese
historian Diogo de Couto (1542–1616) read the account of Marco Polo
and noted its similarities to the story of Barlaam and Josaphat, going
so far as to conclude that the Buddha (whom he calls Budão) was in
fact Prince Josaphat, and that the Gentiles (the Indians) had forgotten the origins of the Buddha's story and then embellished it over the
centuries. De Couto had traveled to India, and reports that during his
visit to the famous Buddhist cave-temple complex of Kanheri (outside modern Mumbai), an old man informed him that it was the palace that King Avenir had built to shield his son from knowledge of the
sufferings of the world.[21]

Any lingering doubts about the connection between Josaphat and
the Buddha are dispelled by the name: Josaphat is Ioasaph in Greek,
Iodasaph in Georgian, Būdāsf in Arabic, Bodhisattva in Sanskrit. A
Middle Persian version of the story seems to have been retold in Arabic in the eighth century, with the title *Kitāb Bilawhar wa Būdāsf*, the
Book of Bilawhar and Būdāsf.[22] In the Arabic story, both the idolater
king and his ascetic son are devotees of "al-Budd," and debate about
which of them practices his true teaching. Scholars speculate that the
Arabic story was turned into a Christian tale by Georgian Christians
in Jerusalem sometime between 800 CE and 900 CE, who called it the
Life of the Blessed Iodasaph. In the late tenth or early eleventh century,
the story was translated into Greek by a Georgian monk, Euthymius
of Athos, who also added many passages from scripture. Then in 1048
the Greek version was translated into Latin. From that point, the
story of Barlaam and Josaphat would become one of the most popular

saints' tales in Christendom, with translations into many European languages, including Icelandic by Prince Hakon in the thirteenth century.

Although never officially canonized, Barlaam and Josaphat were considered saints; their names were included in the *Martyrologium* authorized by Pope Sixtus V, and assigned November 27 in the calendar of saints. In the Eastern Orthodox Church, August 26 was assigned to "the holy Josaph, son of Abener, king of India." The bodhisattva had become a saint.

Yet despite the influence of the Buddhist story on the Christian, much is also different. In the story of Barlaam and Josaphat, the king is not a virtuous man but a tyrant, a worshipper of idols and a persecutor of Christians. Barlaam is a Christian monk who converts the idolatrous prince to the faith in the Living God. Consequently, the work is filled with condemnations of idolaters and declarations of their folly:

•

Thus senseless, then, are also they that trust in idols: for these be their handiwork, and they worship that which their fingers made, saying, "These be our creators." How then deem they their creators those which have been formed and fashioned by themselves? Nay more, they safeguard their gods, lest they be stolen by thieves, and yet they call them guardians of their safety. And yet what folly not to know that they, which be unable to guard and aid themselves, can in no wise guard and save others! "For" saith he, "why on behalf of the living, should they seek unto the dead?" They expend wealth, for to raise statues and images to devils, and vainly boast that these give them good gifts, and crave to receive of their hands things which those idols never possessed, nor shall ever possess.[23]

•

The passage condemns idolatry for its absurdity—that men create idols and then worship them as their creators, that they go to great lengths to protect the idols they have made and then worship them as their protectors, that they expend great wealth to make the idols and then pray to them for wealth. In fact, the idols are dead matter that, when placed in one location, cannot move to another, and are incapable of response. These idols are not gods who were known in the past, who had a covenant with their fathers, but instead are newly concocted.

And we should note that this criticism of idol worship, ascribed to John of Damascus in the eighth century, would be directed specifically at Buddhists centuries later. We find Sir Thomas Herbert (1606–1682), in the 1677 edition of his famous travels, describing an idol in Japan:

•

At *Dabys* such another Coloss of concave Copper was raised: an Idol 24 foot high, notwithstanding his posture was such as his buttocks rested upon his legs after the usual mode of the Orient: But in such remembrances how can I proceed without an exclamation? *Sedulius* furnishes me with one very proper for the occasion.

> *Heu miseri! Qui vana colunt, qui corde sinistro*
> *Religiosa sibi sculpunt Simulacra, suumque*
> *Factorem fugiunt, & quae fecere verentur.*
> *Quis furor est, quae tanta animos dementia ludit?*
> *Ut Volucrem turpemque Bovem, torvumque Draconem,*
> *Semi-hominemque Canem supplex Homo pronus adoret.*

> Poor Wretched Souls! which doat on Vanities,
>   and hallowing dumb Idols in your Heart,
> Fear not your great Creator to despise, by adoring
>   Works of your own hand and Art?
> What fury or what frenzy thus beguiles your minds,
>   foul ugly shapes so to adore,
> With Birds and nasty Bulls and Dragons vile, half dog,
>   half man, prostrate their help t' implore?[24]

•

In 1590, the Jesuits brought a movable-type printing press to Japan. The earliest surviving book from their printing efforts is *Sanctos no Gosagveono Vchinvqigaqi* (*Compendium of the Acts of the Saints*), published in 1591. It contains a full translation into Japanese (written in Roman characters) of *Barlaam and Josaphat*. Based on the life of the Buddha, this story, the story of the conversion of idolaters to Christianity, had been brought to this Buddhist land to convert its idolaters to Christianity.[25]

After Diogo de Couto in the sixteenth century, the parallels between *Barlaam and Josaphat* and the life of the Buddha would go largely unnoticed for three hundred years. In 1853, the great Jewish Sanskrit scholar Theodor Benfey (1809-1881) noted that a parable in *Barlaam and Josaphat* was also found in the *Pancatantra*, a famous collection of Indian fables. The French savant Édouard Laboulaye (1811-1883), best remembered for his books on American politics and law, was the first to draw a direct parallel between the life of Josaphat and the life of the Buddha. He did so in an article in the July 26, 1859, issue of the weekly newspaper *Journal des débats politiques et littéraires*. In 1860, Felix Liebrecht (1812-1890), a German folklorist and translator of the Barlaam and Josaphat story, published an article linking it to a specific Buddhist text, the famously baroque life of the Buddha called the *Lalitavistara*. Liebrecht was in fact mistaken in his association, likely made because the *Lalitavistara* was the first biography of the Buddha to have been translated into a European language at that time; Philippe Édouard Foucaux (1811-1894), a French scholar of Sanskrit and Tibetan and student of the great Burnouf, had translated the text from the Tibetan in 1847. It is almost as if the identity of the Buddha and Prince Josaphat could not be recognized in Europe until the Buddha himself had been elevated, at least in the eyes of some, to the status of a saint. For all but the last two centuries of his long history of contact with Europe and Europeans, the Buddha was not a blessed saint—he was a cursed idol. In order to understand the implications of this appellation, let us briefly consider the history of the term.

Against Idolatry

The condemnation of idols and idolatry has, of course, a long history in Christianity, going back to the Hebrew Bible and the commandments that Moses received from God on Mount Sinai. As set forth in Exodus 20:2-6, those commandments begin:

•

I am the Lord your God, who brought you out of the land of Egypt, out of the house of bondage. You shall have no other gods before me. You shall not make for yourself a graven image, or any likeness of anything that is in heaven above, or that is in the earth beneath, or that is in the water under the earth. You shall not bow down to them or serve them; for I the Lord your God am a jealous God, visiting the iniquity of the fathers upon the children, to the third and the fourth generation of those who hate me, but showing steadfast love to thousands of those who love me and keep my commandments.[26]

•

The passage declares the power that God has shown in delivering the Israelites from slavery in Egypt, and says that God demands two things: first, that the Israelites worship no other gods, and second, that they make no idols representing creatures of the earth, skies, or waters and then worship them. God promises to punish those who reject him and worship others, and to reward those who keep his commandments. In the biblical narrative, these commandments are timely, for after forty days and forty nights on Mount Sinai, Moses descends, carrying the tablets on which the commandments are engraved, only to find the children of Israel worshipping the Golden Calf. They are thus betraying the God who has delivered them from Egypt, and they are worshipping a creature of the earth. And they are punished. Moses smashes the tablets in anger (later returning to the mountain for another set, which would be preserved in the Ark of the Covenant). He burns the Golden Calf, mixes the ashes in water, and makes the Israelites drink it. He then orders the sons of Levi to kill those who had worshipped the idol, leaving three thousand dead. God, as king, father, judge, and deliverer, has been betrayed, and the guilty must be punished.[27]

The passage in Exodus commands that no other gods be worshipped, gods who are worshipped by others, such as Ba'al. It also commands that no idols be made. Although the passage seems to prohibit the making of idols representing various humans and animals—the visible creatures of God—it is clear in Deuteronomy 4:15–19 that the prohibition extends to representations of God:

•

Therefore take good heed to yourselves. Since you saw no form on the day that the Lord spoke to you at Horeb out of the midst of the fire, beware lest you act corruptly by making a graven image for yourselves, in the form of any figure, the likeness of male or female, the likeness of any beast that is on the earth, the likeness of any winged bird that flies in the air, the likeness of anything that creeps on the ground, the likeness of any fish that is in the water under the earth. And beware lest you lift up your eyes to heaven, and when you see the sun and the moon and the stars, all the host of heaven, you be drawn away and worship them and serve them, things which the Lord your God has allotted to all the peoples under the whole heaven.

•

Perhaps the most sustained and influential argument against idolatry in the Bible appears not in Exodus but in the book of the Wisdom of Solomon (also known as the book of Wisdom), part of the Septuagint, the Greek translation of the Hebrew Bible, and included in the Christian Old Testament but not in the Hebrew Bible. It was written in Greek, so scholars speculate that it was composed by an Alexandrian Jew some time between 200 BCE and 100 CE. Its polemic is clearly directed against the idolatry of the Egyptians, but it would be employed to condemn idols everywhere, from Asia to the New World.[28] The fourteenth chapter of the Wisdom of Solomon, verses 15–21, provides an etiology of idolatry, explaining that it all began when a father made an image of his dead child:

•

For a father, consumed with grief at an untimely bereavement, made an image of his child, who had been suddenly taken from him; and he now honored as a god what was once a dead human being, and handed on to his dependents secret rites and initiations. Then the ungodly custom, grown strong with time, was kept as a law, and at the command of monarchs graven images were worshiped. When men could not honor monarchs in their presence, since they lived at a distance, they imagined their appearance far away, and made a visible image of the king whom they honored, so that by their zeal they might flatter the absent one as though present. Then the ambition of the craftsman impelled even those who did not know the king to intensify their worship. For he, perhaps wishing to please his ruler, skillfully forced the likeness to take more beautiful form, and the multitude, attracted by the charm of his work, now regarded as an object of worship the one whom shortly before they had honored as a man. And this became a hidden trap for mankind, because men, in bondage to misfortune or to royal authority, bestowed on objects of stone or wood the name that ought not to be shared.

•

The text goes on to explain that from this innocent source idolatry spread, serving as the cause of all manner of sin, including murder, theft, fornication, deceit, corruption, and debauchery, and calling forth punishment from God.

This prohibition of idols, whether of false gods or true, would be variously interpreted by the Abrahamic religions—more strictly by Jews and Muslims, less so by Christians. The condemnation of idol worship in *Barlaam and Josaphat* occurs in a Christian text, yet images of Jesus, the Virgin Mary, and the saints abound in Christianity. This apparent violation of the second commandment has a long history of contestation, descending at times into violence and destruction. We read in the book of Revelation (21:7-8): "He who conquers shall have this heritage, and I will be his God and he shall be my son. But as for the cowardly, the faithless, the polluted, as for murderers, fornicators, sorcerers, idolaters, and all liars, their lot shall be in the lake that burns with fire and sulfur, which is the second death."

Among incidents of idol destruction by Christians, one of the most famous occurred in 726, when the emperor of Byzantium, Leo III, ordered the destruction of Christ Chalkites, an image that stood above the Golden Gate of the imperial palace in Constantinople. Since the image was considered the protector of the city, its destruction led to a riot; the officer who removed it was killed. In the empty space that was left, Leo placed a cross, beneath which these words were written: "The Lord does not allow a portrait of Christ to be drawn without voice, deprived of breath, made of earthly matter, which is despised by Scripture. Therefore, Leo, with his son the new Constantine, engraved on the gates of the kings the blessed prototype of the cross, the glory of the faithful."[29] This was the opening salvo in what would come to be known as the Iconoclast Controversy. Leo would go on to remove other images (statues, painting, and mosaics) from the churches of his empire, replacing them in some cases with scenes from Constantinople's hippodrome.

The arguments of the iconoclasts, literally, "breakers of images," are preserved largely in the generally derisive writings of their opponents. Setting aside for the moment the political factors at play in the controversy, it appears that the theological position of the iconoclasts (perhaps under some Muslim influence) represented a return to the second commandment, especially as it pertained to depictions of Christ. As the Incarnation of the Word, Christ has two natures, divine and human, which cannot be separated. It is impossible, and therefore blasphemous, to separate out his human nature and then attempt to represent it with lifeless matter. To do so represents the living Christ as dead matter and directs the eye of the viewer only to that which is visible and human, neglecting that which is invisible and divine. In order for an image to be a true image, it must be of the same substance as that which it represents. However, nothing made by human hands can be of the same substance as the divine. The only way that Christ can be represented without succumbing to idolatry is in his own divine substance, which after his resurrection exists only in one material form: the bread and wine that are transubstantiated into the body and blood of Christ through the miracle of the Eucharist. Thus, all images are idols, and those who worship images are idolaters, worshippers of wood and stone.

The defense of the worship of icons was robust, bringing a range of perspectives into the battle. Long before the Iconoclast Controversy, Pope Gregory the Great had defended the use of images as a means of converting pagans to the worship of God by representing the life of Jesus and the saints. He made a commonsensical distinction between the representation and what is represented: "It is one thing to worship a painting, and quite another to learn from a scene represented in a painting what ought to be worshipped. For what writing provides for people who read, paintings provide for the illiterate [*idiotis*] who look at them, since these unlearned people see what they must imitate; paintings are books for those who do not know letters, so that they take the place of books, especially among pagans."[30]

Other arguments in favor of images were more nuanced. The

eighty-second canon of the Quinisext Council, held in Constantinople in 691–92, states:

•

In some depictions of the venerable icons, the Forerunner [John the Baptist] is portrayed pointing with his finger to a lamb, and this has been accepted as a figure of grace, prefiguring for us through the Law the true lamb, Christ our God. Therefore, while these ancient figures and shadows have been handed down as symbols and outlines of the truth passed on by the church, we prefer grace and truth, which have been received as fulfillment of the law. Therefore, so that what is perfect may be depicted, even in paintings, in the eyes of all, we decree that the Lamb of God who takes away the sins of the world, Christ our God, should from now on be portrayed as a man, instead of the ancient lamb, even in icons; for in this way the depth of the humility of the Word of God can be understood, and one might be led to the memory of his life in the flesh, his passion and his saving death, and of the redemption which thereby came to the world.[31]

•

In this remarkable passage, the very doctrine that the iconoclasts had cited against images of Christ is used to defend them: the Incarnation of the Word as flesh in the person of Jesus. The Old Testament prohibition appears to be superseded by the New Testament Gospel, at least in the case of Jesus. The prefiguration of the Incarnation in symbols such as the lamb is no longer necessary when the reality that the lamb symbolizes has already appeared perfectly in the world. The depth of the humiliation of the Word of God has been fulfilled on earth in the person of Jesus. God has become incarnate, and therefore the Incarnation can and should be depicted; the commandment against images of God delivered by Moses to the children of Israel was rescinded when God became flesh. The iconoclasts, however, argued that to make an image of Christ was to limit his divinity. Their opponents responded that God had already circumscribed his divinity and humiliated the Word through becoming incarnate in Christ, making the divine visible to the human eye.

This was essentially the argument made by John of Damascus (circa 676–749), the first to openly counter the iconoclasts of Constantinople, writing from Damascus and, according to his traditional biography, serving the Muslim caliph there. In three works entitled *Apologetic Treatises against Those Decrying Holy Images*, he writes, "When the invisible becomes visible in the flesh, you may depict the likeness of the one seen. When the one who is bodiless and formless, immeasurable and boundless in his own nature, existing in the form of God, takes the form of a servant in substance and in stature and is found in a body of flesh, then you may draw his image and show it to anyone wishing the visual contemplation of it."[32] Indeed, since the fourth century, a tradition held that Jesus had sat for a portrait, the so-called Image of Edessa.

It was in the collected works of John of Damascus that the Greek version of *Barlaam and Josaphat* would be placed, a work attributed to John but actually composed in the tenth century. As we have seen, the story condemns the practice of idolatry; it should not be imagined that theological arguments in favor of the production and veneration of images of Jesus would somehow be extended to false gods.

In other words, the arguments against the iconoclasts and for images of Jesus were not intended as a sanction for the worship of images in general. Any confusion on this point could be solved semantically. As early as the third century, Origen, in his *Homily on Exodus*, distinguished between the icon and the idol. The icon is a truthful representation of what exists; an idol is a false representation of what does not exist.[33] In the Septuagint, more than thirty Hebrew words are rendered by the single Greek work *eidōlon*, or "idol," including *lie, vanity, excrement,* and *abomination,* as well as *statue, image of a living being,* and *cast metal.* The connotation is always negative, and the statues and images are always of false gods, mistakenly worshipped by others.[34]

The opponents of the iconoclasts eventually carried the day, and the icons were restored to the basilica of Hagia Sophia; the mosaic in the apse was unveiled on Easter Sunday 867. On the face of the apse conch, an inscription was added, which read: "These icons the deceivers once cast down the pious emperors have again restored." Since then, this inscription has been effaced, with only the first three and the last nine Greek letters remaining visible. Some six centuries later, the church would fall into the hands of a different group of iconoclasts, and the images of Jesus and of the Blessed Virgin would again be effaced. These iconoclasts would also venture further east, and their iconoclasm would extend to images of the Buddha.

The Roman Catholic position on idolatry was eventually clarified in the thirteenth century by Saint Thomas Aquinas, with his characteristic rigor, in his *Summa Theologica*. He defined idolatry as a form of superstition in which divine worship is paid to something that is not divine, to a creature, when worship should be directed only to the uncreated God. Idolatry is a sin, in some sense the gravest of sins. Thomas explains that worship is paid to idols in a variety of ways. Thus, "Some, by means of a nefarious art, constructed images which produced certain effects by the power of the demons: wherefore they deemed that the images themselves contained something God-like, and consequently that divine worship was due to them."[35] Others worshipped the creature represented by the image, whether a human, beast, or bird, rather than the Creator. Such idolatry originated in one of two ways: through the ignorance of man, as described in the Wisdom of Solomon, or through the deeds of demons, who spoke through idols and won the worship of men.

The Christian is not to offer worship to images of angels and saints, which are simply symbols meant to confirm faith. However, worship may be offered to an image of Christ: "Thus therefore we must say that no reverence is shown to Christ's image, as a thing—for instance, carved or painted wood: because reverence is not due save to a rational creature. It follows therefore that reverence should be shown to it, in so far only as it is an image. Consequently the same reverence should be shown to Christ's image as to Christ Himself. Since, therefore, Christ is adored with the adoration of *latria*, it follows that His image should be adored with the adoration of *latria*."[36]

Latria means "adoration," and for Thomas it is a technical term, referring to a form of reverence to be offered only to the Holy Trinity; even the Virgin Mary is excluded. The important point of the passage, however, is that for Thomas the same adoration one would express to Christ himself may be paid to an image of Christ insofar as it represents him.

The other great explosion of iconoclasm in the history of Christianity occurred during the Protestant Reformation, when, at various moments across western Europe in the sixteenth and seventeenth centuries, Roman Catholic priests were condemned as idol worshippers and images were forcibly removed from churches, sometimes being destroyed in the process. Even the Host of the Eucharist was declared an idol, with Protestant reformers asking whether a communion wafer that has been vomited or excreted should be worshipped as the body of Christ. Of the absurdity of Jesus Christ transubstantiated as the Host, we read, "He lets himself be eaten by rats, spiders, and vermin."[37] Again, the second commandment was invoked. Ludwig Haetzer (1500–1529) cited scripture in support of the view that not only does God forbid the making of images, but that images should be destroyed, and those who destroy them should be glorified.[38] Andreas Bodenstein von Karlstadt (1486–1541) countered the claim that the Incarnation of God in the person of Jesus Christ superseded the Old Testament prohibition by arguing that Christ is the fulfillment of the Law, and that if the second commandment is no longer binding after the coming of Christ, then the other commandments should also be rescinded.[39] The "third man of the Reformation" (after Martin Luther and John Calvin), Ulrich Zwingli (1484–1531), argued that trust in anything other than God is a false religion. Because God is spiritual, he cannot be depicted in material form. Thus, an idol is only an external representation of whatever "strange god" (*der abgott*) that men worship in their hearts.[40] The great Swiss preacher and friend of Calvin, Pierre Viret (1511–1571), described Roman Catholic idolatry as "adultery and fornication between the soul and foreign gods."[41]

But whether Catholic or Protestant, Christians agreed that the Buddha was a foreign god, and that Buddhists were idolaters.

The Animated Idol

Anyone who has visited the Asian art section of any museum in the world will realize that across Asia over many centuries, Buddhists have produced tens of thousands of images of the Buddha, in wood, in metals, and in stone, as well as painted on scrolls and murals. Given the vast number of these representations, we would expect images of the Buddha to figure prominently in Buddhist literature. We would also expect that the relation between the image and the Buddha it represents has been explored by Buddhist exegetes, although perhaps without the political consequences that characterize so much of Christian discourse over icons. Those expectations are correct.

As noted above, around 600 Pope Gregory the Great had written that images of Jesus and the saints should not be destroyed, because they were edifying to the illiterate. Marco Polo's description of the Buddha, or Sagamoni Borcan, as he calls him, was occasioned by a set of footprints on a mountaintop in Sri Lanka, signs of the past presence of a great saint—although what, or who, these images represented was subject to dispute. Of such footprints, which abound in the Buddhist world, the Buddha is reported to have said, "In the future, intelligent beings will see the scriptures and understand. Those of less intelligence will wonder whether the Buddha appeared in the world. In order to remove their doubts, I have set my footprints in stone."[42]

Jesus himself encountered idols, at least according to the Apocryphal Gospels. In the Gospel of Pseudo-Matthew, likely composed in the early seventh century, we find an account that does not appear in the synoptic Gospels, an account of something that happened during the Flight into Egypt, when Mary and Joseph fled from Nazareth with their infant son to escape Herod's slaughter of the innocents. We read in chapters 22 and 23 of that gospel:

•

And rejoicing and exulting, they came into the regions of Hermopolis, and entered into a certain city of Egypt which is called Sotinen; and because they knew no one there from whom they could ask hospitality, they went into a temple which was called the Capitol of Egypt. And in this temple there had been set up three hundred and fifty-five idols, to each of which on its own day divine honors and sacred rites were paid. . . .

And it came to pass, when the most blessed Mary went into the temple with the little child, that all the idols prostrated themselves on the ground, so that all of them were lying on their faces shattered and broken to pieces; and thus they plainly showed that they were nothing. Then was fulfilled that which was said by the prophet Isaiah: Behold, the Lord will come upon a swift cloud, and will enter Egypt, and all the handiwork of the Egyptians shall be moved at His presence.

•

A similar scene is found in the story of the Buddha, with somewhat less destructive results. King Śuddhodana, father of the bodhisattva, the Buddha-to-be, also took his son to the temple. As described in the *Lalistavara*, an elaborate biography of the Buddha probably dating from the third or fourth century CE, "With great royal ceremony and proud display, King Śuddhodana led the prince into the temple of the gods. As soon as the Bodhisattva set his right foot in the temple, the statues of the gods, including Śiva, Skanda, Nārāyaṇa, Kubera, Candra, Surya, Vaiśravaṇa, Śakra, Brahmā, the Guardians of the World, and others, rose from their places and bowed at the feet of the Bodhisattva."[43]

The two stories bear comparison. In the Christian story, it is unclear whether the idols fall at the feet of the infant Savior through their own volition, that is, animated by the gods they represent, or whether they are dead matter, moved by the power of the Christ child to topple from their pedestals and shatter on the ground. Regardless, the idols are destroyed in the process. The Buddhist story is not so much about the Buddhist attitude toward idols as it is about the Buddhist attitude toward the other gods of the day: the Hindu gods, gods who exist and who are represented in matter, in statues of stone, wood, and metal.

This is one of many passages in Buddhist literature in which the gods express their reverence, and their deference, to this man. According to Buddhist cosmology, these gods are not eternal deities but rather sentient beings still bound in the cycle of rebirth, who as a result of their past virtues have been reborn as gods, stations that they will inhabit for many millions of years, but not for eternity. They possess powers beyond those of humans and are able to bestow boons to those who make offerings to them. But they are not omnipotent, and they are not immortal. Eventually, their life in heaven will come to an end, and they will be reborn in a lower realm. The Buddha, however, would eventually find a state beyond birth and death and would teach the path to it. The gods in the temple know that this is the destiny of the child brought before them, and thus the stone statues rise from their altars and bow before the infant. One of the epithets of the Buddha is *devātideva*, the "god beyond the gods."

This, then, would suggest the Buddhist attitude toward statues of gods. They represent deities who have important but limited powers and who can be approached for specific needs. Yet because they remain in the cycle of birth and death, they are not to be considered reliable places of refuge from the sufferings of the world. The only true source of refuge is the Buddha, his teaching (the dharma), and the community of his enlightened followers (the sangha).

But Buddhists made images of the Buddha; as noted earlier, when Buddhism reached China in the first century of the Common Era, it was initially known as *xiang jiao*, the religion of the statues. Exactly when Buddhists began to make statues of the founder is a question that has vexed art historians since the nineteenth century. Moreover, Buddhism may have had its own controversy over whether making images of the Buddha was appropriate. In other words, Buddhism may also have prohibited idol worship.

Asian art historians have noted that although the Buddha had died in the fifth or fourth century BCE, no images of him appear in the archaeological record before the first century BCE, some three hundred years after he passed into nirvana. The earliest extant image of the Buddha is found on the Bimaran Casket, now in the British Museum, a small gold reliquary discovered in eastern Afghanistan in the 1830s; it is tentatively dated to the period between 30 BCE and 10 BCE. In the preceding centuries, Buddhist monuments seem to have represented the presence of the Buddha by his absence: there are footprints, an empty throne, a riderless horse. Elsewhere, the Buddha seems to be represented by symbols: a lotus for his birth, a tree for his enlightenment, a wheel for his teaching (traditionally called his "turning the wheel of the dharma"), a stupa (reliquary) for his death. It is not that these carvings lack figural images; humans and gods abound. It is the Buddha himself who is absent. Art historians have observed this absence and inferred that the Buddha, or his immediate followers, had forbidden the making or worship of his image. And they have speculated that the practice of representing the Buddha in human form—which, depending on one's perspective, might be termed the making of images or the making of idols—had, in fact, been introduced from abroad—from the West, specifically by Greeks in the region of Gandhara (in what is now Pakistan and Afghanistan).

This view that the Buddha prohibited the worship of his form is consistent with the late nineteenth- and early twentieth-century view of the Buddha as a rationalist who never would have condoned idol worship; the practice could have entered his tradition only from abroad as a concession to the masses in the centuries after his passage into nirvana. We might note as well that a century after this aniconism theory was proposed, no proscriptions against making images of the Buddha have been located in what scholars would regard as an early Buddhist text, nor have any prescriptions for his representation been found; such prescriptions become prevalent in some of the Mahāyāna sutras that date from the first centuries of the Common Era. The so-called aniconism debate has persisted, though, with one art historian arguing that in fact there never were such prohibitions; the carvings do not depict events from the life of the Buddha but instead show pilgrimages to and worship of important sites from the Buddha's life depicted sometime after his demise. These sites include the Bodhi tree, and festivals celebrating the key moments in his biography, in which a riderless horse would be led from the city to commemorate his departure from the royal palace on his loyal steed, Kanthaka. But images of the Buddha began to be made, and these images became the Buddha that Europeans would encounter.[44]

And later Buddhist texts do relate how images of the Buddha were made, and the events they purport to recount take place during his lifetime. In a famous story, the Buddha instructs his patron, King Bimbisāra, to send a portrait of the Buddha as a gift to Rudrāyana, king of Kauśāmbī. Thus, just as Jesus is said to have sat for the Image of Edessa, the Buddha sat for the Image of Rudrāyana. However, the painters assigned to the task face a problem similar to that described by the iconoclasts, who argued that it was impossible to capture the divinity of Christ on canvas. The Indian painters are so captivated by the Buddha's beauty that they are unable to paint his portrait. The Buddha then sits in such a way that his shadow is cast on the canvas. He instructs the painters to trace his silhouette and then fill in the details later.

A more elaborate version of the story, important in East Asian Buddhism, describes not the first painting but the first statue of the Buddha. Here, the king of Kauśāmbī is called Udāyana (rather than Rudrāyana). The Buddha's mother had died seven days after his birth, and so did not live to hear her son preach the dharma. She was reborn in the Tuṣita heaven. In the seventh year after his enlightenment, the Buddha uses his magical powers to ascend to the Heaven of the Thirty-Three atop Mount Meru, where his mother, now a male deity, descends to meet him. He spends the three months of the summer rains retreat teaching the dharma to the assembled gods, returning to earth briefly each day to collect alms, then pausing to give his disciple Śāriputra a summary of what he has been teaching the gods. King Udāyana, devastated upon learning that he will be unable to behold the Buddha for three months, approaches Maudgalyāyana, the monk who surpasses all others in supernormal powers, with a request. The king asks the monk to magically transport a five-foot piece of sandal-wood and thirty-two artists to the Heaven of the Thirty-Three, where together they will carve a statue of the Buddha, with each artist re-sponsible for depicting one of the thirty-two marks of a superman (mahāpuruṣa) that adorn the Buddha's body. When they complete their work, the sandalwood statue is brought back to earth. When the Buddha makes his triumphal descent from heaven, the statue rises to meet him, and is therefore a standing image of the Buddha.[45]

According to one tradition, it is this very image that Chinese en-voys brought back to China after Emperor Ming's dream. It is this im-age that the German philosopher Gottfried Wilhelm Leibniz referred to as Infelix Fae Idolatrum, the accursed idol Fo (the Chinese word for "Buddha").[46] Leibniz was one of many European thinkers of the seventeenth century who admired the mandarins of China for their rationality, and so condemned the introduction of idolatry into their realm, blaming it on the Buddha.

Despite its apparent presence in China since the first century, the famous seventh-century Chinese pilgrim Xuanzang (596–664) vis-ited Kauśāmbī during his sixteen-year sojourn in India, and saw the statue there. He reports, "In the old palace in the city there is a great temple more than sixty feet in height that houses an image of the Buddha carved in sandalwood, with a stone canopy suspended over it. It was made by King Udāyana. It often shows spiritual signs and emits a divine light from time to time. The kings of various countries, relying on their might, wished to lift it up, but they could not move it, although a large number of people were employed to do so. Then they had pictures of the image produced for worship, and each of them claimed that his picture was true to life."[47] Xuanzang himself brought a copy of the statue back to China.

In the tenth century, the Japanese monk Chōnen had a sandalwood copy made, which he brought back to Japan. It is said that that copy magically changed places with the original, such that the statue of the Buddha enshrined at Seiryōji temple in Kyoto is in fact the original statue carved in the Buddha's lifetime. The Udāyana statue at Seiryōji has a small compartment in the back. When it was opened in 1954, it was found to contain coins, crystals, scriptures, and miniature internal organs made of silk.

In Thailand, one of the most venerated Buddha images is the Stone Buddha, said to have been created not during the Buddha's lifetime but rather shortly after his death. Seven years, seven months, and seven days after the Buddha's passage into nirvana, King Ajātaśatru had a stone stele of the Buddha carved. When it was completed, he placed the image on a throne, together with a golden casket that contained seven relics of the Buddha. When the monks prayed, "May the relics enter this Buddha image," the relics rose from the casket and miraculously entered the image: one at the head, one at the forehead, one at the chest, two at the shoulders, and two at the knees. The statue then rose into the air before descending back onto the throne.[48]

The most famous Buddha image in Tibet, known simply as "the Lord" (Jo bo) and enshrined in the Jokhang, what European sources call the "Central Cathedral" in Lhasa, was said to have been carved when the Buddha, or Buddha-to-be, was twelve years of age.

But there are tens of thousands of other images of the Buddha that have been produced across Asia over the past two millennia, images that European travelers, beginning in the thirteenth century, identified as idols, dead matter made to represent living beings, dead matter worshipped as a living god.

Idol and *idolatry* have always been used as terms of abuse to describe the religions of others. And thus from the time that Buddhists have been able to understand the connotations, they have rejected these terms as not applying to their tradition. Yet images of the Buddha abound in the Buddhist world, and people are seen prostrating before them and making offerings of flowers, fruit, and lighted lamps. Why do they do so? In order to understand this question, and to engage the charge of idolatry, we must consider the attitudes that Buddhists have expressed toward images of the Buddha. Among the most interesting avenues for such an investigation are the ceremonies performed throughout the Buddhist world to consecrate an image of the Buddha. Like Christians and Muslims in subsequent centuries, Buddhists devoted considerable energy to the question of the status of their dead founder. This Buddhology (as in Christology) would become central to the role of the image of the Buddha.

Early in the tradition, it was declared that Śākyamuni, the sage of the Śākya clan, was not the first buddha to appear in the world. There had been buddhas in the past—Śākyamuni was variously counted as the fourth, seventh, or twenty-fifth—and there would be buddhas in the future. This was a key doctrine, necessary to counter any charges of innovation. Just as the Vedas, the ancient scriptures of the Hindus, were eternal, existing for time immemorial as sound, so buddhas had been achieving the same enlightenment and teaching the same dharma forever. A new buddha did not appear in the world until the teachings of the previous buddha had been completely forgotten, thus accounting for the absence of any memory of his predecessor.

In addition, the path that the Buddha followed to enlightenment did not begin and end over the course of a single lifetime. Millions of lifetimes were required, from the time that he first took the vow to achieve buddhahood out of compassion for the world—becoming at that moment a bodhisattva—to the time that he achieved enlightenment. Thus, both the presence of buddhas, and the careers of individual buddhas, extended over vast epochs.

Furthermore, the death of an individual buddha—or his passage into nirvana—did not mark the end of that buddha's presence. His words persisted in the form of sound, the discourses that monks memorized and recited. Later, they persisted in the physical form of the palm leaves on which those words were inscribed. His body persisted in the form of the relics collected from his funeral pyre and entombed in reliquaries, called stupas. According to the *Great Discourse on the Final Nirvana*, eight shares of relics were apportioned among followers of the Buddha, each of whom enshrined them in a stupa. Later, it is said that the emperor Aśoka broke open those stupas and gathered the relics together, dividing them again and enshrining them in eighty-four thousand stupas, today found across Asia in the form of pagodas.

The body of the Buddha also persisted in the form of statues. Early in the tradition, the question was raised about the practice of refuge, the defining ritual of Buddhism, in which one goes for refuge to the Buddha, the dharma, and the sangha, known as the three jewels.

When one seeks refuge in the Buddha, who is that Buddha, who is the "Buddha jewel"? Because the physical body of the Buddha, at least according to the early tradition, was subject to impermanence and suffering, it was not the Buddha jewel. Instead, various qualities of the Buddha—his love, his compassion, his mastery of deep states of meditation, his knowledge of the nature of reality, his understanding of the inclinations of his disciples—were identified as the Buddha jewel. These qualities, called *dharmas* in Sanskrit, constituted a metaphorical body of the Buddha and were so named: the *dharmakāya*, the corpus of qualities. Thus, there were two bodies of the Buddha—his physical body (*rūpakāya*) and his dharma body (*dharmakāya*).

With the rise of the Mahāyāna some four centuries after the Buddha's death, a more elaborate theory of the Buddha's bodies would develop. In its classic formulation, the Buddha had three bodies. Most exalted of all was the *dharmakāya*, still an invisible body, but now transformed into a kind of eternal principle of enlightenment in which all buddhas of the past, present, and future partake, and from which all forms of the Buddha flow. The second body was called the "enjoyment body" (*saṃbhogakāya*), a magnificent physical form that did not appear on earth but only in special realms reserved for the instruction of advanced bodhisattvas. Neither of these first two bodies was visible to the eyes of humans in this world. The third body of the Buddha was the body that appeared in India twenty-five hundred years ago, achieved enlightenment under the Bodhi tree, and taught the four noble truths. Yet this body was called the "emanation body" (*nirmāṇakāya*), with the Sanskrit term having the sense of something created or conjured. Just as in the first centuries of Christianity the Docetists claimed that Jesus' physical body was an illusion, and so he did not suffer and die on the cross, Mahāyāna sutras, most famously the *Lotus Sutra*, would declare that the Buddha had been enlightened long before he sat under the Bodhi tree, and that he had only pretended to pass into nirvana; in fact, his life span was measureless. The Buddha who appeared was an emanation, a display.

There were also other forms in which a buddha could appear. A buddha could appear as a god, a human, or an animal. A buddha could appear as an artist, or a work of art that subdues the passions of those who see it. A buddha could appear as a bridge, a path, or a cooling breeze. And thus the Buddha, the historical Buddha, was himself a physical representation of a reality beyond human sight.

A buddha could also appear in the form of a statue—and numerous texts from across the Buddhist world extol the virtues of making images of the Buddha, often having the Buddha himself recommend the practice. Hence in a Thai text entitled the *Meritorious Blessing for Making Buddha Images* (*Ānisong Kān Kosāng Phraphuttharūp*), the Buddha says, "Whoever is full of faith and makes an image of the *tathāgata* [a buddha] from a leaf will receive meritorious blessings for five eons; those full of faith in the Triple Gem who make an image of the *tathāgata* by painting it on cloth, will receive meritorious blessings for ten eons." He then continues through various materials from which an image can be made—clay, wood, tusk, brick, stone, tin, copper, silver, pollen, gold, and gems—in each case increasing the number of eons of blessing by five. He concludes, "Those who build an image of the *tathāgata* from sandalwood or *bodhi* tree will receive meritorious blessings for seventy eons or will receive meritorious blessings forever."[49]

A statue of the Buddha, whether painted or sculpted, is not considered finished until it has been animated in a consecration ceremony. It is this ceremony that turns the dead material of the statue—be it wood, bronze, or stone—into a living buddha. This appears to be a very ancient practice. Some of the oldest Buddha images that survive (dating from the first four centuries of the Common Era) contain a small hole at the top of the *uṣṇīṣa*, the "crown protrusion" on the Buddha's head; art historians speculate that this hole originally contained a relic.[50] The ceremonies vary across the Buddhist world, but the most ubiquitous is called "opening the eyes of the Buddha," in which the eyes of the image are painted. In Sri Lanka, it is a ceremony rich in power and fraught with danger. Prior to the painting of the eyes, a white cloth is placed in front of the face of the image, and a monk places a relic in a hole in the back of the statue. The artist who is to paint the eyes then mounts a scaffold. However, when he paints the eyes, he does not look directly into the face of the image. Instead, he averts his gaze into a mirror held by an assistant while his brush paints the eyes. After he has opened the eyes of the Buddha, the eyes of the artist are closed; he is blindfolded and led outside to purify himself by slashing a tree with a sword, washing his face with milk from a bowl, and breaking the bowl on the horns of an ox, which is then driven away.[51]

The ritual of the opening of the eyes is indeed powerful; it transforms a piece of wood into a living buddha. As a Thai text explains, "If one constructs a buddha image and chants as written in this text, it will be the same as though the Buddha himself was present. The monastery will prosper and will be firm in faith."[52]

Thai ceremonies for the consecration of buddha images are typically held between October and May, although one text specifies that they are to be consecrated on the full moon night of the fourth lunar month, the anniversary of the Buddha's achievement of enlightenment. Over the course of that night, monks perform a series of rituals that reenact the Buddha's enlightenment.[53] In one of these rituals, the assembled monks recite the events of the Buddha's life in order to animate his form, like reading a diary to a person emerging from a coma.

In Tibetan Buddhism, the interior of the image is typically filled with rolls of mantras wrapped around a wooden dowel, called the "life stick," that runs from the crown of the head to the base of the image. Often, incense or the soil from a sacred place is added as well, before the bottom of the image is sealed shut and marked with the sign of a crossed *vajra* (ritual implement). Paintings are marked with mantras, often the letters *oṃ āḥ hūṃ* on the reverse of the scroll, aligned with the head, throat, and heart of the figure on the front. A consecration ceremony, sometimes brief, sometimes quite elaborate, is then performed, the purpose of which is to cause the deity represented in the image (most commonly a buddha) to enter into and thus animate the image. One such ceremony includes this prayer:

•

Just as all the buddhas from their abode in Tuṣita, entered the womb of Queen Māyā, may you, the protector, always reside here with the image. To create the aspiration to enlightenment, and for the sake of the patron, please accept whatever wealth I have and these offerings and flowers. May you regard me as well as my disciples with affection. It is fitting that you bless all these and dwell in this very [image].

May all the buddhas and bodhisattvas in the ten directions care for me. As long as the realms of sentient beings, as vast as space, have not gathered in the unlocated nirvāṇa, I pray that you remain steadfastly, without passing into nirvāṇa. In particular, as long as these abodes of body, speech, and mind are not destroyed by damage from earth, water, fire, and wind, I pray that you act immeasurably for the welfare of sentient beings and remain steadfast [in the image].[54]

∙

According to the Mahāyāna, a buddha is said to reside in what is called the unlocated nirvana (apratiṣṭhitanirvāṇa), because he abides in neither the maelstrom of saṃsāra nor the solitude of the arhat's nirvana. The consecration rite thus causes the buddha to move from the unlocated nirvana to become located in the physical image. The image has to be transformed into a buddha in order that it become localized as a site of merit making. In the ceremony, the unconsecrated image is (in the visualization of the person performing the consecration) made to dissolve into emptiness (which is its true nature) and then reappear as the deity itself, often through the use of a mirror, which reflects the ultimate nature of the deity into the conventional form of the image. The consecrated image of the Buddha thus is not a symbol of the Buddha but, effectively, is the Buddha, and there are numerous stories of images speaking to their devotees.

The Accursed Idol Fo

This Buddhist theory of images did not go unnoticed by European travelers and missionaries. In 1667, the Jesuit scholar Athanasius Kircher (1602–1680), whom we will meet again in subsequent chapters, published *China Illustrata*, based on the reports of Jesuit missionaries to Asia. There, he provides a striking condemnation of Buddhist meditation, and the relation between the Buddhist adept and the idol:

∙

Those who are better trained, or perhaps I should say, more insane, in their philosophy, say that a man by thinking is really able to achieve the desired object, that a man can stop all activity to the point that no life remains in him. They think that he does this not only by his intellect and his will power, but also by his cognitive, appetitive, and imaginary powers. They add that when a man has made such intellectual progress, he falls into ecstasy and an unmoving stupor. Then finally he can be said to have arrived at the greatest possible happiness and he is said to be among the gods in the pagodas. The images in the pagodas, although they do not seem to see or hear or make use of anything in the material world, nevertheless are said to hear and see in their own way. A deity is thought to have been seized or absorbed into them. They defend the life of the idols and pagodas by ridiculous reasoning when answering those who say that the idols don't exist.[55]

•

Reading through Father Kircher's rhetoric, we find here a relatively accurate representation of Buddhist practice, both the practice of meditation and the practice of image consecration.

In Amsterdam between 1723 and 1743, a nine-volume work was published with the title *Cérémonies et coutumes religieuses de tous les peuples du monde*. It was published in English between 1733 and 1739 as *The Ceremonies and Religious Customs of the Various Nations of the Known World: Together with Historical Annotations, and Several Curious Discourses Equally Instructive and Entertaining*. It was the work of the French bookseller Jean-Frederic Bernard and Bernard Picart, the greatest engraver of the day. Although remembered especially for Picart's superb engravings, the work was highly influential in its day and remains an invaluable compendium of information on the religions of the world as they were understood during the French Enlightenment.[56] There, in a chapter entitled *"On the RELIGION of the People of LAIES, LANGIENS, or LAOS,"* we find an account that mentions the three buddhas that preceded Śākyamuni (called Xaca here), and how after his entry into nirvana (Nireupan) his spirit continues to reside in his idols:

•

BEFORE this Restoration of the Earth to its primitive State, four Deities condescended to govern and preside over it. Three of them, weary at last of the important Charge, resigned their Guardianship, and went higher towards the North, to taste the uninterrupted Joys of Solitude and Retirement. Now the sole acting God that remained, and who, as they insist, was *Xaca*, was still to live and reign for some thousands of

Years. This *Xaca*, being fully determined to attain to the highest Pitch of Perfection imaginable, sunk at last into that happy State of Annihilation: But he took particular Care beforehand to direct, that Mankind should build Temples and Idols in Commemoration of his godhead; promising at the same Time, that he would fill those sacred Edifices, set apart for Divine Worship, with an Emanation of his Virtue, which should amply make amends for the Want of his personal Appearance, and would effectually breath into the Idols some Degree of his divine Influence. Thus these Statues participated of the divine Nature of *Xaca*, pursuant to his gracious and express Promise, when he sunk down into *Nireupan*, or the ever-blessed State of Annihilation. From hence the Worship of Images, and such other Objects, in which the divine Spirit, as they imagined, delighted to reside, was first instituted and anointed. This Idea is not so extravagant, but that something very much resembling it has imperceptibly crept into divers other Religions. . . .

So far are they from entertaining the least sacrilegious Thought of pillaging this Statue of all its costly Decorations, that they impoverish themselves to testify their Zeal and Veneration for it. What a pity 'tis, that a people so pious, and so well disposed, should be blind, and so confirmed in Ignorance and Error![57]

•

Such condemnations of Buddhism as a form of idolatry persisted into the nineteenth century. In fact, well into that century, European (Christian) authors divided the world into four nations or peoples: Christians, Jews, Mohametans (Muslims), and Pagans or Idolaters; Daniel Defoe, for instance, entitled his dictionary of religion, published in 1704, *Dictionarium Sacrum Seu Religiosum: A Dictionary of All Religions, Ancient and Modern, Whether Jewish, Pagan, Christian, or Mahometan*. These four groups could be further subdivided into three, based on their attitude toward the truth. Christians worshipped the true God and recognized Jesus as the Messiah. Jews worshipped the true God but failed to recognize Jesus as the Messiah. Muslims worshipped the true God but followed a false prophet, Muhammad. Thus, the first three had all encountered the truth and had either accepted it (Christians) or rejected it (Jews and Muslims). All were monotheists, none idolaters. The last group, the Idolaters or Pagans, was vast and various, worshipping a host of false gods, in most cases because they had not yet heard the Gospel. In a sense, they were less blameworthy than Jews and Muslims, who had had the opportunity to recognize the Messiah, but had refused to do so. The idolaters were simply ignorant of his existence.[58] Thus, there was reason to believe that the idolaters would be converted if they heard the Gospel. The problem was that there were so many of them.

The estimation of the number of idolaters in the world was a persistent concern. In 1614 we find the English mathematician Edward Brerewood (1565?–1613) providing the following information in his *Enquiries Touching the Diversity of Languages, and Religions, through the Chiefe Parts of the World*:

•

And yet in Asia idolaters abound more then in Afrique, even as Asia is larger then Afrique for the continent, and for the people, better inhabited, for Asia also, very neere about the one halfe, or rather a little more is possessed by idolaters. For first if we consider the maritime parts, all from the river of *Pechora*, Eastward to the Ocean, and then turning downeward, to the most Southerly point of *India*, (and of all Asia) the cape of *Cincapura*, and from that point Westward, by the South coast, to the outlets of the river *Indus*, all that maritime tract I say, is entirely possessed by idolaters. Saving only, that in the neerer part of *India*, betweene *Indus* and *Ganges*, there is among them some mixture both of Mahumetans and Christians: and in the further part, the city and territory of *Malacca*, is held by Portugals, and some part of the sea coast of the kingdome of *Siam*, by Mores. So that by this account, a good deale more then halfe the circumference of Asia, is possessed by Idolaters.[59]

•

And once their chief idol was identified with the Buddha, he became the object of particular condemnation. Accordingly, in the late seventeenth century, Fernão de Queyroz (1617–1688), a Portuguese missionary to Sri Lanka, would write of the Buddha, "For he who considers the extensive regions which venerate him, at least will doubt whether he leads more to perdition than shameful Mahomet, whom he preceded by more than 1400 years."[60]

In his *History of All Religions, as Divided into Paganism, Mahometan-*

ism, Judaism, and Christianity of 1824, David Benedict (1779–1874), a Baptist pastor in Pawtucket, Rhode Island, provided a chart of "Tabular and Statistical Views of All Religions." There, speaking of idolaters, he writes, "This class of mankind are found in almost all parts of the world, but the great body of them reside in Hindostan, China, Tartary, Japan, and neighboring regions of the east."[61] With the exception of India (Hindostan), in 1824 these regions had large Buddhist populations; *Tartary* was a term used since the Middle Ages to designate regions under the control of the Mongols; it included Turkestan, Mongolia, Manchuria, and in some cases Tibet. Elsewhere, Benedict considers the extent of idolatry:

•

If the whole world, as known to us, were divided into thirty-two parts, not less than *nineteen* of these parts are still inhabited by pagans and idolaters. They possess, at this day, more than one half the extent of the immense continents of Asia and Africa, together with considerable parts of Europe and America. Different estimates have been made of the total number of pagan nations, and most accounts agree that they are somewhere from four to five hundred millions.

Many have doubted whether all these millions of the human family are deserving the odious name of idolaters; they suppose there are multitudes among them, who have correct views of the character of God, and render him an acceptable worship. Efforts are now making to explore all parts of the pagan world, and certainly nothing will afford greater pleasure to missionaries or their supporters, than to find multitudes of this description in pagan lands.

But until evidences can be obtained to justify the palliations and excuses which many are so anxious to make for the heathen, we may consistently consider them idolaters, without God and without hope in the world; and we ought to pity their deplorable condition, and continue and increase our efforts to bring them to the knowledge of God, and the gospel of his Son.[62]

•

The view that Buddhists were idolaters and that the Buddha was an idol thus had spread across the Atlantic to America, and had extended into the nineteenth century, where, just two decades after Reverend

Benedict published these words, the view of the Buddha would radi-
cally change, as we shall see in chapter 4.

The history of Christianity, from the Iconoclast Controversy that
pitted iconoclast (icon smashers) against iconoclude (supporter of
icons), to the Protestant Reformation, demonstrates a rich and complex theology of the representation of the divine. An equally sophisticated, although a good deal less contested, theology is to be found in
Buddhism, a religion that, like Christianity, developed a rich artistic
tradition for the representation of its founder and its saints. Yet that
sophistication remained, like the divine nature of Christ, invisible to
the eyes of the Christians who encountered images of the Buddha.
In one sense, this had to be the case. They could not understand the
ceremonies they witnessed. They could not read the Buddhist texts
in which this theology was expressed. But perhaps in fact they could
see something, and to imagine that they could not is to miscalculate
how much we understand now, and how little they understood then.
Robert Knox, held captive in Sri Lanka from 1659 to 1679, wrote this
about the making of a Buddha image:

·

Some being devoutly disposed, will make the Image of this God at their
own charge. For the making whereof they must bountifully reward the
Founder. Before the *Eyes* are made, it is not accounted a God, but a lump
of ordinary Metal, and thrown about the Shop with no more regard
than anything else. But when the *Eyes* are to be made, the Artificer is
to have a good gratification, besides the first agreed upon reward. The
Eyes being formed, it is thenceforeward a *God*. And then, being brought
with honour from the Workman's Shop, it is dedicated by Solemnities and Sacrifices, and carried with great state into its shrine or little
house, which is before built and prepared for it.

Sometimes a man will order the *Smith* to make this Idol, and then
after it is made will go about with it to well-disposed People to contribute toward the Wages the Smith is to have for making it. And men will
freely give towards the charge. And this is looked upon in the man that
appointed the Image to be made, as a notable piece of Devotion.[63]

·

Yet for Knox, who here describes with some accuracy the ritual of consecration, the image of the Buddha was still an idol. Buddhists were consequently condemned as idolaters for centuries. They worshipped images made of wood, or stone, or gold. They were idolaters because they worshipped the material thing itself rather than the spirit that it represented, as Saint Thomas explained in his defense of icons of Jesus.

Buddhists did indeed worship the material thing (after it had been properly consecrated, that is, animated), and so perhaps they were idolaters—if only the term could somehow be rehabilitated, somehow purged of the pejorative. As we have seen, Buddhists had sophisticated theories for their idolatry, with rituals that brought about their own version of transubstantiation, changing a wooden statue into the "form body" of the Buddha. For Buddhists, the statue is the Buddha, just as much as the Host of the Eucharist is the body of Christ. The iconoclasts of Byzantium argued that only the Host is a suitable icon, because it is not a symbol but a substance. Buddhists make a similar claim.

But *idolatry* cannot be rehabilitated and somehow made a neutral term of description rather than a polemical term of abuse, because most exegeses of the term, whether Jewish, or Christian, or Muslim, specify that idolatry is the worship of a false god—that is, the god of someone else. For Europe, over much of its long history of contact with Buddhism and Buddhists, the Buddha was that god.

And so, from another perspective, the theology of icon and idol, expressed with such care by the fathers of the church at their councils and by the firebrands of the Reformation from their pulpits, may have itself also been a representation that masked the invisible—not the invisible that is divine but the invisible that is most human, the politics of power. In the course of promoting iconoclasm, Emperor Leo III the Isaurian (circa 685–741) seized control of the property of Sicily and southern Italy, formerly held by the pope, whom he accused of condoning idolatry; the pope, Gregory II, had refused to pay taxes to Constantinople. The Beeldenstorm, the destruction of icons in the Low Countries in 1566, was one of the events that led to the Eighty Years' War, which in turn led to the independence of the (Protestant) Dutch Republic from (Catholic) Spain. Political concerns also motivated the conquest of Buddhist Asia, with missionaries (whether Catholic or Protestant) accompanying various European armies, ready to save the souls of the idolaters. In fact, Christian missionaries met with relatively little success among the Buddhists of Asia. Some exceptions would include Japan in the late sixteenth century, Sri Lanka in the nineteenth century, and Korea in the twentieth. But the most devastating attack on the idolatrous Buddhists was not made by Christians.

This is not to say that Christians who encountered idols did not sometimes smash them. The most famous case occurred in 1560, when a Portuguese armada of ninety-nine ships under the command of Don Constantino da Bragança (1528–1575) attacked the Buddhist kingdom of Jaffna in northern Sri Lanka. They took the crown prince hostage and sailed back to their headquarters in Goa, on the southwest coast of India, with their prisoner in chains covered in crimson velvet. They also carried a greater prize, a tooth of the Buddha, mounted in gold. The king of Pegu in Burma heard of this great theft and sought its return. In 1561, he sent a delegation to Goa, authorizing it to offer three hundred or four hundred *cruzados*, a vast sum, to the Portuguese in exchange for the tooth. During the negotiations, the Buddhist delegation from Pegu proposed an alliance with the Portuguese, under the terms of which it would provision the Portuguese base at Malacca on the Malay Peninsula. Knowing that their own treasury was depleted, the Portuguese commanders and noblemen were inclined to accept the offer. However, the recently arrived archbishop of Goa, Don Gaspar de Leão Pereira, intervened, protesting that returning the tooth would further encourage idolatry among the heathens, allowing them to offer homage to a tooth, homage that was rightfully due only unto God. A council of the officers of the military and the church was convened, deciding in the end that the needs of the state to replenish its treasury were outweighed by the need to prevent the worship of false gods. In an elaborate ceremony, at which the delegation from Pegu was apparently present, the archbishop placed the tooth in a mortar and smashed it to powder. After burning the powder in a brazier, the ashes were cast into the Gomati River.[64] Shortly thereafter, the tooth reappeared in Sri Lanka. It is said that at the moment that it was about to be destroyed, it magically disappeared, reappearing on a lotus blossom in Kandy, where it is today enshrined.

For the Portuguese who encountered images and relics of the Buddha in the sixteenth century, the Buddha must ever be an idol and Buddhists ever idolaters, deserving only conquest and conversion. In fact, the Buddha had been an idol and Buddhists idolaters once before, with devastating consequences for Buddhists and profound consequences for Buddhism and how it would be understood in Europe. As a result, even if we might wish to "reform" the term *idolatry*, to reinstate it, lifting it from the ground and replacing the image on its pedestal, the fact remains that for the Abrahamic religions, the idol is not only to be rejected as a false god; it must also be smashed to pieces, like the Golden Calf. Images of the Buddha were likewise smashed, with far-reaching and unexpected consequences.

The Idol in India

By the time the Portuguese explorer Vasco da Gama landed in Calicut on the southwest coast of India in 1498, Buddhism, at least as an active religious presence, had disappeared from the subcontinent, although it was a strong presence offshore on the island of Sri Lanka. Like the vacant throne of the Buddha in early Buddhist art, there were symbols of Buddhism in India, but no Buddhists. Evidence of the absence of Buddhism there is found in the account of the French astronomer Guillaume Joseph le Gentil, who in 1761 participated in an international scientific project to measure the distance from the earth to the sun by observing the path of Venus across the sun from various points on the globe; over one hundred observers were dispatched.

Le Gentil was assigned to the French colony of Pondicherry on the east coast of India. But by the time he arrived, the British had captured the colony. On June 6, 1761, the date that the observations had to be made, he was at sea, and the rolling of the ship made it impossible to make accurate observations. Undeterred, he decided to remain in Asia until Venus returned, eight years hence. By this time, Pondicherry was back in French hands. Le Gentil built an observatory and waited for the appointed day, June 3, 1769. It was cloudy. Driven almost to madness, he eventually returned to Paris, where he found himself declared dead and his wife remarried. In 1780, he published an account of his travels in two volumes, the title of which translates as *Voyage in the Seas of India, Made by Order of the King, on the Occasion of the Passage of Venus Across the Disk of the Sun on June 6 1761 and on the 3rd of the Same Month 1769.* In the passage below, he describes something he saw near Pondicherry:

•

There was then in those parts of India, and principally on the Coromandel Coast and in Ceylon, a form of worship about whose dogmas we are absolutely ignorant. The god Baouth, of whom nothing more than the name is known today in India, was the object of this worship; but it has been completely abolished; although some families of Indians might still be found, separated from and scorned by the other castes, who remain faithful to Baouth, and who do not recognize the religion of the Brames [brahmans].

I have not heard that there are these families in the vicinity of Pondichéry; yet there is something most noteworthy, which none of the travelers who discuss the Coromandel Coast and Pondichéry have noticed, found a short league south of the town, on the plane of Virapatnam, and rather near the river, a granite statue very hard and very beautiful: this statue, around three feet to three and a half feet in height, is sunk in the sand up to the waist, and doubtless weighs many thousand; it is as if it was abandoned in the middle of this vast plain. I cannot give a better idea of it than to say that it exactly conforms to and resembles the Siamese *Sommonacodum*; its head is the same shape, it has the same facial features, its arms are in the same attitude, and the ears are absolutely similar. The form of this divinity, which has certainly been made in this country, and which does not resemble in any way the present-day divinities of the Gentiles [Hindus], struck me when I passed this plain. I found various information about this singular figure; the Tamoults [Tamils] all assured me that it was Baouth, who was no longer looked to and whose worship and festivals ceased after the Brames made themselves masters of the peoples' belief.[65]

•

Thus, by the time le Gentil was in South India awaiting the arrival of Venus, the Buddha had been buried in the land of his birth, sinking slowly beneath the sands, his name remembered, but not much else. The absence of the Buddha, and Buddhism, in India at the time of the arrival of the Europeans would have profound effects on the image of the Buddha that we worship today. As the Tamils informed le Gentil, the Hindu brahmans ruled the religion of the region. But another religion was already well established in India at that time. The earliest and most devastating condemnation of the Buddha as an idol came not from Christians but from Muslims.

The Qur'an does not specifically condemn idolatry in the way that the Hebrew Bible does, but the worship of idols is among the gravest of sins in Islam. It is a form of *shirk*, literally "association," the ascribing of equals to God. To give God human attributes or to give the names and attributes of God to anything other than God is *shirk*. Any expression or act of worship directed at any being other than God is *shirk*. This is the most heinous of sins, and God has sent the prophets to warn humanity against it. Those who do not heed that warning are to be punished. The Qur'an states at Sura 9:5, "So when the sacred months have passed away, then slay the idolaters wherever you find them, and take them captives and besiege them and lie in wait for them in every ambush, then if they repent and keep up prayer and pay the poor-rate, leave their way free to them; surely Allah is Forgiving, Merciful."[66]

The Prophet Muhammad died in 632, and Muslims had gained control of parts of modern-day Pakistan by the end of that century. Raids into what is now northern India began in earnest in the eleventh century. Mahmud of Ghazni defeated the king of Gandhara, long an important Buddhist center, in 1001. Between 1005 and 1027, Mahmud sent expeditions from Afghanistan into India every other year after the mountain passes were clear of snow, extending further and further into the east, sacking and destroying Hindu temples and Buddhist monasteries.

In 1011, Mahmud of Ghazni had declared, "The religion of the faithful inculcates the following tenet: 'That in proportion as the tenets of the prophet are diffused, and his followers exert themselves in the subversion of idolatry, so shall be their reward in heaven'; that, therefore, it behooved him, with the assistance of God, to root out the worship of idols from the face of all India."[67] Buddhists were among those regarded as idolaters. Indeed, the Persian word *bot*, a common term for *idol*, was derived from *buddha*. This is not to suggest that Muslim scholars had no knowledge of the Buddha. One of the most detailed descriptions of the Buddha in an Arabic source is that of 'Abd al Karīm ash-Shahrastānī (1086–1153) in his *Kitāb al-milal wan-niḥal* (*The Book of Sects and Creeds*), a compendium of the doctrines of Muslim and non-Muslim religious sects and philosophical schools, composed around 1125. In a section entitled "Ārā' al-hind" ("The Views of the Indians"), we read:

•

The Buddha, in their opinion, means a person who is not born, who never marries nor eats food nor drinks nor grows old nor dies. The first Buddha appearing in the world was named *Shākamīn*, which means "the noble master." Five thousand years have elapsed from the time of his appearance and the time of the *hijra*. . . . This group maintains that the Buddhas came to them according to the number [of branches] of the Kīl River [that is, the Ganges, with seven branches], bringing them knowledge of the sciences and appearing to them in different kinds and as different individuals. Further, on account of the nobility of their substances, the Buddhas appeared only in the families of kings. They claim that there is no difference among the Buddhas with respect to what has been reported of them about the eternity of the world and about their assertion concerning reward [and punishment in the afterlife] already noted. The appearance of the Buddhas has been limited to India, however, due both to the wide variety of its creatures and climates and also to the many Indians who are intent on spiritual exercises and exertion. There is no one comparable to the Buddha as they have described him—if they are right about that—except al-Khiḍr [a legendary Muslim saint], whom Muslims recognize.[68]

•

In 1193, Muslim troops under the command of Muhammad bin Bakhtiyar Khalji attacked Nālandā, the most famous of all the great monasteries of India. At its height it housed some ten thousand monks and was considered the greatest center of Buddhist learning in the world, drawing students from across Asia. Its library was said to contain hundreds of thousands of manuscripts. The Muslim forces apparently mistook it for a fortress. According to Muslim historians, "Great plunder fell into the hands of the victors. Most of the inhabitants of the place were brahmans with shaven heads. They were put to death. Large numbers of books were found there, and when the Muhammadans saw them, they called for some persons to explain their contents, but all the men had been killed. It was discovered that the whole fort and city was a place of study [*madrasa*]. In the Hindi language the word Behar [*vihar*] means a college."[69] According to a well-known story, when there was no one left to identify the contents of the manuscripts, a soldier asked Bakhtiyar Khalji what should be done with them. He reasoned that if the books agreed with the Qur'an, there was no reason to keep them, since the Muslims already had the Qur'an. If they did not agree with the Qur'an, there was no reason to keep them, because they were books of a false religion. He therefore ordered that the library be burned.[70]

In 1235, the Tibetan pilgrim Chag lo tsa ba visited Bodh Gaya, the place of the Buddha's enlightenment and the holiest site in the Buddhist world. He found only four monks, all from Sri Lanka rather than India, serving as caretakers. Fearing that the statue of the Buddha inside the main temple would be destroyed, they would wall up the entrance and hide in the jungle whenever Muslim troops were in the vicinity.[71] The famous monastery of Vikramaśīla was razed so effectively that its precise location has yet to be determined.

Buddhism had been in decline in India—at least in certain regions—for centuries; the seventh-century Chinese pilgrim Xuanzang reports seeing stupas in ruins. It had been persecuted by various Hindu kings over the centuries, with its *sanctum sanctorum*, the Bodhi tree itself, cut down, only to miraculously return, like the Buddha's tooth. It has also been argued that the religious life of India, and the life cycle rituals at its center, were increasingly controlled by Hindu priests, depriving Buddhist monks of the lay support they relied on in order to survive. The intellectual vitality of the monastic tradition came to depend on large monastic universities, whose fortunes waxed and waned based on royal patronage. If these monasteries were destroyed, it would be difficult for Buddhism to survive in India.

The monastic universities of North India became favored targets of Muslim troops, but the extent of forced conversions of Buddhists to Islam is unclear. In many cases, Muslim armies seemed more interested in the material wealth of Buddhist monasteries. The Buddhists, however, clearly regarded Muslim forces with a combination of fear and contempt, blaming them for the decline of the dharma in India.

A famous eleventh-century text, the *Kālacakra Tantra*, describes barbarians who drink camel blood and cut off the ends of their penises
(that is, practice circumcision), followers of one Madhumati (a Sanskrit approximation of "Muhammad," literally meaning "Mind of
Mead," that is, wino). The same text foretold of an apocalyptic war in
which Buddhist armies would sweep south out of the Himalayas to
defeat the barbarians and restore the dharma to India.

Regardless of the reasons for its disappearance, Buddhism did
disappear from India, as Muslim sources confirm. Abū-al Faz'l ibn
Mubārak (1551-1602) was the vizier of Mughal emperor Akbar. He
composed the *Akbarnāma*, or *History of Akbar*. Its third volume, entitled *Ā'īn-i Akbarī*, contains an "account of the Hindu sciences," including a description of the Buddha:

•

It came to pass that he turned his mind from the affairs of the world,
and made the choice of a life of retirement. He visited Benaris, Rajgird,
and several other fire temples. He then travelled to Cashmeer, where
he made many proselytes; and he also gained followers from people
of Hind, the seaports, Tibbet, and Khatai. From his birth to this time,
which is the 40th year of his Majesty's reign, is a period of 2962 years.
They say that he had the gift of prophecy; and could change the course
of nature. He died at the age of one hundred twenty years. The learned
among the Persians and Arabians call the priests of this religion *Buk-
shee*, and in Tibbet, they are stiled *Lama*. For a long time past there
have not been any traces of them, excepting in Peigu, Dehnasiry, and
Tibbet.[72]

•

And thus the labeling of Buddhists as idolaters had profound consequences for the fate of Buddhism in India, far beyond the fate of
monasteries and the images enshrined within them. This ancient religion, which perhaps initially prohibited images of the Buddha, with
the place for the Buddha on the throne left empty, came under attack
by a more violent prohibition of images; the Buddha, or at least his
followers, became absent once again. The idol remained, often broken
or buried, but the idolaters were gone. By the thirteenth century and
its demise in India, Buddhism was well established across Asia in all

directions—in China, Korea, Japan, Tibet; in Sri Lanka, Thailand, and Burma—and it was Christians who would dub the Buddhists in these lands idolaters. But for Buddhism, India was a burial ground, a dead zone, no longer the vibrant center of the tradition, the destination of pilgrims. For Buddhists elsewhere in Asia, India became a relic to be worshipped from afar.

Beginning in the late fifteenth century, a different kind of pilgrim began to arrive in India, this time from Europe. Then, as we shall see in chapter 4, in the nineteenth century a new relic of the Buddha would be discovered in India, a relic that would be worshipped by Europeans. It would be Europeans who would transform that relic into an idol of their own making, and place him on the vacant throne.

Good Idols, Bad Idols

But as this chapter draws to a close, we would be mistaken to conclude that all the Christians who encountered Buddhism in Asia held identical views of idolatry. Ippolito Desideri (1684–1733), an Italian Jesuit missionary to Tibet from whom we will hear more in the next chapter, discerned a difference between "the other Asian paganisms" (by which he likely meant the Hindu deities he had seen during his time in India) and "the special paganism of Tibet," Buddhism (though he never used the term). He wrote:

•

It is quite true that all offer up their prayers and incense to false and fictitious saints, but there is still a vast difference between them. The other Asian paganisms commonly recognize, preach about, and admire the unusual powers and extraordinary abilities of their objects of worship, yet at the same time they represent them as impotent figures, as liars, or as intriguers, now frothing with rage and fury, now shameless and adulterous, much as the ancient Romans did Jove, Venus, Mars, Mercury, and Pluto. Such is not the case with the Tibetans. It is true that the powers and miracles that the Tibetans admire with such astonishment and wonder in their idols are but the bright colors and varnishes of fantastic invention, yet these colors and varnishes are so pure and so good that they are capable of captivating and astonishing, if not the healthiest and clearest eyes, at least weakened eyes that see things

indistinctly. Nevertheless, while the Tibetans' indistinct sight may be
dazzled, at least they are not nauseated to the pit of their stomachs by a
rotten, putrid, and corrupt vision together with the revolting filthiness
of execrable wickedness and pernicious examples. This, therefore, is
the difference between the paganism of the rest of Asia and the special
paganism of Tibet: the former burn incense to, revere, and worship
vice and unbridled passions, while the Tibetans worship a virtue that
is certainly imaginary but nonetheless purged of revolting vices and
free from all unbridled passion.[73]

•

This remarkable statement would go unread until the twentieth century, because Desideri's works were placed on the Vatican's index of
banned texts after the suppression of the Jesuits by Pope Clement XIV
in 1773.

Desideri had spent a year in India before traveling north to Tibet,
and he likely encountered images of various Hindu deities. And by
the time of his arrival at the Society of Jesus (Jesuit) headquarters
in the western Indian state of Goa, various European travelers had
gathered many stories of the Hindu gods, sometimes in garbled versions, stories where anger, lust, and jealousy abound—not unlike the
stories of the gods of Mount Olympus, to which Desideri alludes.

For Desideri, the idolaters of Tibet differ from those of India in two
ways. First, the Tibetan idols represent virtuous figures with admirable qualities (he apparently had not seen or failed to mention the
famous *yab yum* deities depicted in sexual union), while the Hindu
idols represent wicked and pernicious gods. The Tibetan images that
he has in mind, and whom he mentions by their Tibetan names, are
such important figures for Tibetan Buddhism as the historical Buddha Śākyamuni ("Sciaccià-Thubbà" for Desideri), the bodhisattva
of wisdom Mañjuśrī ("Giam-yang" for Desideri), the bodhisattva of
compassion Avalokiteśvara ("Cen-ree-szi"), and the Indian tantric
master Padmasambhava ("Urghièn"). His imagery is of vision and its
effects on digestion. The Tibetan idols are clearly false and superficial,
form without substance, all bright colors and varnish, and yet they
are also so pure and good as to be captivating, at least to those with
weak eyesight; those who see clearly would surely recognize their
artifice. Still, the goodness of these idols is such that their ultimate

falsity does not corrupt the Tibetans; it is a falsity that is visual, not visceral, not descending to the stomach to nauseate the Tibetans with "the revolting filthiness of execrable wickedness," as, he implies, it does the idolaters of India.

The second difference between India and Tibet has to do with the nature of the deities. The Indian idolaters worship what they consider a supreme being, yet that deity is "false, fictitious, unholy, monstrous, and execrable." The Tibetans, on the other hand, do not acknowledge a supreme being. Instead, they offer obeisance only to figures who embody qualities they deem honorable.

Indeed, one might ask whether the Tibetans are idolaters at all. Desideri writes, "They preferred not to recognize any supreme creator of the world with absolute and independent power over it and human beings rather than assent to one in the way that was deceptively proposed to them. That being so, I say that according to their religion or sect, the Tibetans not only completely dismiss the existence of the true deity, but also they do not recognize any false and monstrous divinity either, as many other idolatrous nations of Asia do."[74]

This difference between Tibetans and other heathens raised a special challenge for the missionary. It was generally felt that heathens who worshipped a supreme deity offered an opportunity for conversion, if that supreme deity could be deposed and supplanted by the true God. From this perspective, the Hindus should be easier to convert than the Tibetans. The Tibetans—like all Buddhists, although this was unknown to Desideri—did not worship a supreme deity, and yet they were disposed to virtue. As we shall see in the next chapter, Desideri developed his conversion strategy accordingly.

Yet the larger point suggested by the passage is that for the Europeans in Asia who encountered Buddhism—which they considered simply a form of idolatry—there seemed to be degrees of falsity among the false gods. A certain differentiation among the idols began to take place. This became possible because Europeans, and especially Catholic missionaries, began to learn the languages of the lands they sought to convert. They began to hear, and even read, some of the stories told about the idol.

CHAPTER TWO. The Myth

Christian missionaries to Asia in the sixteenth and seventeenth centuries accepted the chronology of the world as presented in the Bible. Thus, all the peoples they encountered were the distant descendants of Noah. They also believed that over time, many of these peoples had forgotten about God, degenerating almost to an animal state. We find such a description by Joannes Boemus (circa 1485–1535) in a work entitled *The Manners, Lavves, and Customes of All Nations*:

•

The short and vntimely alienation of the children from their progenitors, (of whose life and manners they had little taste) was cause of all the diuersity which insued; for *Cham* [meaning Noah's son Ham] beeing constrained to flye with his wife and children, for scorning and deriding his father, seated himselfe in that part of Arabia, which was afterwards called by his name, where hee left no religious ceremonies to his posterity, as hauing receiued none from his Father: whereof insued, that, as in tract of time, diuerse companies beeing sent out of that coast, to inhabite other countries, and possessing diuerse partes of the world, (for the reiected seede did exceedingly increase) many of them fell into inextricable errors, their languages were varyed, and all knowledge and reuerence of the true and living God, was vtterly forgotten and abolished, in so much as many of them might well bee sayd to liue a life so vnciuill and so barbarous, as hardly could there any difference bee betwixt them and brute beasts.[1]

•

Yet the missionaries who set out across the seas were not only seeking those who had strayed over the centuries, to return the once lost to the fold of believers in the one true God. They were also bringing news of something that had occurred long after Noah and the great flood: the birth, gospel, death, and resurrection of Jesus. They were following Jesus' own exhortation, made to the disciples after his resurrection, as described in Mark 16:14–16: "Afterward he appeared to the eleven themselves as they sat at table; and he upbraided them for their unbelief and hardness of heart, because they had not believed those who saw him after he had risen. And he said to them, 'Go into all the world and preach the gospel to the whole creation. He who believes and is baptized will be saved; but he who does not believe will be condemned.'" And so after the Pentecost, the apostles set out, as instructed by Jesus (in Acts 1:8): "And you shall be my witnesses in Jerusalem and in all Judea and Samaria and to the ends of the earth."

In the story of the Christian encounter with the Buddha, the most important of the apostles was Thomas—he who had doubted the risen Christ and who, according to some traditions, was his twin brother. In the Apocryphal Acts of Thomas, a work probably composed sometime in the first half of the third century CE, the apostles cast lots to decide who will go where to spread the Gospel. Thomas is assigned India but refuses, saying, "I am a Hebrew man. How can I go amongst the Indians and preach the truth?" (1:1) Then the risen Christ appears in the marketplace of Jerusalem and sells Thomas into slavery to an envoy of Gundaphorus, "king of the Indians," whom Thomas eventually converts before being martyred.

In 1854, the British archaeologist Alexander Cunningham (1814–1893), remembered especially for his excavation of Buddhist stupas, identified ancient coins that had been unearthed bearing the name of the king Gondophares. Subsequent scholarship has identified a dynasty of kings with this name who ruled what is known as the Indo-Parthian kingdom (which included modern Pakistan as well as parts of Afghanistan and northern India) from capitals at Taxila and Kabul. One of these kings, Gondophares IV, or Sases, reigned for twenty-six years in the middle of the first century CE, overlapping what would have been Thomas's lifetime. The story of the apostle's sojourn in India had gained further credence centuries earlier, when the Portuguese arrived on the west coast of India (Vasco da Gama landed in 1498) to discover "Thomas Christians." The Chaldean breviary of the Malabar Church, located far to the south of the former empire of Gondophares IV, contains the line, "By St. Thomas were the errors of idolatry banished from among the Indians."[2] During the Gondopharid dynasty, as it is called, Buddhism had a strong presence in northern India. Had he actually made the long journey from Jerusalem, Saint Thomas would have been the first Christian, an early Christian indeed, to encounter an idol of the Buddha.[3]

Other Christians were present elsewhere in Asia. At the Council of Ephesus in 431, Nestorius, archbishop of Constantinople, was excommunicated for his suggestion that the Virgin Mary be referred to as Christotokos, "Bearer of Christ," rather than Theotokos, "Bearer of God." Nestorius was exiled to Egypt, but his followers traveled east to Persia, where they established what would be known as the Church of the East. It eventually spread as far east as China, and enjoyed particular success among the Mongols. In the eleventh century, twenty thousand members of the Kerait tribes were baptized.

In China, a community of Nestorian Christians had flourished during the early Tang dynasty, until its suppression (along with Buddhism) by Emperor Wuzong, a patron of Daoism, in 845. In 781, the Nestorian monk Jingjing (Adam in Syriac) composed a Chinese inscription in the Tang capital of Chang'an (modern Xi'an). In eighteen hundred characters, it describes the tenets of the "Luminous Religion" (*jingjiao*) and its establishment in China (which it dates to 635) and concludes with a list, in Syriac, of bishops and monks. It says, in part, describing Jesus: "He threw open the gate of the three constant (virtues), thereby bringing life to light and abolishing death. He hung up the bright sun to break open the abodes of darkness. By all these things the wiles of the devil were defeated. The vessel of mercy was set in motion to convey men to the palace of light, and thereby all intelligent beings were conveyed across (the intervening space). His mighty work being thus completed, at noonday He ascended to His true (place)."[4] We might note in passing that there is no mention of the Crucifixion or the Resurrection.

This is not the only evidence of Christianity in China during this period. A number of Christian texts from the Tang dynasty, in Chinese (sometimes referred to as the "Jesus Sutras"), were discovered in the early twentieth century in the cave temple complex at Dunhuang in western China. They show knowledge of, and rivalry with, Buddhism. One passage suggests that the true Buddhist must acknowledge the existence of God: "If there be any persons, who, though they have already 'received the precepts' [in other words, converted to Buddhism] do not fear the Lord of Heaven, then, they cannot be counted among those who have 'received the precepts' in spite of professing that they rely on the teaching of Buddha. They are, in reality, traitors."[5]

Rumors of the existence of these Christians in the East provided some comfort to Christians in the West, especially after the Holy Land fell into the hands of the Muslims. Beginning in the twelfth century and continuing for several more, legends were told of Prester John, descendant of one of the three Magi (the wise men from the East who paid homage to the newborn Jesus) and ruler of a fantastic kingdom, variously said to be located in India, Mongolia, and eventually Ethiopia. In 1165, a letter from Prester John (later shown to be a forgery of European origin) began to circulate widely through Europe. Translated into a number of languages, including Hebrew, it described the wonders of his realm, which included the Fountain of Youth as well as a huge mirror in which all of his kingdom's activities were reflected. It also declared his wish to lead an army to the Holy Sepulcher of Christ in Jerusalem and defeat the enemies of the Cross. As late as 1667, the Jesuit scholar Athanasius Kircher reported evidence of Prester John in Tibet: "Certainly our Fathers Albert de Dorville and Johannes Grueber testify that right up to the present day there remain traces of Prester John in the royal kingdom of Tanchut, which the inhabitants call Lassa and the Saracens call Barantola, and which they crossed while returning from China to Europe in 1661."[6]

Then in the thirteenth century, European Christians encountered Buddhism in the courts of Mongol princes. These travelers included Franciscan priests such as William of Rubruck and John of Plano Caprini. They also included traders; it was at the court of the Mongol prince, later Chinese emperor, Kublai Khan that Marco Polo would hear the story of Sagamoni Borcan. Knowing the stories of Saint Thomas and of Prester John, they expected to find Christians in the East, and they often did. Sometimes they were Nestorians, whom the European Catholics regarded with a certain ambivalence: they were fellow Christians, but they were also heretics, and were described with contempt. William of Rubruck characterizes those he met at the court of Karakorum: "The Nestorians there know nothing. They say their offices, and have sacred books in Syrian, but they do not know the language, so they chant like those monks among us who do not know grammar, and they are absolutely depraved. In the first place they are usurers and drunkards; some even among them who live with the Tartars have several wives like them. When they enter the church, they wash their lower parts like Saracens; they eat meat on Friday, and they have their feasts on that day in Saracen fashion."[7]

Although William and other travelers to Asia of the thirteenth century encountered Buddhists and images of the Buddha, their depictions of these idolaters and their idols remained relatively superficial, making little attempt (apart from the life of the Buddha recounted by Marco Polo) to connect the idol to a living figure—whether human or divine—or to relate the events of his life or the elements of his doctrine. His life and teachings would start to appear in European accounts in the seventeenth century, and largely in the writings of the Jesuits. The Jesuit devotion to scholarship, especially in contrast to that of the other religious orders, is sometimes overstated. Yet it is the case that European knowledge of the religions of Asia, including Buddhism, was advanced through the efforts of Jesuit missionaries who learned the languages of the lands they sought to evangelize, whether the Chinese of Matteo Ricci, the Sanskrit of Roberto de Nobili, or the Tibetan of Ippolito Desideri.

A Case of Mistaken Identity

In the previous chapter, we encountered the idol of many names. In this chapter, the many names will remain, although a smaller number will recur with some frequency: Sommona-Codom, Xekia, Fo, Sciaccià-Thubbà, Buddu. Here, too, stories associated with this idol will be told. The stories will vary widely, their sources in Buddhist texts and traditions not always easy to discern. Yet despite how strange the stories may have seemed to the Christians who told them, sometimes there was an uncanny familiarity about them, a familiarity that was more than a remnant of heretical Christians or of Prester John. There were signs of presence—a shadow, a footprint, a mirror image, a dream—that were also signs of absence. Something was missing that should have been there, and what was there was wrong. There had been some kind of mistake—whether accidental or willful—and it had resulted in all manner of woes.

As we shall see, for the Catholic priests of the sixteenth and seventeenth centuries, the Buddha was an idol. He would be condemned not only as an idol but as a purveyor of idolatry, coming from the West—whether Egypt, India, or Siam—to spread the pestilence across East Asia. But for a brief moment, the Buddha was not an idol but a smasher of idols, who proclaimed the existence of the one true God.

In December 1547, the Jesuit priest Francis Xavier was in Malacca on the Malay Peninsula when he met Anjirō (often appearing in the other works as Yajiro), an illiterate Japanese who had fled to Malacca on a Portuguese ship after being accused of murder in his homeland. He spoke some Portuguese, and so described his native Japan to Father Xavier. Anjirō was then sent to the Jesuit headquarters in Goa, where he was baptized as Paulo de Santa Fe. There, he gave a detailed report about Japan and its religion, which was committed to writing by the Italian priest Nicolò Lancilotto, who had been sent to St. Paul's College in Goa to teach Latin grammar. From Anjirō Father Lancilotto learned that the Buddha (called Sciacca in the original and Shaka in the translation here) is not an idol. He is a destroyer of idols:

•

All adore one single God whom they call in their language *Denychy*; and he says that they sometimes paint Denychy with only one body and three heads. They then call him Cogy. But this man said that he did not know the meaning of those three heads; but he knew that all were one, Denychy and Cogy, as with us God and Trinity. . . .

This man also told the history of a man who is regarded among them as a saint and who is called *Shaka* by them, and the account runs as follows:

He says that there is a land on the other side of China towards the west called Chencigo. In it there was a king who was called Jombondaiuo, and he was married to a woman by the name of Maiabonym. This king, when he was once sleeping during the day, dreamed that a boy appeared to him who said that he must enter into the body of his wife; and this boy appeared to him three times on the same day and each time spoke the same words to him. And this king immediately told his wife what had happened to him. Since they were so frightened by the dream, they no longer had any marital relations with each other; and in the same month she discovered that she was pregnant without having had any relations with anyone. At the end of nine months she bore a son whom they called Shaka; and, immediately after the child's birth, its mother died and its father had Shaka brought up by a sister of the mother of the boy.

He says that when this Shaka was born, two large snakes with wings miraculously appeared. They came in the air over the boy, and they spewed water out of their mouths upon the said boy. And he says that this boy got on his feet at the end of three months and took three steps and lifted a hand to heaven and pointed the other to the earth and said, "I am one alone above in heaven, and one alone on earth." This Shaka grew until he reached the age of nineteen and his father ordered him to marry against his will. And when he reflected upon the misery of mankind, he did not wish to unite himself with his wife and fled at night and came to a very high and barren mountain, where he remained for six years and practiced great penance. After this he went forth and began to preach to those inhabitants, who were still pagans, with great eloquence and enthusiasm. Through this he gained such a reputation for the greatest sanctity and virtue that he renewed all the laws and gave to that people a law and a new kind of divine worship. And he says that he won over eight thousand disciples who led the same life of perfection as he. Some of his disciples came to China, where they preached their laws and their kind of divine worship and thus converted the whole of China and had all the idols and pagodas that were in China destroyed. And they came from China to Japan and did the same. And he says that in all of China and Japan are found pieces of old statues as in Rome. This Shaka taught all these peoples to worship one single God, the Creator of all things; and he ordered that he be painted, as has been said above, with one single body and three heads. . . .

This Shaka, who gave laws to these people of China and Japan, ended his life as follows. He called all of his disciples and the people in general together and preached to them and said at the end that he would soon die. And he stepped into a marble tomb which he had ordered to be built and died before the eyes of all. His disciples then burned his body, and as they were placing his ashes in the same tomb, Shaka himself, in the presence of all, appeared in the air above a white cloud with a cheerful countenance and a marvelous aspect and thus went up to heaven and was seen no more. He was ninety years old.[8]

•

It is difficult to say whether this odd account derives from Anjirō's ignorance of Buddhism, his desire to please the Catholic fathers in Goa, or some combination of the two. Or perhaps something was lost in translation. A few of the elements here derive from traditional biographies of the Buddha, such as the early death of the Buddha's mother. However, he took seven steps (not three) immediately after his birth (not when he was three months old). According to some versions, two serpent deities (called *nāgas*) did indeed appear in the sky and send down a stream of water. But Anjirō's version of the story seems far more Christian than Buddhist. And thus we should not be surprised that one of the first scholars in Europe to read this account would conclude that not only was the Buddha a smasher of idols but he was also a Christian—in fact, the Buddha was Christ himself. The scholar's name was Guillaume Postel (1510–1581), one of the most important biblical scholars of the sixteenth century.

Father Postel subscribed to the theory of Divine Simplicity, according to which God created a single human race to be united in a single faith, a universal religion based on the worship of the one true God. Diversity, including the diversity of languages and the diversity of religions, was the work of man. For Postel, Hebrew was the original language, spoken by Adam and Eve. He thus devoted much of his life to studying the Hebrew Bible and Kabbalah, so much so that his critics accused him of being a Jew. Postel believed that if the Bible could be translated into other languages, the entire world would naturally convert to Christianity. Because the Ottomans ruled so much of the world of his day, he studied Arabic so that he could translate the Bible for the Muslims.

A friend of Ignatius Loyola, Postel joined the Society of Jesus in Rome in 1544, only to leave the order the following year, though he remained a priest. In 1547, he went to Venice, where he served at a small hospital for the sick and indigent. There he became the confessor of Madre Zuana or Mother Johanna, a pious woman who had founded the hospital. Postel eventually became convinced that she was a prophet, and called her the "Virgin of Venice," the "Mother of the World," the "Female Pope," "La Personele Iervsalem," the "Personal Jerusalem," and the "New Eve." She revealed to him that it was God's will that all humanity be united into a single flock; when all were joined into a single religion, the salvation of all would follow.

Postel claimed that in 1552, he had received two gifts from Mother Johanna in the form of two garments, one white and one red, which gave him a new spiritual body and perfected his reason and intelligence. He called this transformation his "immutation." He began to preach and write about his divine ordination, which led to his being summoned by the Inquisition. In 1555, he was declared mad, dangerous, and delirious. And because his delirium could lead to heresy, he was condemned to life imprisonment at the Ripetta prison in Rome. However, after serving only four years, Postel escaped with the other inmates after the death of Pope Paul IV. He returned to his native France to continue his mission, and was eventually confined to the monastery of Saint Martin des Champs. This confinement became stricter after 1566, when he proclaimed that the exorcism of a young woman in Laon had been a miracle and a sign of his own restitution. No longer able to preach or publish under his own name, he wrote under a pseudonym and contributed anonymously to the famous Polyglot Bible, published in Antwerp in eight volumes between 1568 and 1573, with the scriptures rendered in Hebrew, Greek, Latin, Syriac, and Aramaic.[9]

This description of Postel's life and vision is important in order to appreciate his comments on Buddhism. Lancilotto's report on Japan and its religion was sent back to Europe, where it found its way to Postel. He published it, with his own interlinear commentary, in *Des Merveilles du Monde* (*Wonders of the World*) in 1552, shortly after his "immutation." Mistaking the identity of Anjirō, he ascribes the report to a Jesuit priest and to "M. Paul, gouverneur du collège de sainte-Fois." But for Postel, it was the Japanese who were mistaken. Centuries before the German Jesuit and theologian Karl Rahner set forth his notion of the "anonymous Christian," Postel describes the religion of Japan as "the most marvelous religion in the world, which remains without knowing its author, who is Jesus Christ, his name unknown." This circumstance arose because Japan's priests "slowly converted the truth of Jesus into the fable of Schiaca." Yet for Postel, the signs are unmistakable. The central figure of the report was born in a country beyond China called Cegnico (that is, Tenjiku, the Japanese name for India), which Postel identifies with Judea. His father is Jambon Daino (Jōbon Dai Ō in Japanese), and his mother was Magabonin (Maya Bunin in Japanese); for Postel they are clearly Joseph and

Mary. He continues in this way. Postel's comments on Lancilotto's report appear in italics in his text:

•

To this king *to Joseph or to all of the Judaic or Abrahamic Church* [came]
in a dream *this is the Gospel, speaking of Joseph,* I know not what small
child *According to ancient sources, the angel was the cherubim, that is to
say, they were like small children, announcing and speaking in the name of
God, who sent them* appeared in a dream or in a vision saying, I want to
be born and will be born from your wife *For this is what the virgin was
called* and this vision came to him three times. He was most astonished
and after he told the Queen he decided not to touch her for that month
or ever again, and in this way, without the deed of a man, she found
herself pregnant. *This is the divine incarnation known by the astronomy
of the Magi, who were neighbors of that place, as from here to Jerusalem.*
And after she gave birth she died *in this way the false is joined to the true
as we see in the Old Testament where holy things are told through fables.*
When the father saw this he sent the child to be brought up by his sister. He was called Schiaca, and as soon as he was born two serpents of
extraordinary size came to him and bathed him in water. *This is confused with the memory of baptism, of which all are baptized, in the survival
of this fable, and the serpents are from the memory of Satan, who appeared
first in a serpent and was condemned under the name of serpent.* And his
legs and limbs grew so that he could stand up in his third month *which
signifies his divine nature.* Holding one hand to Heaven and the other to
the earth he said, I was the sole emperor of Heaven and earth *these are
the very words where he said: the complete power of Heaven and earth is
given to me.* He was nineteen years old when his father wanted to force
him to marry, but when he considered human misery, he did not want
to obey his father or know a woman. In the night he fled to a mountain.
*For most of the life and the teaching of the Savior took place in the moun-
tains.* There he spent six years in penance. After he left the mountain,
he began to preach with such marvelous devotion that the people who
were idolaters benefitted so much that they admired him immediately
and he changed their laws, teaching them all the way to worship God.
He assembled eight thousand disciples who followed his way of living *a
number that is certainly uncertain* and from among whom a certain number went into the land of the Chinese *who are the ancient Sines or their*

neighbors where they preached his holy laws so that they converted them all to their teaching and doctrine *and their words went out to the ends of the earth* and broke their idols and destroyed their temples and the places where they were worshipped, they did not hesitate to ruin them *by this we see with certainty that the fable of Sciaca, or if we read the letter x in the Spanish way, Xaca, is nothing other than a dark cloud drawn from the Gospel story. For there have never been but two destroyers of idols and their temples, one without sword and force, but only the goodness of his life and the truth of his teaching, the other by the sword and a most evil and vicious life. The first is Jesus Christ, the second is Mohammed, of whom it is most certain that such a fable could not be composed, for he has in all the Orient a world of devotees who know his story through the Coran. But in the Orient, before books or doctrine confirmed by councils could be joined to the good and miraculous life, tyrants and the false priests of idols and heretics destroyed the good principles, and so Jesus appeared as the omnipotent conservator of order and of life, even though they had no knowledge of the doctrine of the Gospels as such.* Having arrived in Giapan, they did the same, so that even up to our time, you can see bits and pieces of statues and idols on that aforementioned island. This Xaca taught that there is one God, creator of all things, and he had him painted with one body and three heads. *This shows us clearly, not simply by the image but by doctrine and signification that he was Jesus Christ, who alone revealed the doctrine of God Three in One, against which principally the bastards and half-Jews, the Ismaelites, have, through their Muhammad, raised themselves as much as they are able.*[10]

•

And so, Xaca destroyed idols, whose remnants can still be seen in Japan. And because there have been only two destroyers of idols in history—Jesus and Muhammad (it is unclear why the Hebraist Postel does not mention Moses)—one who did so with his goodness and one who did so with his sword, and because Xaca apparently destroyed idols peacefully, it follows that Xaca is Jesus. This is the reasoning of Postel, a reasoning perfected by the gift of the Virgin of Venice. He ends the passage by condemning the Muslims (descendants of Ishmael, son of Abraham and the slave Hagar, hence "bastards and half-Jews") for their rejection of Jesus.

The view that the Buddha is not an idol but a smasher of idols would quickly change after Francis Xavier arrived in Japan in 1549. He would describe the Buddha (whom he also called Xaca) as "the pure invention of demons."[11] Anjirō had explained to Father Xavier that the Japanese believed in a god who was the creator of the universe and who rewarded the good and punished the evil. This god, he said, was named Dainichi. Dainichi, literally "Great Sun" in Japanese, is the name of the important buddha Vairocana, central to the Shingon sect of Japanese Buddhism. Upon Francis Xavier's arrival in Japan, he began preaching about Dainichi, proclaiming in the streets, *Dainichi wo ogami are* (Pray to Dainichi). This attracted the interest of Shingon priests, who seemed to regard the Jesuits as Buddhist monks from India. Xavier soon became suspicious when the priests appeared uninformed concerning the incarnation and passion of Christ; he then instructed his Portuguese companion, Brother Fernández, to go into the streets and tell the people that Dainichi was an invention of the devil, and to shout, *Dainichi na ogami asso* (Do not pray to Dainichi). Both statements seemed to confuse the Japanese, since in the slang of the day, *dainichi* was also a term for the female genitalia. From that point onward, the Jesuits used a word of their own invention for God: *Daiusu*, their attempt to render the Latin *Deus* into Japanese. Again, they encountered problems, because *daiusu* sounded like *dai usō*, "great lie" in Japanese. Children began throwing rocks at the priests. Yet despite these embarrassments, the life of the Roman Catholic mission to Japan in the sixteenth and seventeenth centuries—a life that was short and ended in a violent death—would be one of the most successful in Buddhist lands, when success is measured in the number of converts.[12]

In 1582, Matteo Ricci (1552–1610) arrived on the Chinese island of Macau. The founder of the Jesuit mission in China was his colleague Michele Ruggieri (1543–1607). Father Ruggieri had established good relations with the governor-general of Guangdong and Guangxi Provinces, who suggested that the Christian fathers adopt the garb of Buddhist monks in order to look less foreign. As we will see, Europeans thought that Buddhist monks looked like Catholic priests. In addition, it seems that the Chinese thought that Catholic priests looked like Buddhist monks, even in their own garb. And from the Chinese perspective, the similarities were not simply superficial. Both religious orders were celibates who taught a foreign religion that had come from the West. And so the Jesuits cropped their hair and shaved off their beards and donned the robes of Buddhist monks, providing themselves with visible markers that would be understood in China, hoping that the Chinese would mistake them, at least initially, for Buddhist monks. And it is likely that they were initially regarded as such, an impression reinforced by the plaque on their residence in the city of Zhaoqing that read: "Pure Land of the West" (*xilai jingtu*), a term that would evoke for the Chinese Western Pure Land (*xifang jingtu*), the pure land of the buddha Amitābha. The priests were referred to by the Chinese as *heshang* and *seng*, two terms used for the monks. And they introduced themselves as "Buddhist monks from India" and "Buddhist monks from the Western Pure Land," perhaps leaving ambiguous whether the latter referred to Amitābha's heaven or their street address in Zhaoqing.

Thirteen years later, in 1595, at the urging of his Chinese scholar friends and with the permission of his superior, Ricci and the Jesuits abandoned the dress of Buddhist monks—whom, he reports, the Chinese held as "vile and lowly"—for the long beard and silk robes of the Confucian scholar.[13] From that point onward, Ricci's slogan would be *qin ru pai fo*, "Draw close to Confucianism and repudiate Buddhism." In 1603, he would condemn Buddhism in his catechism, *Tianzhu shiyi* (*The True Doctrine of the Lord of Heaven*), written in Chinese. No longer wishing to be mistaken for a Buddhist monk, he argues in these pages that the very presence of Buddhism in China was a case of mistaken identity. He recounts the famous story, discussed in chapter 1, of the dream of Emperor Ming and the delegation sent to the West to retrieve the teachings of the Golden Man. In describing Jesus, he writes:

•

When His work of preaching was complete He ascended to Heaven in broad daylight at a time forecast by Himself. Four saints recorded the deeds he had performed whilst on earth, as well as His teachings. These were transmitted to many countries, and large numbers of people from all quarters believed in Him, keeping his commandments from one generation to another. From this time onwards many nations in the West took great strides along the road to civilization.

When we examine Chinese history we find that Emperor Ming of the Han dynasty heard of these events and sent ambassadors on a mission to the West to search for canonical writings. Midway these ambassadors mistakenly took India to be their goal, and returned to China with Buddhist scriptures which were then circulated throughout the nation. From then until now the people of your esteemed country have been deceived and misled. That they have not heard the correct Way is truly a great tragedy for the field of learning. Was it not a disaster?[14]

•

So it had all been a mistake. The emperor's dream in fact foretold the coming of Christ to China, not the coming of the Buddha. The Christian missionaries were therefore carrying out the emperor's instructions as his own envoys had not, by bringing the teachings of the Golden Man from the West to China. Furthermore, any similarity that the Chinese might discern between Buddhism and Christianity, such as the fact that both assert the existence of heaven and hell, was the result of a more willful error: "Things may be similar in one or two respects yet quite different in reality. The Religion of the Lord of Heaven [meaning God] is a very ancient religion, and Sakyamuni lived in the West. He must secretly have heard of this teaching. Anyone wishing to promote his own school of thought must insert two or three elements of orthodoxy into it otherwise no one will believe him. Sakyamuni borrowed the doctrines concerning the Lord of Heaven, Heaven and Hell [from us] in order to promote his private views and heterodox teachings; we transmit the correct Way."[15]

Elsewhere in his text, Ricci describes the Buddha as a small man who, illumined by the light of the Lord of Heaven, possessed some talent. But the Buddha became arrogant and boastful, feeling that he was as worthy of worship as the Lord, teaching such benighted doctrines as reincarnation and the prohibition against killing animals. If the Lord of Heaven did not want men to kill animals for food, Ricci argues, why did he make their flesh taste so good?[16]

Matteo Ricci died in Beijing on May 11, 1610. In the two years before his death, he began writing, at the request of the General of the Society of Jesus, a history of Christianity in China. This work was later found unfinished in his desk. In late 1611, the Flemish Jesuit Nicolas Trigault (1577–1628) arrived in Beijing. However, he was quickly recalled to Europe to serve as procurator for the Jesuits' China mission. On the voyage home, he began the task of translating Ricci's manuscript, composed in Italian, into Latin. Trigault also edited and expanded it, into a book he called *De Christiana expeditione apud sinas ...* (*The Christian Expedition among the Chinese undertaken by the Society of Jesus from the commentaries of Father Matteo Ricci of the same Society ... in which the customs, laws, and principles of the Chinese kingdom and the most difficult first beginnings of the new Church there are accurately and with great fidelity described*). He added, "authored by Fr. Nicolas Trigault, Flemish, of the same Society." First published in Latin in 1616, *De Christiana expeditione apud sinas* proved immensely popular, being translated into French, German, Spanish, Italian, and English by 1625.

Father Trigault returned to China in 1619 and would spend the rest of his days there, developing great proficiency in Chinese, even translating *Aesop's Fables*. But his knowledge of the language led to his unhappy end: he apparently committed suicide over a dispute about how to translate *God* into Chinese. He favored the traditional Chinese term *Shangdi*, "High Sovereign."

Because of Trigault's contributions, *De Christiana expeditione apud sinas* is sometimes referred to as "Ricci-Trigault." The passage below concerning Buddhism, however, derives entirely from Matteo Ricci. Writing about "the second sect" of China, what we call Buddhism, he saw further evidence of the sin of plagiarism:

•

It is historically clear that this doctrine was brought into China at the identical period in which the Apostles were preaching the doctrine of Christ. Bartholomew was preaching in upper India, namely in Hindustan and the surrounding countries, when Thomas was spreading the Gospel in lower India, to the South. It is not beyond the realm of possibility, therefore, that the Chinese, moved and interested by reports of the truths contained in the Christian Gospel, sought to contact it and to learn it from the West. Instead, however, either through error on the part of their legates, or perhaps through ill-will toward the Gospel on the part of the people they visited, the Chinese received a false importation in place of the truth they were seeking.

It would seem that the original authors of the teachings of this second sect had drawn certain of their ideas from our philosophers of the West. For example, they recognize only four elements, to which the

Chinese, rather foolishly, add a fifth. According to the latter, the entire material world—men, beasts, plants, and mixed bodies—is composed of the elements of fire, water, earth, metal, and wood. With Democritus and his school, they believe in a multiplicity of worlds. Their doctrine of the transmigration of souls sounds like that of Pythagoras, except that they have added much commentary and produced something still more hazy and obscure. This philosophy seems not only to have borrowed from the West but to have actually caught a glimpse of light from the Christian Gospels. The doctrine of this second sect mentions a certain trinity in which three different gods are fused into one deity, and it teaches reward for the good in heaven and punishment for the wicked in hell. They make so much of celibacy that they seem to reject marriage entirely and it is a common custom with them to abandon their homes and families and to go on pilgrimage to beg alms. In some respects their profane rites resemble our own ecclesiastical ceremonies, as for instance their recitation in chant which hardly differs from our Gregorian. There are statues in their temples and the vestments worn by those offering a sacrifice are not unlike our copes. In reciting prayers they frequently repeat a certain name, which they pronounce Tolome but which they themselves do not understand. Again, it might possibly be that in doing this they wish to honor their cult with the authority of the Apostle Bartholomew.

Whatever ray of truth there may be in their doctrine is, however, unfortunately obscured by clouds of noisome mendacity. Heaven and earth are quite confused in their ideas, as are also a place of reward and one of punishment, in neither of which do they look for an eternity for souls departed. These souls are supposed to be reborn after a certain number of years in some one of the many worlds which they postulate. There they may do penance for their crimes if they wish to make amends for them. This is only one of the many nonsensical doctrines with which they have afflicted the unfortunate country.[17]

•

Here, Ricci finds all manner of things that remind him of the true faith, but which are somehow false. The three gods fused into one (perhaps the three bodies of the Buddha) remind him of the Holy Trinity; other missionaries saw it in the three-headed idols. Buddhist monks are celibate like Catholic priests, they go on pilgrimage, and their chants sound Gregorian. The religion of the idolaters looks like and sounds like Christianity, and may indeed derive from it.

Ricci goes on to note that the priests recite prayers that they themselves cannot understand, called *tolome*. He is referring to the Chinese term *tuoloni*, which represents the Sanskrit *dhāraṇī*, the long mantras found in many Mahāyāna sutras, often incomprehensible even in Sanskrit and thus rendered phonetically in Chinese. But for Ricci, *tuoloni* sounds like *tolome*, and *tolome* sounds like *Bartholomew*. And indeed, according to a tradition—reported in the fourth century by such distinguished doctors of the church as Saints Jerome and Ambrose—the apostle Bartholomew had, like Doubting Thomas, gone to India, leaving there the Gospel of Matthew written in Hebrew. Perhaps the Buddhist monks were unwittingly chanting some version of that. But the similarities evoke in Ricci not feelings of kinship but rather a sense of annoyance, wondering how the idolaters could have gotten things so wrong. They speak of heaven and hell, but these are places of temporary rebirth, not the permanent abodes of the blessed and the damned; everything is mendacious and confused.

European travelers to Asia consistently noted similarities between Buddhist monks and Catholic priests, and were either outraged or amused by these similarities, depending on whether they themselves were Catholic or Protestant. The English travel writer (and Protestant) Samuel Purchas (1575?-1626), describing Sri Lanka, suggests that the influence may have flowed in the other direction:

•

In Vintane, is a *Pagode* or Idol-temple, the compasse whereof is an hundred and thirtie paces: it is very high, and all white except on the toppe, which hath the spires thereof gilded, in so much that men are not able, when the Sunne shineth, to looke thereon. It hath a Tower or square Steeple of excellent workmanshippe. There are many other Temples, and a Monasterie also of Religious persons, which are attired in yellow, have their crownes shaven, with Beads in their hands, and always seem to mumble over somewhat of their devout orisons, being in high estimation of sanctitie with the vulgar, and freed from publike labours and burthens. Their Monasterie is built after the manner of the Popish, being also gilded with gold. In their Chappells are many Images of both sexes, which they say represent some of their Saints: they are set on the Altars, and are cloathed with garments of gold and silver. . . . Any man that should see it (saith our Author) would thinke, our Westerne Monkes had hence borrowed their Ceremonies.[18]

·

It was during this period that accounts of the life of the Buddha, more detailed than the one provided by Marco Polo, began to appear. These accounts, often by missionaries, in other cases by diplomats and various and sundry travelers, derived not from the direct translation of Buddhist texts but rather from oral reports, likely heard with varying degrees of comprehension. Accordingly, Simon de la Loubère, the envoy of Louis XIV to the king of Siam in 1687 complains, "'Tis no fault of mine that they gave me not the life of *Sommona-Codom* translated from their Books, but not being able to obtain it, I will here relate what was told me thereof."[19] He then goes on to provide a fairly lengthy account of the life of the Buddha, or Sommona-Codom, as he calls him, including the following: "'Tis said, that he bestowed all his Estate in Alms, and that his Charity not being yet satisfied, he pluck'd out his Eyes, and slew his Wife and Children, to give them to the *Talapoins* of his Age to eat. A strange contrariety of Idea's in this People, who prohibit nothing so much as to kill, and who relate the most execrable Parricides, as the most meritorious works of *Sommona-Codom*."[20] *Talapoin* is the term used by the Europeans—first the Portuguese, then the French, then more generally—to refer to a Buddhist monk, especially the Theravāda monks of Southeast Asia. The French claimed that the name derived from the palm-leaf fan that monks often carried, called *talapat*. However, it likely derives from an old Burmese form of address to a monk, *tala pôi*, "my lord."

De la Loubère, after expressing his dismay at not receiving a full translation of the life of Sommona-Codom—the Thai version of a standard epithet for the Buddha in Sanskrit, Śramaṇa Gautama, or the "Ascetic Gautama"—presents a rather muddled version, apparently confusing the famous story of Prince Vessantara, actually the Buddha in a previous life, who displayed his extraordinary generosity by giving away his wife and children. In de la Loubère's version, he first kills them and then feeds them to monks.

Reading de la Loubère's *Du royaume de Siam*, published in Paris and Amsterdam in 1691 and two years later in English as *A New Historical*

Relation of the Kingdom of Siam, one is struck by the fact that his description of the life of the Buddha is only one-third as long as his description of the life of "Thevetat," or Devadatta, the Buddha's cousin. The reason derives from perhaps the most consequential case of mistaken identity in the history of the European encounter with Buddhism.

The Enemy of My Enemy

In the stories of the Buddha's life, there are two villains: one divine, one human. The divine villain is Māra, the Buddhist deity of desire and death. It is Māra who attacks the Buddha under the Bodhi tree, trying to prevent his achievement of buddhahood. It is Māra who extracts from the Buddha the promise to enter nirvana when his work is done, rather than live "for an eon or until the end of the eon." The human villain is in many ways a more interesting figure. He is Devadatta, the Buddha's cousin.

After his enlightenment, the Buddha returned to his home city of Kapilavastu, where he preached the dharma to his family and kinsmen. Several of his relatives joined the order of monks, including two of his cousins: Ānanda, who would eventually become the Buddha's personal attendant, and one of the most beloved figures in the history of Buddhism; and Devadatta, who would become the Buddha's chief antagonist, and one of the most reviled figures in the history of Buddhism.

According to the legends of the Buddha's previous lives, the "birth" stories, or *jātaka*, Devadatta's animus toward the Buddha extended back over many lives. At the end of each story, the Buddha identifies the characters therein with one of his contemporaries. The hero of the story is the Buddha; his companion is often Ānanda or his disciple Śāriputra. The villain is often Devadatta.

Yet in accounts that may date from a period closer to the actual events, Devadatta is a more complicated figure. He became a monk when the Buddha returned to his home city after his enlightenment (according to some accounts, one year afterward), and seems to have been a dedicated monk for decades. It was only when the Buddha grew old that the trouble began. Eight years before the Buddha's passage into nirvana, Devadatta went to him and suggested that in light of the Buddha's advanced age (he was seventy-two years old), leadership of the order of monks should be turned over to him. In front of the entire assembly of monks, Devadatta rose, threw his upper robe over his shoulder, approached the Buddha, and with his palms joined as a sign of respect said, "Lord, the Blessed One is now old, burdened with years, advanced in life and come to the last stage. Let the Blessed One now rest. Let him dwell in bliss in the present life. Let him hand over the order of monks to me. I will govern the order of monks." The Buddha refused. Yet he often refused a first request, only to agree the third time. When Devadatta asked the third time, the Buddha again refused, adding, "Why would I turn over the order to a clot of spittle like you?"[21]

Smarting from this public humiliation, Devadatta sought revenge; he plotted to assassinate the Buddha. First he hired sixteen archers to kill him, but the Buddha ended up converting each of them. Next, Devadatta decided to kill the Buddha himself, by pushing a large boulder down Vulture Peak as the Buddha was walking back and forth in its shade. Two large outcroppings miraculously rose out of the mountain to block its path, but a splinter of rock broke off and struck the Buddha's toe, causing it to bleed. (That he was injured at all was said to be the residual effect of having murdered his brother in a previous life in order to inherit the family fortune.) After he attempted to kill the Buddha, Devadatta was berated by the nun Utpalavarṇā. She was an *arhat*, that is, someone who has achieved enlightenment and will enter nirvana at death. Devadatta became enraged and murdered her. He then tried a third time to murder the Buddha, by sending a mad elephant to trample him. But when the beast reached the Buddha, it knelt before him and the Buddha stroked its head, a scene widely depicted in Buddhist art.

Unable to kill the Buddha, Devadatta determined to win the allegiance of the order of monks. He recommended that all monks follow five rules: (1) they should live their entire lives in the forest and not live in villages; (2) they should live entirely on the alms they received from begging and not accept invitations to dine in the homes of the laity; (3) they should wear only robes made from discarded rags and not accept offerings of cloth for robes from the laity; (4) they should dwell at the foot of a tree and not under a roof; (5) they should not eat fish or meat. Hearing of this, the Buddha declared that any monk who wished to obey these rules (apart from living under a tree during the rainy season) was free to do so, but he would not make these practices obligatory. Devadatta then denounced the Buddha for being lax in the practice of asceticism, apparently gaining a substantial following of newly ordained monks in doing so, for they departed with Devadatta. But these monks were quickly persuaded to return. Devadatta vomited blood at the news of their desertion. Knowing that his end was near, he set off to see the Buddha one last time. According to some accounts, he was sincerely contrite. According to others, he smeared poison on his fingernails for a final assassination attempt. As he rested at the shore of a pond where he had stopped to bathe, he was slowly swallowed by the earth—first his feet, then his knees, then his chest, then his neck. When only his head remained and his jawbone touched the ground, he declared:

•

With these bones, with these vital airs, I seek refuge in the Buddha,
Preeminent among men, god of gods, charioteer of untamed humanity,
All-seeing, endowed with the auspicious marks of a hundred virtues.

•

But Devadatta disappeared, descending to Avīci, where he suffered a horrible fate. The Avīci (Incessant) hell is the most horrific of the sixteen Buddhist hells (eight hot, eight cold). It is located at the greatest distance beneath the surface of the earth, with the longest life span and the most terrible sufferings. In the other hot hells, the denizens undergo various forms of gruesome torture, but here their bodies become indistinguishable from a fire that never goes out. All that remains is their voice. According to Buddhist doctrine, there are five deeds, called "deeds of immediate retribution," that cause one to be reborn immediately in Avīci, without an intervening lifetime elsewhere. They are (1) killing one's father, (2) killing one's mother, (3) killing an arhat, (4) wounding a buddha, and (5) causing dissension in the monastic community. Devadatta committed the third, fourth, and fifth of these.

Thus, Devadatta suffered a particularly horrible fate. Once in hell, his body grew to be a hundred leagues tall, such that his head touched the top of the vast chamber of Avīci, and his feet sunk up to his ankles into its surface of solid iron. His head was placed inside an iron helmet that held him motionless. Then, as the commentary to the *Dhammapada* explains, "An iron stake as thick as the trunk of a palmyra tree proceeded forth from the west wall of the iron shell, pierced the small of his back, came forth from his breast, and penetrated the east wall. Another iron stake proceeded forth from the south wall, pierced his right side, came forth from his left side, and penetrated the north wall. Another iron stake proceeded forth from the top of the iron skull, pierced his skull, came forth from his lower parts, and penetrated earth of iron. In this position, immovable, he suffers this mode of torture." Devadatta is thus impaled for eons, unable to move. As the text says, "Since he sinned against an unchanging Buddha, let him endure torture unchanging."[22]

We find an accurate rendering of Devadatta's infernal state in Simon de la Loubère's *De royaume de Siam*, in a section entitled "The Life of Thevetat, Translated from the Balie," that is, the Pāli, the canonical language of the Theravāda tradition of Buddhism practiced in Sri Lanka and Southeast Asia. In de la Loubère's account, Devadatta becomes Thevetat (in the 1693 English translation; Tévétat in the original French), Avīci is Avethi, and the Buddha is Sommona-Codom. But otherwise, the rendition is quite faithful:

•

Mean while *Thevetat* was buried in the Earth, and even to Hell where he is without possibility of removing, for want of having loved *Sommona-Codom*. His Body is the heighth of a *Jod*, that is to say, Eight Thousand Fadom: he is in the Hell *Avethi*, 650 Leagues in greatness: on his head he has a great Iron pot all red with fire, and which came to his Shoulders: he has his Feet sunk into the Earth up to the Ankles, and all inflamed. Moreover a great Iron Spit which reaches from the West to the East, pierces through his Shoulders and comes out at his Breast. Another pierces him through the sides, which comes from the South, and goes to the North, and crosses all Hell. And another enters through his Head, and pierces him to the Feet. Now all these Spits do stick at both ends, and are thrust a great way into the Earth. He is standing, without being able to stir, or lye down.[23]

•

But why was the French legation to the court of Siam so interested in the story of Devadatta? Alexandre, chevalier de Chaumont (1650–1710), was the first ambassador sent by Louis XIV to Siam. In the account of his embassy of 1685, he briefly describes the religion of Siam, referring to the Buddha as Nacodon, apparently an abbreviation of Sommona-Codom:

•

The last of these three *Talapoins* is the greatest God called Nacodon, because he has been in five thousand bodies; in one of these Transmigrations, of *Talapoin* he became a Cow, his brother would have killed him several times; but there needs a great book to describe the miracles, which they say, Nature, and not God wrought for his preservation. In short, his Brother was thrown into Hell for his great sins, where Nacodon caused him to be crucified; and for this foolish reason they abominate the Image of Christ on the Cross, saying we adore the image of this Brother of their God, who was crucified for his Crimes.[24]

•

The chevalier de Chaumont was accompanied by two priests, the Abbé du Choisy and the Jesuit Guy Tachard (1651–1712). The former, a noted diarist and transvestite, was more interested in the idols and especially how much gold they contained.[25] But Father Tachard, to whom we will return below, provides a detailed description of the life of the Buddha, in the course of which he laments the connection with Devadatta:

•

Tho there be many things that keep the *Siamese* at a distance from the Christian Law, yet one may say, nothing makes them more averse from it than this thought. The similitude that is to be found in some points betwixt their Religion and ours, making them believe that Jesus Christ, is the very same with that *Thevathat* mentioned in their Scriptures, they are perswaded that seeing we are the Disciples of the one, we are also the followers of the other, and the fear they have of falling into Hell with *Thevathat*, if they follow his Doctrine, suffers them not to hearken to the propositions that are made to them of embracing Christianity. That which most confirms them in their prejudice, is that we adore the

image of our Crucified Savior, which plainly represents the punishment of *Thevathat*. So when we would explain to them the Articles of
our Faith; they take us always up short, saying that they do not need
our Instructions, and that they know already better than we do, what
we have a mind to tell them.[26]

·

And so Simon de la Loubère asked for and received a Pāli account
of the life of Devadatta, which he then had translated into French.
Giving new meaning to "the enemy of my enemy is my friend," the
French may have felt that they might learn something from the life
of the Buddha's antagonist as they themselves sought to save the
Siamese from perdition and convert them from idolatry to the true
faith.

The Thai Buddhists at court must have immediately been struck by
the fact that the French priests were wearing little statues of Devadatta around their necks. But even if the most famous case of crucifixion in Buddhism had not involved the monk who tried to murder
the Buddha, Buddhists likely would have found it odd that anyone
would honor a being who had suffered such a fate. What horrible deed
could such a being have committed to deserve that punishment as its
karmic effect? And if he were a being worthy of worship, why did he
lack the powers to escape the cross? At that early point in the history
of Buddhist-Christian dialogue, it is unlikely that the fine points of
the theology of the Lamb of God could have been conveyed effectively
from French into Thai.

From another perspective, the Siamese suspicion seems to have
been well founded. Devadatta's only sin was his greed for power.
He did not doubt the efficacy of the Buddha's teachings, he did not
question that the Buddha was, indeed, the enlightened one. He simply wanted to succeed him as head of the order after the Buddha
had grown old. But those who came from Europe wearing crucifixes
around their necks would declare the teachings of the Buddha to be a
lie, and insist that the Buddha's followers reject them and worship instead the one who had suffered the fate of Devadatta. Even in the late
eighteenth century, we find the claim that the story of Devadatta was
not original to Buddhism, but had been concocted by the Buddhists

after the arrival of the Portuguese in India in 1498, in an effort to prevent conversion to the Roman Catholic faith. We read the following in a footnote in the Scottish (and Protestant) physician Francis Buchanan's important essay, "On the Religion and Literature of the Burmas," published in *Asiatick Researches* in 1801: "The *Siammese* painter beforementioned told me, that DEVADAT, or, as he pronounced it, TEVEDAT, was the god of the *Pye-gye*, or of *Britain*; and he conceived, that it is he who, by opposing the good intentions of GODAMA, produces all the evil in the world. I am inclined to believe, that the legend of TEVEDAT, of which M. LOUBERE has given us a translation, has been composed since the arrival of the *Portuguese* in *India*, in order to prevent the propagation of their religion, so well adapted, by its splendour and mysteries, to gain the belief of an ignorant people."[27]

Lives of the Idol

The French interest in Devadatta did not mean, however, that they were uninterested in his antagonist. Guy Tachard, mentioned earlier, was a French Jesuit and a member of both the 1685 and the 1687 delegations of Louis XIV to the court of Siam. Among the host of fascinating figures who visited Buddhist lands and wrote about the Buddha, Tachard is one of the most colorful and the most infamous — widely despised, it seems, by all who knew him. His fellow missionary and member of the second delegation to Siam, Bénigne Vachet (1641–1720), wrote in his memoirs, "It would need a blacker ink than mine to paint the true portrait of Fr. Tachard. If I were to say he was an ecclesiastic, a host of witnesses would rise up against me to say he was unworthy of this glorious name. If I call him a Jesuit, I would do injustice to the Company which suffers him to remain in its fold after all the accusations formulated against him. If ever a man were imbued with foolhardiness to a degree beyond which it would not be possible to proceed, it is Fr. Tachard."[28] Despite these flaws in his character, Tachard spent much time in Thailand, and in the company of Thais (he accompanied a Thai embassy to the Vatican in 1688 and translated the Thai king's letter to Pope Innocent XI) — learning their language, learning about their religion, and learning about the founder of their religion:

•

The Religion of the *Siamese* is very odd, and cannot be perfectly understood but by the Books that are written in the *Balis* [Pāli] Language, which is the Learned language, and hardly understood by any, except some of their Doctors. Nor do these Books . . . always agree amongst themselves. This following account of their Religion is the most exact that possibly I could attain to.

The *Siamese* believe a God, but they have not the same notion of him that we have. By that word they understand a being perfect after their manner, consisting of Spirit and Body, whose property it is to assist men. That assistance consists in giving them a Law, prescribing them the ways of living well, teaching them the true Religion, and the Sciences that are necessary unto them. The perfections which they attribute unto him are all the moral virtues, possessed by him in an eminent degree acquired by many acts, and confirmed by a continual exercise in all the Bodies he hath past through.

He is free from passions, and feels no motion that can alter his tranquillity; but they affirm that before he arrived at that State, he made so prodigious a change in his Body by struggling to overcome his Passions, that his blood is become white. He hath the Power to appear when he pleases, and also to render himself invisible to the eyes of men; and he hath such wonderful agility, that in a moment he can be in any place of the world he pleases.

He knoweth all without having ever learnt any thing from men, whose Doctor and Master he himself is, and that universal knowledg is inherent in his state, having possessed it from the instant that he was born God; it consists not as ours does, in a train of consequences, but in a clear, simple and intuitive vision, which all at once represents to him the Precepts of the Law, Vices, Virtues, and the most hidden secrets of Nature, things past, present and come, Heaven, Earth, Paradice, Hell, this Universe which we see, and even what is done in the other Worlds which we know not. He distinctly remembers all that hath ever befallen him from the first transmigration of his Soul, even to the last.

His body is infinitely more radiant than the Sun, it lights that which is most hidden, and by the help of the light that it diffuses, a man here below upon Earth, might, that I may make use of their expression, see a grain of Mustard seed placed in the Highest Heavens.

The happiness of the God is not compleat, but when he dies never to be born again: for then he appears no more upon the Earth, nor is he any more subject to Misery. They compare that death to a torch extinct, or to a sleep that renders us insensible of the Evils of Life, with this difference that when God dies, he is exempted from them for ever, whereas a man asleep is but free from them for a certain time.

This reign of every Deity lasts not eternally, it is confined to a certain number of years, that's to say, until the number of the elect who are to be sanctified by his Merits be accomplished; after which he appears no more in the World but slides into an Eternal repose, which was thought to have been a real annihilation, because they were not rightly understood. Then another God succeeds to him, and governs the Universe in his place, which is nothing else but to teach men the true Religion.[29]

·

Tachard provides a remarkably accurate description, albeit in his own vocabulary, of buddhahood, never naming the Buddha by his Thai name but simply referring to him as "the God." The Buddha is indeed often described as perfect, and his primary purpose is to benefit the world, which he accomplishes largely through teaching the dharma, a term that, among its many meanings in Sanskrit, also means "law." The Buddha is said to be endowed with ten perfections (*pāramī*) in the Theravāda tradition of Thailand: giving, ethics, renunciation, wisdom, effort, patience, truthfulness, resolution, love, and equanimity. These are indeed "moral virtues, possessed by him in an eminent degree." And they are "acquired by many acts." The bodhisattva is said to practice infinite forms of these ten perfections over the course of billions of lifetimes on the path to buddhahood.

Tachard also accurately describes some of the wondrous powers of the Buddha, such as the ability to appear anywhere in the world through the use of his mind-made body (*manomayakāya*). It is also true that a buddha achieves enlightenment without relying on a teacher; rather, he is one "whose Doctor and Master he himself is." It is not the case, however, that a buddha is fully endowed with universal knowledge from the moment of his birth; this knowledge is achieved at the moment of his enlightenment. Yet Tachard is correct that the mind of a buddha operates always through direct perception and not through our processes of thought. And he is said to know the past, present, and future, everything that is occurring everywhere in the universe, and the events of each of his countless past lives.

Tachard next describes a buddha's passage into nirvana (without using the word), noting that when a buddha dies, unlike the death of ordinary men, he is never reborn and is forever free from suffering; passing into nirvana is often described as being like a flame going out. Thus, the God is not eternal. It is said that the Buddha could have lived "for an eon or until the end of the eon" had he been asked to do so; but shortly after his enlightenment, he agreed to enter nirvana after he had taught everyone there was to teach, "the number of the elect who are to be sanctified by his Merits." Tachard then notes, almost in passing, that the eternal repose of nirvana has been mistaken as "a real annihilation." As we shall see, this mistake, if in fact it is a mistake, would appear again and again in European descriptions of the Buddha and his teaching. Tachard ends his account by noting that after one buddha has passed into nirvana, "another God succeeds to him, and governs the Universe in his place." Here he is referring to the buddha of the future, Maitreya.

This, then, is Tachard's description of a buddha and the state of buddhahood, presented as relatively disinterested reportage. He then goes on, in a very different tone, to relate the life of the Buddha himself. Another of Tachard's detractors, the noted cardinal Carlo Tommaso Maillard de Tournon (1668–1710), patriarch of Antioch, apostolic visitor, and papal legate to the Indies and China (and, admittedly, no friend of the Jesuits), described his fellow priest in his memoirs as "an idolater and abominably superstitious."[30] Yet clearly, this idolater was no admirer of the Buddha, as the following passage from Tachard attests:

•

I thought fit to premise all these things before I came to speak of *Sommonokhodom* (so the *Siamese* call the God whom at present they adore) because they are necessary to the understanding of this History. That History, after all, is a monstrous mixture of Christianity and the most ridiculous Fables. It is at first supposed that *Sommonokhodom* was born God by his own virtue; and that immediately after his Birth, without the help of any Master, to instruct Him, he acquired by a meer glance of his Mind, a perfect knowledge of all things relating to Heaven, the

Earth, Paradice, Hell, and the most impenetrable Secrets of Nature; that at the same time he remembred all that ever he had done in the different Lives he had led; and that after he had taught the People those great Matters, he left them written in Books, that Posterity might be the better for them.

In these Books he reports of himself, that being become God, one day he desired to manifest his Divinity to Men by some extraordinary Prodigy, He then Sate under a Tree called *Ton ppô*. . . . He adds, that presently he found himself carried up into the Air in a Throne all shining with Gold and precious Stones, which came out of the Earth in the place where he was; and that at the same instant Angels coming down from Heaven, rendered him the Honours and Adorations that were due unto him. His Brother *Thevathat* and his Followers could not without extream Jealousie behold the Glory and Majesty that environed him. They conspired his Ruin, and having stirred up the Beasts against him, engaged with him in a War. Though he was all alone, he was not terrified by that multitude of Enemies, he resisted all their Attempts without being shaken, and by virtue of his good works which defended him, the shafts they darted at him, were changed into so many Flowers, which far from hurting him, served only to encrease his Honour. In the mean time he confesses that in the brunt of the Battle, when he was most in danger, it was but in vain that he had his recourse to the good works he had done in keeping the Nine first Commandments of the Law, which he found were not sufficient to defend him in this pressing Necessity. But being armed with the tenth Command, which he had inviolably observed, and which enjoyns the practice of Charity towards Men and Beasts, he easily triumphed over his Enemies; and in this manner he obtained that victory. The Female Guardian-Angel of the Earth (for we have already distinguished two Sexes amongst the Angels) coming to him, at first adored him, then turning towards *Thevathat* and his Adherents, she made known to them that *Sommonokhodom* was really become God. She told them, that she had been a Witness of his good Works; and to convince them of that shewed them her own Hair still dripping with the Waters that he poured out in the beginning of his good Actions. . . . In fine, she exhorted them to render him the Adorations that he deserved; but finding them to be hardned and obstinately resolved not to hearken to her remonstrances, she squeezed her wet hair, and pressed out of them an Ocean of Water, wherein they were all drowned.

It is also found written in the books of *Sommonokhodom*, that from the time he aspired to be god, he had returned into the World five hundred and fifty times under various shapes; that in every Regeneration, he had been always the Chief, and, as it were, Prince of the Animals under whose shape he was born; that many times he had given his Life for his Subjects, and that being a Monkey, he had delivered a Town from a horrible Monster that wasted it; that he had been a most potent King, and that seven days before he obtained the Sovereign Dominion of the Universe, he had retired in imitation of some Anchorites, with his Wife and two Children into remote Solitudes; that there he was dead to the World and his Passions in such a degree that without being moved he suffered a *Baramen* who had a mind to try his Patience and carry away his Son and Daughter, and torment them before his face. Nay his mortification went a great deal farther, for he even gave his Wife to a poor Man that begged an Alms, and having put out his own eyes he sacrificed himself by distributing his flesh amongst the Beasts, to stay the hunger that pressed them. From thence they take occasion again to find fault with the Christian Religion, which enjoyns not Men to comfort and assist Beasts in their necessities. These are the rare actions which the *Talapoins* in their Sermons propose to the people for imitation, and the examples they make use of to encline them to virtue.[31]

•

Tachard sees the life of the Buddha as "a monstrous mixture of Christianity and the most ridiculous Fables." There is in fact little that seems Christian here, apart perhaps from the angels; and Tachard himself offers a mixed-up version of the traditional account of the Buddha's enlightenment, or, in the Jesuit missionary's words, his manifestation of "his Divinity to Men by some extraordinary Prodigy." When the Buddha sat down under the Bodhi tree (called *ton pho* in Thai), he did not rise into the air on a golden throne at that time. In some accounts, it is said that in the third week after his enlightenment, in order to demonstrate his attainment to the gods, he created a golden bridge in the air and walked back and forth on it. The Buddha had yet to teach the dharma and thus had no disciples at this time. Thus, the attack on the Buddha that Tachard describes was mounted not by Devadatta (Thevathat) but rather by Māra, the Buddhist deity of desire and death. Knowing that the bodhisattva was seeking to discover a state beyond birth and death, Māra tried to stop him, but the various arrows and spears fired by Māra's army turned into flowers.

Māra eventually sought to unseat the bodhisattva by challenging his right to occupy the spot of earth under the tree. The bodhisattva replied that because he had practiced the ten perfections (enumerated above; Tachard calls them "commandments"), and especially the perfection of giving, over many lifetimes, he had the right to sit there. Then the bodhisattva famously touched the earth with his right hand, calling on the goddess of the earth to bear witness to his virtue over his former lives. She responded with a tremor, and Māra withdrew. However, this story receives a dramatic elaboration in Thailand and Laos, where it is said that the goddess of the earth, called Thorani, appeared and began to wring water from her hair. This was all the water that the bodhisattva had offered each time he performed a virtuous deed over the course of his past lives—so much that the water she wrung from her hair caused a great flood that swept away Māra and his army.

Tachard next turns to the stories of the Buddha's former lives, the famous *jātaka*, or "birth" stories. He correctly reports that the bodhisattva was often reborn as an animal; when he was among other animals, he was their virtuous leader. He was indeed a monkey king who saved not a town but his tribe of monkeys from a water demon in one lifetime; in another lifetime as a monkey he saved his fellow simians from the archers of the king of Banaras.

Tachard ends his description of the life of the Buddha by summarizing the story of Prince Vessantara, the Buddha's last human rebirth before his birth as Prince Siddhārtha. Vessantara did not renounce the world but was banished into the forest with his wife and two children. In an extraordinary, and heartbreaking, display of the perfection of giving, he did indeed give away his children to an evil brahman (*Baramen*) and later gave away his wife. He did not, however, pluck out his eyes and cut off his flesh to feed animals, although such gifts of the body (*dehadāna*) abound in other stories of the Buddha's former lives. Like Matteo Ricci before him, Tachard is perturbed by the Buddhist injunction against killing animals, illustrated by stories of the Buddha's kindness to animals in his former lives.

Despite the fantastic and fanciful elements that Tachard identified in the story of Sommonokhodom, the French delegation to the court of Siam seems to have at least entertained the possibility that the God of the Siamese was not an entirely mythological figure, that he was once a man. Thus, it sought to determine when he might have lived and where he had come from. Tachard's compatriot and fellow missionary, Nicolas Gervaise (circa 1662–1729), spent the years 1681–85 in Siam, traveling widely and holding frequent conversations with the Siamese emissaries to the French court. Father Gervaise seemed to recognize that in some sense, both the Siamese and the Chinese practiced the same religion, and he sought to determine its historical origin—whether a historical figure stood behind the fantastic myths:

•

The era of this religion is very vague, and one cannot tell very exactly when it began nor in what manner it was established. Common opinion says it is about two thousand years old, and the Siamese would like to believe that it originated in their country. Those who have voyaged along the Coromandel coast think that this religion came from the Brahmins by reason of the great similarity that exists between them and the Siamese in religion. The Chinese maintain that the glory is due to their country. It is seen in their books, which are exceedingly old, that Sommonokodom was Chinese. An emperor of China, they say, had sent his ambassador to Siam, and he acquitted himself so well that the King of Siam gave him his daughter in marriage and made him his successor. After having reigned several years to the people's liking, this ambassador voluntarily abdicated his sovereign power and retired to the woods, where the austerity of his life did not, however, prevent his being followed by a great number of people who placed themselves under his guidance. He taught them, not only by his own example, but also by means of precepts full of admirable wisdom. After his death his disciples spread his teaching, and, in order to immortalize their gratitude and his memory, they built temples in his honour and erected statues to him. As century followed century these statues served to cast the Siamese into the practice of idolatry, and led them to look upon Sommonokodom as a God, and, finally, in order to justify their worship of him and to legalize their errors, they invented those stories which their unfortunate posterity have received as fixed truths and articles of faith.[32]

•

In fact, this is not the Chinese story of the origin of the Buddha; it was clear to the Chinese that the Buddha was not from the Middle Kingdom but from the West. Nor did the Siamese think that the Buddha was from their country; like many Buddhist lands, theirs had stories of his magical visitations, when he often left footprints in stone, but it was understood that the Buddha was from India. Yet despite the inaccuracy of his account, Gervaise's discussion is notable for its lack of condemnation; he simply laments that the statues of a man who taught "precepts full of admirable wisdom" eventually came to be worshipped as idols and that the man became a god—a sentiment that would be felt by Europeans for centuries to come.

The garbled versions of the life of the Buddha presented by the French missionaries to Siam may result from an inadequate grasp of Pāli, the canonical language of Theravāda Buddhism. As Guy Tachard writes, the religion of the Siamese "cannot be perfectly understood but by the Books that are written in the *Balis* [Pāli] Language, which is the Learned language, and hardly understood by any, except some of their Doctors." The information that the French possessed appears to have been gleaned from conversation. The situation with regard to Buddhist languages was different in China, where a number of Catholic missionaries, beginning with Matteo Ricci and his party, learned to read Chinese. In his *True Meaning of the Lord of Heaven*, published in Beijing in 1603, Ricci mentions the *Lotus Sutra* by name, although it is unclear whether he read the text himself. However, it is clear that by the time of the Jesuit mission to Siam, Jesuit missionaries in China read Chinese well.

And they learned other languages. Adriano di St. Thecla (1667–1765), an Italian missionary to Vietnam and a monk of the Discalced (or Barefoot) Augustinian Order, arrived in what is today the northern part of that country on April 29, 1738. He quickly gained the ability to read Hán, classical Chinese with Vietnamese pronunciation, as well as to speak vernacular Vietnamese. In his Latin work *Opusculum de Sectis apud Sinenses et Tunkinenses* (*A Small Treatise on the Sects among the Chinese and Tonkinese*), he provided a brief account of the life of the Buddha. Here, the prince is the son of a king who for three years has failed to pay tribute to another king. In order to avoid punishment for his father and his kingdom, the prince volunteers to deliver the

payment to the other king, winning his favor as well as the hand of
his daughter in marriage:

•

When he returned to his father, he was received with the deepest gratitude and exultation of all [the people of the kingdom], and his father
bestowed upon him a special honor by giving him an oriental palace to
live in. But, indeed, he, to cover his name with even more glory, left the
court secretly, keeping his father ignorant, and retreated to the mountains. There he met two demons on the road called A la la (Aluoluo) and
Hác la la (Heiluoluo), and for many days they taught him a doctrine,
which later he passed on to members of his sect, who called him with
a new name, Thích Ca Mâu Ni Phật (Śākyamuni Buddha); having at the
same time accepted [this] new name from those who called themselves
Di Đà (Mituo) and Di Lặc (Milei). He was sitting between the two devils,
who, from the left and from the right, were giving him instructions as
[his assistants]; he listened to [the instructions] and wrote them down
in forty-two treatises, according to the testimony collected in the next
article, and not forty thousand, as some [people] wrote in the books of
the Christians.[33]

•

Here, before returning to the more traditional account of the life
of the Buddha, Father St. Thecla tells a story similar to that recounted
by Gervaise about Prince Siddhārtha serving as envoy, but with certain variations. In Buddhist accounts, after Prince Siddhārtha leaves
the palace and embarks on the path to a deathless state, he studies
with two meditation teachers of the day, Ārāḍa Kālāma and Udraka
Rāmaputra. However, he quickly equals their attainments and goes
on to practice with five ascetics, eventually being abandoned by them;
left alone after six years of searching, he achieves buddhahood. Thus,
the Buddha did not receive instructions from his former teachers—
who are never described as devils—that he then conveyed to others,
as St. Thecla states, but instead taught what he had understood himself as a result of his enlightenment. St. Thecla goes on to state that
the Buddha is flanked by Di Đà (Mituo) and Di Lặc (Milei). These are
Amitābha, the buddha who presides over the pure land of Sukhāvatī,
and Maitreya, the buddha of the future. Śākyamuni is in fact some-

times depicted with them, but they do not offer him instructions, and he does not take dictation. In China, however, the Buddha is regarded as the author of the *Scripture in Forty-two Sections*, to which St. Thecla alludes.

In 1687, the Portuguese Jesuit Fernão de Queyroz (1617–1688), who lived in India from 1635 until the year of his death, completed *The Temporal and Spiritual Conquest of Ceylon*. The title of the work, which seems to imply a history, denotes a prophecy. In 1645, Pedro de Basto, a Portuguese lay brother of the Society of Jesus, died in Cochin in India. Although he had performed only menial duties for the order during his years in the India missions, he was respected for his deep piety and for his visions of Jesus, in which he received prophecies. He predicted, for example, that as punishment for their sins, the Portuguese would lose Ceylon to the Dutch, which in fact occurred after his death, in 1656. But Brother Pedro also predicted that the Portuguese would regain the island from the Dutch. This prophecy never came true, but in preparation for it, Father Queyroz wrote a book about Ceylon that could be used by his compatriots in their conquest.

The Temporal and Spiritual Conquest of Ceylon would not be published in Portuguese until 1916 (with an English translation in 1930). It contains one of the most detailed biographies of the Buddha to be produced by a missionary, written not by Queyroz in India but by another Portuguese Jesuit, Tomás Pereira, in China. Father Pereira was one of the most famous of the Padres da Corte, the Jesuits who served the emperor in Beijing. He served the Kangxi Emperor and instructed the ruler's children in European music. A skilled musician, he wrote a book in Chinese entitled *The Elements of Music*, and performed on both the clavichord and the organ. Pereira built a large organ for the church of Beijing Xuanwumen, described with wonder by many Chinese writers of the day. In 1689, the emperor sent him to Russia to help negotiate the Treaty of Nerchinsk. Upon Pereira's death in Beijing in 1708, the emperor ordered special honors at his funeral.

At the request of his compatriot in Sri Lanka, Queyroz, Pereira had procured a three-volume biography of the Buddha with the assistance of a recent Chinese convert, himself a former Buddhist monk, or, as Queyroz describes him, "a Bonze converted to our Holy Faith, who had been a Prelate among them."[34] From this, and likely with the help of the former Buddhist monk, Pereira produced an eight-thousand-word summary, at the time the most extensive biography of the Buddha in a European language, although it would not be read until the twentieth century. Queyroz included the biography in his account of Sri Lanka, under the title "Account which the Missionaries of China give of the Idol Buddu." Before the biography proper, Pereira provides this note of explanation to Queyroz. He refers to the Buddha by his Chinese name Fô, calling him "the principal Pagode," the principal idol:

•

In order to satisfy the desire of Your Reverence without being irksome, I took no small pains on account of the awkwardness of the Chinese style, so contrary to ours, to put things as far as I could in our own way, for their style would certainly cause great confusion, although as a political nation they do not fail to observe the substantial and common rules of historical composition. For this purpose I thought it best and more to the purpose to give a full account of what the bonzes here believe of their Fô, the principal Pagode out of many others, drawn from the writings, the most authoritative among them, although in everything they are blind and deceived by the Devil. I took this resolution, because I thought that by comparing the fables, many of them invented by those people, with the notices which Your Reverence will find there, any of them would be found to be conflicting, and you would be able by comparision [sic] to discover the falsity of the—for them—infallible Scriptures. It is really unworthy of so cultured a people to deviate so widely from the truth, but when the light of the true Faith does not shine, the saying of St. Paul—*Tradidit illos Deus in reprobum sensum* [Romans 1.28: "God abandoned them to experience depravity"], I very clearly verified.[35]

•

Pereira's account of the life of the Buddha is a fascinating text. It paraphrases many famous stories from the life of the Buddha, but not without comment. Throughout, the Jesuit scholar offers all manner of asides, often with biting sarcasm, and finds occasions to take a swipe at Calvin, to claim that a passage in a Buddhist text is taken from the Qur'an, and to claim that Tibetan monks convince "barren women that they will be fruitful if they touch their [presumably the monks'] genital parts." Particularly painful to Buddhists is the fact that Pereira renders the name of Ānanda (Anan in Chinese), the beloved attendant of the Buddha, as "Onan," well known from the book of Genesis as the man whom God struck dead for spilling his seed on the ground and who is forever associated with the sin of masturbation. And there are frequent references to the devil and his machinations. Thus, when the Buddha, approaching death, describes the potency of his relics with the words, "And as my eternal essence is united to my material body, their merits will be infinite," Pereira notes, "From all this one can see how the Devil counterfeited the mysteries of the Incarnation."[36]

At the conclusion of his rendition of the life of the Buddha, Pereira expresses his suspicions about its origin:

•

This is the substance of their Scripture, printed with great authority and engraven in the Palace in large-sized letters, figures and engravings, which illustrate what is related in each chapter. They say that this translation was made with great authority by Bonzes from India and by learned Chinese, who held conferences and settled the foregoing. But to my mind there is no doubt that the greater part of it is fiction, first of the Devil, and secondly of Chinese cunning, because there are many things which are peculiar to China and are unused in India, which have been adapted to their taste, as for instance the rhymes which are imagined at every step in praise of Fô, for the highest wisdom of the Chinese consists in that, and they end where the Europeans begin, and with their so many thousand letters they do not go further than our students of Rhetoric.[37]

•

The Doctrine of Nothing

Queyroz's book, and hence Pereira's account of the life of the Buddha, would not be published until 1916. At the time it was written, it had been one of the few accounts of the Buddha drawn, albeit indirectly and with sarcastic commentary, from Buddhist sources. Other accounts of the life of the Buddha had been and would be written by other Jesuits. And beginning in the seventeenth century, they consistently referred to "the doctrine of nothing." Here is an example from Louis le Comte (1655–1728), a Jesuit missionary to China:

•

No body can well tell where this Idol *Fo*, of whom I speak, was born; (I call him Idol and not Man, because some think it was an Apparition from hell) those who with more likelihood say he was a Man, make him born about a thousand years before JESUS CHRIST, in a Kingdom of the *Indies* near the Line, perhaps a little above *Bengala*. They say he was a Kings Son. . . .

When this Monster was first born he had strength enough to stand alone, and he made seven steps, and pointed with one Hand to Heaven, and the other to the Earth. He did also speak, but in such a manner as shewed what Spirit he was posses'd withal. *In Heaven or on the Earth, says he, I am the only person who deserve to be honoured.* At seventeen he married, and had a Son, which he forsook as he did all the rest of the World, to retire into a Solitude with three or four *Indian* Philosophers, whom he took along with him to teach. But at thirty he was on a suddain possessed, and as it were fulfilled with the Divinity, who gave him an universal knowledge of all things. From that time he became a God, and began by a vast number of seeming Miracles, to gain the Peoples admiration. The number of his Disciples is very great, and it is by their means that all the *Indies* have been poysoned with his pernicious Doctrine. Those of *Siam* call them *Talapoins*, the *Tartars* call them *Lamas* or *Lama-sem*, the *Japoners Bonzes*, and the *Chinese Hocham*.

But this Chimerical God found at last that he was a Man as well as others. He died at 79 years of Age; and to give the finishing stroke to his Impiety, he endeavoured to persuade his Followers to Atheism at his Death, as he had persuaded them to Idolatry in his Life time. Then he declared to his Followers that all which he had hither told them was enigmatical; and that they would be mistaken if they thought there was any other first Principle of things beside nothing; *It was,* said he, *from this nothing that all things sprang, and it is into this nothing that all things must return. This is the Abyss where all our hopes must end.*

Since this Impostor confessed that he had abused the World in his life, it is but reasonable that he should not be believed at his death. Yet as Impiety has always more Champions than Virtue, there were among the *Bonzes* a particular Sect of Atheists, formed from the last words of their Master. The rest who found it troublesome to part with their former prejudices, kept close to their first Errors. A third sort endeavoured to reconcile these Parties together, by compiling a body of Doctrine, in which there is a twofold Law, an interior and an exterior. One ought to prepare the mind for the reception of the other. It is, say they, the mould which supports the material 'till the Arch be made, and is then taken away as useless.[38]

•

Among the tenets of Buddhism is the famous doctrine of emptiness (śūnyāta), which for centuries Buddhist scholars have sought to demonstrate is *not* a doctrine of nothing. It is associated especially with the second-century-CE Indian master Nāgārjuna and his Madhyamaka, or "Middle Way," school of Indian Buddhist philosophy. However, although the Madhyamaka and its doctrine of emptiness would be highly important in Tibet, they were less influential in China. It is noteworthy that Pereira in his life of the Buddha, composed around the same time as le Comte's observations and based on Chinese Buddhist sources, does not mention this so-called nothing. Yet this doctrine, based largely on Jesuit rather than Buddhist sources, would be associated with Buddhism for centuries to come.[39]

It is likely, therefore, that for his account le Comte was drawing not from a Buddhist source but from the work of a fellow Jesuit—and one who had served not in China but in Japan, where the Zen sect was strong.[40] The answer to a famous Zen koan, "Does a dog have the Buddha nature?" is, in Japanese, *mu*, which means "no" or "nothing."

Many Jesuits would recount what they believed to be the Buddha's doctrine of nothing, and the story of his deathbed confession. One of these was Cristoforo Borri (1583–1632), missionary to Cochin China, in what is now Vietnam. Born in Milan, he joined the Society of Jesus in 1601 and soon distinguished himself in mathematics and astronomy. He was an advocate of the theories of Copernicus, Kepler, and Galileo, which countered the Ptolemaic system supported by the church. As a result, he drew the ire of the General of the Society of Jesus, who demanded his public penance. Seeking to devise a new method to determine latitude by using magnets, Father Borri requested permission to go to India. In 1615, he departed for Asia, arriving in what is today Vietnam two years later. There, along with his missionary duties, he continued his work as an astronomer, recording comets and eclipses of the sun and the moon. He left Vietnam in 1622 and returned to Europe in 1624. In his 1631 account of the religion of Vietnam, we find one of the most beautiful, and least polemical, accounts of the Buddha in the vast literature of the missionaries, an account in which the Buddha gains enlightenment not by meditating under a tree but by contemplating the heavens from a mountaintop:

•

The end of all sects is either the god they adore, or the glory and happiness they expect; some believing the immortality of the soul, others concluding that all ends when the body dies. Upon these two principles the eastern nations build all their sects; all which took their origin from a great metaphysician of the kingdom of Siam, whose name was Xaca, much more ancient than Aristotle, and nothing inferior to him in capacity, and the knowledge of natural things. The acuteness of this man's wit exciting him to consider the nature and fabric of the world, reflecting on the beginning and end of all things, and particularly of human nature, the chief lady of this worldly palace; he once went up to the top of a mountain, and there attentively observing the moon, which rising in the darkness of the night, gently raised itself above the horizon to be hid again the next day in the same darkness, and the sun rising in the morning to set again at night, he concluded that moral as well as physical and natural things were nothing, came of nothing, and ended in nothing. Therefore returning home, he wrote several books and large volumes on the subject, entitling them, "Of Nothing"; wherein he taught that the things of this world, by reason of the duration and measure of time, are nothing; for though they had existence, said he, yet they would be nothing, nothing at present, and nothing in time to come, for the present being but a moment, was the same as nothing. . . .

Having established this doctrine of nothing, he gathered some scholars, by whose means he spread it throughout all the east. But the Chinese, who knew that a sect which reduced all things to nothing was hurtful to the government, would not hearken to it, nor allow there was no punishment for wicked men, or that the happiness of the good should be reduced only to being free from sufferings in this world, and the authority of the Chinese being so great, others following their example rejected his doctrine. Xaca dissatisfied that he was disappointed of followers, changed his mind, and retiring wrote several other great books, teaching that there was a real origin of all things, a lord of heaven, hell, immortality, and transmigration of souls from one body to another, better or worse, according to the merits or demerits of the person; though they do not forget to assign a sort of heaven and hell for the souls of departed, expressing the whole metaphorically under the names of things corporeal, and of the joys and sufferings of this world....

The Japanese and others making so great account of this opinion of nothing, was the cause that when Xaca the author of it approached his death, calling together his disciples, he protested to them on the word of a dying man, that during the many years he had lived and studied, he had found nothing so true, nor any opinion so well grounded as was the sect of nothing; and though his second doctrine seemed to differ from it, yet they must look upon it as no contradiction or recantation, but rather a proof and confirmation of the first, though not in plain terms, yet by way of metaphors and parables, which might all be applied to the opinion of nothing, as would plainly appear by his books.[41]

•

This is a remarkable passage, in both its tone and its content. It explains that Xaca—not a demon but a philosopher to rival Aristotle himself—developed his doctrine of nothing (which Borri describes in more detail than can be presented here) in his native Siam. But when he took it to China, the Chinese objected that it was "hurtful to the government." Thus, Xaca devised a more conventional doctrine featuring what the Jesuits most commonly associated with Buddhism (in addition to idol worship): the system of transmigration of souls based on virtuous and sinful deeds. He then apparently traveled to Japan, which was more amenable to his original doctrine of nothing. And thus, as he lay dying, he declared that it was his true teaching, and that his subsequent accommodation in his second doctrine should be understood metaphorically.

There is much to ponder here. The precise Buddhist source for this doctrine of nothing remains mysterious; it sounds something like the Buddhist doctrine of emptiness, and also vaguely like the more pervasive doctrine of impermanence. Yet Father Borri probably learned of it not from a Buddhist text but from a fellow Jesuit of the previous generation who had served in Japan. As in China, Nāgārjuna's emptiness was not a strong presence in Japan. At the time of Francis Xavier's mission there, however, the Zen school was flourishing.[42] The story of the Buddha adapting his teachings to his various audiences—Siamese, Chinese, and Japanese—sounds something like the famous doctrine of *upāya*, the Buddha's skillful methods of teaching what is appropriate to each audience, reserving his highest teaching for his most qualified disciples. But according to Buddhist sources, the Buddha was born and died in India, and he made no deathbed revision of his teachings. As in so many cases of European accounts of the Buddha, some element of the traditional story seems to lie below the surface, but is blurred almost beyond recognition. In some cases the distortion seems to have been simply a matter of linguistic error; in others, it seems to have been more willful.

Borri's fellow Jesuit missionary and successor in what is now Vietnam, Alexandre de Rhodes (1591–1660), gave a sinister twist to the same story. Here the Buddha, whom he calls by his Vietnamese name, Thicca, has a violent and malignant nature and devotes himself to magic. At the urging of two demons, he abandons his wife and young son and goes into solitude, where the demons instruct him in atheism. Returning to his father's palace five years later, he tries to teach atheism to his subjects, but cannot find a single follower:

•

Thicca, thus vexed at seeing his enterprise rejected, decided to take the counsel of his familiar demons for another pernicious plan that would disseminate a certain history and fabulous genealogy of the gods, and under the cloak of these fables, proclaimed the practice of the most monstrous vices and introduced the belief in various divinities. He succeeded at this such that in the forty years of his reign that he toiled at this impious plan, using his authority as much as the illusions of his magic, he established and spread across all of India the superstitious worship of idols, which had been previously unknown there. . . . But the devils who controlled the mind of this unfortunate prince, not unaware that atheism is worse and more pernicious than idolatry, as it is that which serves as the stage for all manner of vices, persuaded this impious mind to recant at the end of his days.[43]

•

In China as in Siam, then, Jesuit missionaries encountered the Buddha, and found him deeply disquieting. He was an idol, but an idol believed to have walked the earth, and to have practiced virtue. The presence of virtue among the pagans was itself not the issue; the Jesuits were well versed in the classics of Greek and Roman thought, citing them often in their works. But the pagan philosophers had preceded the coming of the Christ. Many of the missionaries believed that the Buddha, if he had been a historical figure at all, had lived after Jesus. And yet so many elements in the life story of this idol were similar to the story of Jesus. The truth had been copied, and being copied, it had become false. It was an inversion, a perversion, something demonic. Issues of truth and falsity, of accommodation and condemnation, appeared yet again in a Jesuit mission less famous than those of Francis Xavier to Japan, Matteo Ricci to China, and Guy Tachard to Siam. It is the mission of Ippolito Desideri to Tibet.

The Original and the Copy

Desideri was born in 1684 in the town of Pistoia in Tuscany. He entered the Jesuit order in 1700, studying at the Collegio Romano. Following two years of instruction in theology, he requested permission to become a missionary. After audiences with Pope Clement XI and the Grand Duke of Tuscany, Cosimo III de' Medici, he made his way to Genoa, where he sailed for India on November 23, 1712. Braving high seas and Turkish pirates, the ship made port five months later in Goa, the Portuguese colony on India's west coast. Assigned to the Tibet mission, Desideri and another priest, the Portuguese Manoel Freyre, eventually set off on the trip north—first by ship up the Indian coast, then on foot and horseback through Jaipur, Delhi, and Lahore, through the Himalayas to Kashmir, and then to Leh, the capital of Ladakh, the westernmost Tibetan domain. They remained in Leh for fifty-two days. Desideri wished to found the mission there, but Freyre, his superior, insisted that they continue eastward to Lhasa. They were able to survive the difficult seven-month journey thanks to the protection of a Mongolian princess, who allowed the two priests to join her caravan. They reached Lhasa on March 18, 1716.

After just a month in Lhasa, Freyre decided to return to India, leaving Desideri the only European, and the only Christian, in Tibet. The country was ruled at that time by a Mongol warlord, the Lhazang Khan, and Desideri was soon granted an audience. Apparently impressed by the Tuscan's determination to teach Tibetans the route to heaven, and his wish to remain in Tibet for the rest of his life, the khan granted Desideri permission to stay. Desideri set to work studying the Tibetan language and the Tibetan religion.

Less than a year later, on January 6, 1717, he presented the khan with an exposition of Christianity, written in Tibetan verse. It was not insubstantial, filling 128 short Tibetan pages. Desideri clearly conceived it as the first of a series of works, calling it *Tho rangs mun sel nyi ma shar ba'i brda* (*The Dawn, Sign of the Sun that Dispels the Darkness*).

The khan, himself a Buddhist, proposed a debate between Desideri and a learned Tibetan monk, but suggested that Desideri first undertake further study. He arranged for the Jesuit to live at Ramoche, one of the oldest Buddhist temples in Lhasa, and then at Sera, a monastery of some 5,500 monks on the outskirts of the city and one of "three seats" of the Geluk sect. Desideri's notes from his studies, preserved in the Jesuit archives in Rome, trace his course from a young monk's textbooks on elementary logic through the masterworks of the tradition.

Desideri's studies at Sera were interrupted by war. A rival faction of Mongols invaded Lhasa in December 1717, assassinating the Lhazang Khan and pillaging the city. Desideri fled east to a small Catholic hospice in Dakpo, selected in part because the surroundings had a few grapevines that could be used for making communion wine. There he continued his studies until missionaries of the Capuchin order, who had arrived in the fall of 1716, finally received an official letter from the Propaganda Fide ordering Desideri to leave Tibet. He reluctantly did so, arriving in Kathmandu on January 20, 1722. He would remain in India for five more years before departing for home.

Desideri arrived in Rome on January 23, 1728, during the final stages of what came to be known as the Rites Controversy. Jesuit missionaries to China, most notably Matteo Ricci, had adopted forms of the local culture in order to proclaim the Gospel, drawing a distinction between what was religious and what was civil. There was no question that Buddhism and Daoism were religions; they were "the sects of idolaters and sorcerers" and as such were condemned. The practice of "ancestor worship," however, was deemed civil by the Jesuits, and because it was not immoral or in conflict with Christianity, they permitted it among Chinese converts. The practice, as the Jesuits understood it, involved participation in seasonal ceremonies honoring Confucius and rituals of bowing, lighting incense, and offering food at a funeral, a grave, or a family altar where stone tablets were arranged, each inscribed with the name of a departed ancestor and the characters for "seat of the spirit."

Should Chinese converts to Christianity be allowed to make offerings at festivals honoring local gods, and could Roman Catholic masses be said for heathen ancestors of Christian converts? A range of opinions on these and related issues arose among the Jesuits. Positions became polarized when the Spanish Dominican Juan Bautista de Morales left China and returned to Rome in 1643, where he condemned the Jesuit practice of accommodation. Arguments circulated back and forth, in China and in Rome, throughout the remainder of the seventeenth century. Then on November 20, 1704, the Holy Office issued a decree prohibiting the practice of Chinese ceremonies. Pope Clement XI had already dispatched Cardinal Carlo Tommaso Maillard de Tournon (who had described Guy Tachard as an idolater) as the highest level of papal legate, *legatus a latere*, to inform the Kangxi Emperor that Chinese Christians were no longer permitted to practice ancestor worship. Cardinal Tournon stopped briefly in India, where he issued a decree against the so-called Malabar Rites (used so successfully by the Jesuit Roberto de Nobili in South India in the early seventeenth century) before continuing to China, arriving in Beijing on December 4, 1705. When word of the Vatican's official decree on ancestor worship reached the cardinal in China, he issued his own decree on January 25, 1707, instructing all missionaries in China to abolish the practice of these rites or risk excommunication. When the emperor received word of the ban, he ordered that Tournon be imprisoned in Macao, where he died a few months later. Papal bulls confirming the church's position against the practice of Chinese rites were issued by Clement XI in 1715 and Benedict XIV in 1742.[44]

As a Jesuit, Desideri was on the losing side of the Rites Controversy. His situation was made more difficult by the Capuchins' charges that their failure to successfully evangelize Tibet stemmed from the errors of the Jesuits who had preceded them there. The last years of Desideri's life were consumed with composing long defenses of his work, as well as the captivating account of his time in Tibet, the *Relazione de' viaggi all' Inde e al Thibet* (*Report of Travel to India and Tibet*), to which we will turn below. He died in Rome on April 13, 1733. His works would remain unread and unknown for almost two hundred years.

Before Desideri left Tibet, he dispatched appeals to the Vatican, imploring the Holy Father to allow him to continue his work there. While he awaited a response that never arrived, he continued writing what he considered his most important work: a refutation, composed in excellent Tibetan, of the central Buddhist doctrines of rebirth and emptiness. Desideri carried this manuscript with him back to Rome, where it languished in the Jesuit archives, read neither by the Tibetan audience for whom it was intended, nor by anyone else. The work's title is *Inquiry into the Doctrines of Previous Lives and of Emptiness, Offered to the Scholars of Tibet by the White Lama called Ippolito* (*Mgo skar gyi bla ma i po li do zhes bya ba yis phul ba'i bod kyi mkhas pa rnams la skye ba snga ma dang stong pa nyid kyi lta ba'i sgo nas zhu ba*).

It is an extraordinary text in many ways. First, it is the most sophisticated work ever written in the Tibetan language by a European. Second, it reveals a deep and nuanced understanding of Tibetan Buddhist doctrine and philosophy, one that would not be matched by European scholarship until the late twentieth century. Third, it contains the most beautiful, and beautifully crafted, Tibetan poetry composed by a Westerner; the work begins with a long poem in praise of Jesus, written with such sensitivity to Buddhist metaphor that it could easily be mistaken as a hymn to the Buddha. Hence Desideri's prayer to Christ looks like a prayer to the Buddha. Here is an excerpt:

> In order to rouse from sleep and dispel all darkness from all beings,
> Forever beclouded by the gloomy darkness of delusion,
> Sleepwalking mindlessly in their ignorance,
> You act as the sun whose light pervades everything.
>
> In order to compassionately search for and lead
> Those who have blithely entered evil paths,
> Wandering toward the abyss and toward danger,
> You lovingly appeared in this world

As a single being who, without abandoning your indestructible
  nature,
Came to be united with a human nature.

To those sunk in the mud of false religions,
Constantly indulging in misdeeds,
To those bound in the prison of wrong views,
You extend the hand of the peerless true religion,
In order to compassionately lead them out and untie them.
You are forever free of fear,
Yet you know how to free others from fear.

In order to cure those tormented
By dangerous diseases incurable by others,
Negative deeds like desire and hatred,
You became a physician for us common beings.
You became a raincloud of blessings
Quelling the ever burning flames
Of pride, jealousy, and lust, so difficult to douse.

For those humans who do not know nor do they seek the source of
  refuge,
You are like a mother, because you give birth to all good deeds,
You are like a wet nurse, because you give the milk of virtue,
You are a friend, because you turn back all harm.[45]

Although this is a poem in praise of God, the imagery is Buddhist.
These are some of the allusions: The literal meaning of *buddha* in Sanskrit is "awakened," and the commentaries explain that the Buddha
is so called because he has awakened from the sleep of ignorance. The
benighted sentient beings in the six realms of saṃsāra are asleep,
waiting to be roused by the Buddha. The Buddha has two bodies: the
truth body, or *dharmakāya*, and the form body, or *rūpakāya*. The truth
body is a kind of cosmic principle of enlightenment, sometimes defined as the Buddha's omniscient consciousness. The form body is
the form of the Buddha that physically manifests in the world out of
compassion for suffering sentient beings. A Sanskrit text called the

Satyakaparivarta describes the Buddha as rescuing sentient beings from prison:

> When he sees the many beings whose minds
> Are ever enshrouded by the dark gloom of ignorance,
> Locked in the prison of saṃsāra,
> The Excellent Sage feels compassion.[46]

The Buddha is repeatedly praised as the teacher of the truth, destroying the wrong views of all rival religions. His teaching is often called "the lion's roar" (*siṃhanāda*); just as the roar of the lion silences the other animals, the Buddha's teaching silences all other teachers. The Buddha is often compared to a skilled physician. Just as the best of doctors knows the appropriate remedy for each of the vast array of afflictions, so the Buddha uses his skillful methods to teach what is most appropriate for each person, based on his or her capacity and disposition. Elsewhere, his teaching is compared to the rain that nourishes all plants without discrimination. And he is said to love each sentient being as a mother loves her only child.

Thus, the Tibetan reader of Desideri's poem would read it as a paean to the Buddha. It is only at a few points that Desideri uses imagery that would be unfamiliar to a Buddhist, but immediately familiar to a Roman Catholic:

> You are never tainted by impurity.
> We are ever stained by impurity.
> In order to free us from defilement,
> Each day you transform your blood
> Endowed with the power to cleanse and completely dispel
> All impurity from every mind.[47]

Desideri's *Inquiry into the Doctrines of Previous Lives and of Emptiness* is a philosophical refutation, not a polemic. He speaks directly to "the scholars of Tibet" in their own language and on their own terms. He regards Buddhist monks as learned and worthy interlocutors, and he sees in Tibetan Buddhism a commitment both to rational philosophy and to ethical practice. He thus discerns the possibility for reasoned argumentation on key points of doctrine; he also clearly feels that he will eventually win that argument and convert the Tibetan people to the truth of the Gospel.

To do so, he must first establish the value of studying another religion, even for those committed to their own. Here, Desideri seems to anticipate by 150 years the Victorian Orientalist Friedrich Max Müller's famous dictum of comparative religion, "He who knows one religion, knows none." But Desideri uses the naturalistic imagery so common to Buddhist texts to make his point:

•

To encounter another tradition that accords greatly with one's own tradition and understand them both is like having two butter lamps burning in a single room, or one gold or silver ring shining with the light of two diamond studs. Again, if a tree receives the appropriate amount of water from separate sources, rainwater and water from a stream, its roots will grow large, and the tree will be more and more firmly fixed in the earth. In the same way, by moistening one's mind with the complete instructions and essential points of one's own religion as well as another religion that accords with it, one's body, speech, and mind will become most conducive to religion and one will, like a thick nail, abide with a firm aspiration to religion.[48]

•

Acknowledging that someone might say there is no reason to study another religion when one's own is clearly superior, Desideri says that although iron and wood are clearly inferior to gold, they can be used to make a tool with which to dig up more gold to make beautiful jewelry.

Among the myriad doctrines of Tibetan Buddhism, Desideri chose only two to explore in his *Inquiry*, the two which arguably stand at the very foundation of the Buddhist philosophical tradition: the doctrine of rebirth and the doctrine of no self, or emptiness; unlike in China, the doctrine of emptiness was of paramount importance in Tibet, especially in the Geluk sect, at whose monasteries Desideri studied. He recognized that the doctrine of rebirth (and its attendant doctrine of karma) presented two problems for the Christian faith: a challenge to the view of heaven and hell as the final domains of the blessed and the damned, and a challenge to the idea of a creator God who blesses and damns his creatures. The doctrine of emptiness is in some ways even more consequential, for it entails the negation of a transcendent and preexistent deity as well as the negation of a First Cause. Desideri seems to understand that if he can undermine, or even call into question, the validity of these two doctrines, then his task of establishing the existence of a fundamental and eternal ground of all existence, God, becomes possible.

Yet despite his final aim, Desideri's text is entirely Tibetan, in style, in concept, in terminology. He uses Buddhist terminology extensively, and accurately, quoting from Buddhist scriptures to argue against Buddhist views. And he presents his arguments in the classical form of Tibetan debate, one that he observed on the debating courtyards of Sera monastery outside Lhasa.

In his *Inquiry*, writing in Tibetan for Tibetans, Desideri rarely mentions the Buddha. Here, his approach is again typical of Tibetan scholastic literature, where the omniscience of the Buddha and his authorship of the sutras are assumed, with disputation concerned more with what is and is not logical than with overarching worldviews. Desideri assumes that Buddhist worldview and then seeks to find inconsistencies within it.

Upon his return to Rome, he wrote for a different audience, in a different language, in a different tone. In his *Relazione*, he describes the religion of Tibet, in Italian, to his fellow Roman Catholics. Here also, he rarely mentions the Buddha, whom he refers to not as the Buddha but as Sciacchiá-Thubbá, his rendering of Shakya thub pa, the Tibetan version of Śākyamuni, the Buddha's epithet, "sage of the Śākya clan." Desideri identifies him as the "Lawgiver of the Thibettans," much as Moses gave the law to the children of Israel. He seems to regard Sciacchiá-Thubbá only as the founder of the religion of the Tibetans, although he knows he was born in "Hindustan." Desideri had read Kircher and other Jesuits, but he does not identify Sciacchiá-Thubbá with the Xaca of the Japanese, the Fo of the Chinese, or the Sommona-Codom of the Siamese.

In his relatively brief description of the life of the Buddha, Desideri is particularly interested in the nativity accounts. In the passage that follows, he describes a famous moment in the life story. The Buddha has perfected himself over millions of lifetimes as bodhisattva. In his penultimate lifetime, the lifetime before he achieved buddhahood, he is reborn, as all buddhas are, as a god (*lha* in Tibetan) in a heaven called Tuṣita, or Joyous; it is called Ganden (Dga' ldan) in Tibetan. As the moment for his final birth approaches, he surveys the world to decide where he should be reborn, in what caste, to which parents. This is Desideri's description of that scene:

•

Then, remembering our lowly world, he regarded each region most attentively and pondered how it had been reduced to a most deplorable condition of spiritual ruin by the blindness, the passions, and wickedness of human beings, beyond any help or redress. He then generated the highest compassion for them and decided to come to earth himself and be reborn as a human being to deliver humankind from evil and to lead them to eternal salvation. . . . The Tibetans' lawgiver describes how he glanced down upon the world and resolved to leave Kaa-n-den and the supremely happy state of a Lhà and descend to earth and be reborn in the human condition. He employs a manner of speaking and tone in making his decision and expresses such thoughts as he had on that occasion and subject that make it seem as if it were the Devil himself speaking in the guise of a man, or through the mouth of a man, and that he had undertaken to behave, as we say, like a monkey, by fully imitating everything our ascetics and contemplatives are wont and capable of expressing in order to make us comprehend the decree of the Most Holy Trinity for the salvation of mankind which the Divine Word accepted in coming to earth and becoming a man, in order to be our Savior, at the cost of his degradation, his passion, and his holy death.

After a long series of very tender and moving speeches, the Tibetans' lawgiver adds that once he had made his resolution, he glanced over the world another five times to determine the five special qualities of his advent: his caste or tribe, his country, his time, his family, and the woman from whom he would be born and take a human body. The special gifts and perfections he sought in the woman whom he had to choose as his mother are also like another copy made by the said infernal monkey of what our ascetics and contemplatives are wont to say about the Divine Word's election of the Most Holy Virgin to be elevated to the great dignity of the Mother of God Incarnate. Another copy is his moving speech of how, before coming to be born into the world as a man and embarking on the great task of leading the world to the good and to salvation, he offered to endure insults, pains, hardships, and whatever might serve the goal that he had undertaken.[49]

•

In the story of the Buddha's descent into the world and the choice of his mother, Desideri sees affinities with the Christian doctrine of incarnation, of how the Word became flesh. And the description of Mahāmāyā, the Buddha's future mother, with all her virtues, reminds him of the Blessed Virgin, chosen to be the mother of God. Desideri is appalled by this similarity, seeing it as the aping of the "infernal monkey," the devil. Here, without using the term, he evokes the Christian doctrine of demonic plagiarism, articulated by Justin Martyr and other church fathers during the second and third centuries, according to which similarities between elements of the church and rival cults are attributed to Satan. In some cases, Christian rituals had in fact been derived from these same rival cults.[50] The doctrine of demonic plagiarism allowed the church to claim, falsely, that the original was theirs, that anything else was a copy, and a copy made by the devil.

This doctrine was invoked often by Roman Catholic missionaries after the Counter-Reformation. Indeed, almost a century before, in 1667, the illustrious German Jesuit Athanasius Kircher also saw the work of the devil in Tibet—not in the person of the Buddha but in the Dalai Lama: "Before him the visitors fall prostrate and place their heads on the ground. They kiss his feet with incredible veneration, as if he were the Pope. Thus, even by this the deceitfulness of the evil spirit is marvelously shown, for veneration due only to the vicar of Christ on earth, the Pope of Rome, is transferred to the heathen worship of savage nations, like all the other mysteries of Christianity. The Devil does this with his natural malevolence."[51]

There is, of course, another possible reason for the similarities between Buddhism and Christianity, a reason more human, less demonic. Desideri raises the question himself: "whether Christianity had at any time in the distant past ever been established in these parts, or if any of the apostles ever reached there." He acknowledges evidence of an ancient Christian community in China, and he mentions the mission of Saint Thomas to Hindustan (India). Regarding the Tibetans, he writes:

•

When we learn from their books of the many prodigies and extraordinary marvels attending the incarnation and birth of their lawgiver
Sciacchiá-Thubbá . . . and other similar things, one might wonder
whether these people in former times had knowledge of the incarnation, birth, and ascension into Heaven of Our Lord Jesus Christ and of
the lives and miracles of the saints of the Old and New Testaments. . . .

Notwithstanding all of the foregoing I state that neither the history,
recollections, nor traditions of the Tibetans give any indication that
the holy faith or any apostle or evangelic preacher had ever been there
at any time.[52]

•

For the larger question of the European portrayal of the Buddha
as an idol, Desideri is an important figure here as well, because he
understood Tibetan Buddhist literature so well. As we have seen, in
earlier portrayals, knowledge of the Buddha comes from a garbled
story transmitted orally from an Asian language to a European one,
possibly mistranslated or misunderstood. Or it comes from an account written at the request of the European, such as the story of
Devadatta provided to the French. Even for those missionaries such
as Matteo Ricci whom we esteem for their linguistic skills, they often did not read Buddhist texts in the original but instead relied on
digests, often composed by a convert. The French Jesuit Jean Crasset
(1618-1692) explains in his 1689 *Histoire de l'eglise du Japon* (in the 1705
English translation, *The History of the Church of Japan*), "These Books
are Wrote in such a manner, that it is absolutely impossible for anyone to know this Impostor's meaning."[53] Thus, we are not so surprised
when the portrayals of the Buddha are so negative. But Desideri read
large sections of the Tibetan canon, and he seems to have understood
it. And still the Tibetans were idolaters, the Buddha was an idol, his
biography the work of Satan.

Among Desideri's Tibetan works preserved in the Jesuit Archives in
Rome are his notebooks. There, we find that on September 14, 1717, he
began to make extensive notes, in Tibetan, on the most famous work
of Tsong kha pa (1357–1419), founder of the Geluk sect: the *Great Expo-*

sition of the *Stages of the Path to Enlightenment* (*Byang chub lam rim chen mo*), a work Desideri would later translate into Italian (since lost). He copied long passages of the text into his notebook, including the passage below. Here, in the chapter on the Buddhist practice of "going for refuge" to the three jewels (*triratna*)—the Buddha; the dharma, his teaching; and the sangha, the community of the enlightened—Tsong kha pa is explaining the qualities of a person who is a suitable source of refuge from the sufferings of saṃsāra: "In brief, one who is himself free from all fear, who knows the means to free others from fear, who acts with great compassion for all without discrimination, seeking the welfare of everyone, whether or not they have helped him, such a person is suitable as a refuge. The Buddha alone has [those qualities]; God does not. . . . Therefore, without being requested to do so, moved by great compassion, he comes to our aid, he is not lazy about this, he is the auspicious and peerless place of refuge, he is your own protector. Knowing this, go to him for refuge."⁵⁴

This is very much the language that Desideri uses in his Tibetan prayer to Jesus. In it, he writes, "You are forever free of fear, / Yet you know how to free others from fear." Here plagiarism takes a more human form.

One Idol, Many Names

Through Desideri's extensive reading of Tibetan texts, he came to recognize that the religion of the Tibetans had come to Tibet from India. More than a century before, from the time of Ricci, Roman Catholic missionaries to China had understood that the religion they encountered in China, the religion we call Buddhism, had also originated in India. As Ricci wrote:

•

The second important sect among the Chinese is known as Sciequia or Omitose. The Japanese call it Sciacca and Amidabu, the sect being quite similar in character in both countries. The Japanese also call it the Lex Totoqui. This code of law was brought to China from the West, in the year sixty-five of the Christian era. It was imported from the region of Thiencio, also called Shinto, which was formerly two kingdoms but today is known by the single title of Hindustan, lying between the rivers Indus and Ganges. A written record is extant that the King of China sent legates to this country, after being enlightened in a dream to do so. These messengers brought back the books of the laws and also interpreters to translate them into Chinese. The founders of the sect had died before the doctrine found its way into China. From this it would appear quite evident that this doctrine passed from the Chinese to the Japanese, and it is not at all clear why the Japanese followers of this creed assert that the Sciacca or the Amidabu was introduced into Japan from the kingdom of Siam, where they say it had its origin. It is made quite evident in the books of the followers of this doctrine that Siam was too well known to the Chinese to be mistaken from the far-distant Thiencio in a matter of this kind.

It is historically clear that this doctrine was brought into China at the identical period in which the Apostles were preaching the doctrine of Christ. Bartholomew was preaching in upper India, namely in Hindustan and the surrounding countries, when Thomas was spreading the gospel in lower India, to the South. It is not beyond the realm of possibility, therefore, that the Chinese, moved and interested by reports of the truths contained in the Christian Gospel, sought to contact it and to learn it from the West. Instead, however, either through error on the part of their legates, or perhaps through ill-will toward the Gospel on the part of the people they visited, the Chinese received a false importation in place of the truth they were seeking.[55]

•

Sciequia is Śākya, short for Śākyamuni; Omitose is the buddha Amitābha—yet further evidence that Roman Catholic missionaries encountered the Buddha in many lands, that they saw him in many forms, and that they heard him called by many names. From our perspective, they were seeing not different idols but simply regional variations of images of a single figure; not many gods but a single (admittedly extraordinary) man. In the Buddhist cultures of Asia, he was not known by three hundred different names (see appendix 1). The names that the Europeans tried to spell were various regional pronunciations of just a few names and epithets: Buddha, Gautama Buddha, Śākyamuni, Śramaṇa Gautama. Who was the first European to figure this out? One candidate is the Portuguese Jesuit Fernão de Queyroz, who in the year before his death completed *The Temporal and Spiritual Conquest of Ceylon*. At the end of Pereira's long account of the life of Buddha (discussed above) that Queyroz included in his book, he writes:

•

And as it has been observed that the Ganezes of Ceylon, the Talpoys of Arracan, Pegu, Siam and other neighbouring Realms, as well as the Lamazes of Tartary agree with the Bonzes of China and Japan in the essentials of their sect and profession, it is easy to understand that the Buddum of Ceylon, the Fô of China, the Xaka of Japan is the same as the Xekia of India, for the word Buddum is only an adapted name, and in Ceylon it means Saint by antonomasia. And if those who had read the documents of Ceylon had been more curious and had not been weary of giving us more detailed information, we could have shown more clearly from what they relate of his life the additions made by Chinese malice.

If intelligent Europeans wonder, considering what it is that such intelligent people embrace as true, let them remember what heathen Europe so pertinaciously believed and worshipped. The fact is the Devil has forestalled everything. When we preach to the heathens of hither India, they reply that they also have a Trinity, and that their Vixnu incarnated himself times out of number; if we preach to those of farther India and of Ceylon (for this Sect has disappeared from many parts of India wherein it began), they reply that their Buddum or their Fô or their Xaka also took the shape of a man, though he was an eternal being. And as the Religious of this Sect have a great reputation outside China, it is a very difficult matter to convert any of his sectaries, which has been the experience especially in the Kingdoms of Arracan, Pegû, Siam, Laos and others of lesser name.[56]

•

Thus, the Jesuits across Asia had seen enough to conclude that the religion practiced by monks in Sri Lanka, in Burma, in Tibet, in China, and in Japan was essentially the same, and thus the figure that they worshipped, known by different names, was the Buddha.[57] If the Portuguese had been more diligent in studying the documents they found in Ceylon while the island was still under their control (Colombo had fallen to the Dutch in 1656), they would have known more about the Buddha and would have been able to tell which elements the Chinese had added to his story. Writing as he is at the end of Pereira's long account of the life of the Buddha, Queyroz cautions his readers not to judge the heathens too harshly; the Europeans had also been heathens not so long ago.

Although we would consider this an advance in historical knowledge, a collapsing of many idols into one, we do not see a similar advance in historical perspective. It is still all the work of the devil. When Queyroz says that "the Devil has forestalled everything," he means that Satan has anticipated everything, creating demonic doubles that await the missionaries at the end of their long journey. Thus, when Christian missionaries preach the Trinity and the Incarnation, the heathens tell them that they do not require the Trinity and the Incarnation. They already have their own. And so the Buddha was often regarded with a certain resentment by Europeans.

One of the most spiteful Jesuit biographies of the Buddha came from perhaps the greatest Jesuit scholar of the seventeenth century, Athanasius Kircher, whom we will encounter again in the next chapter. In his *China Illustrata*, he writes:

•

The first creator and architect of the superstition was a very sinful brahmin imbued with Pythagoreanism. He was not content just to spread the doctrine, but even added to it so much that there is scarcely any one who is able to describe the doctrine or to write about it. He was an imposter known all over the East. The Indians called him Rama, the Chinese Xe Kian, the Japanese Xaca, and the Turks Chiaga. This deadly monster was born in central India in the place which the Chinese call Tien Truc Gnoc. His birth was portentous. They say his mother had a dream and saw a white elephant come first from her mouth and then from her left side. Hence the white elephant was held in great esteem by the kings of Siam, Laos, Tonchin, and China. These kings value white elephants more than their kingdoms. They think themselves blessed if one of these beasts is given them by a gift of the gods. We will discuss the apotheosis of this elephant later. So Xaca was born and he was the first who is said to have killed his mother. Then he pointed one hand toward heaven and the other down to the earth and said that except for him, there was none holy, not in heaven nor in earth. Then he betook himself to the mountain recesses and there he instituted this abominable idolatry with Satan's help. Afterwards he infected the whole Orient with his pestilent dogmas. The Chinese Annals say that when he emerged from his solitary hermitage, a divine, (or more likely, a satanic) spirit filled him. He gathered together about 80,000 disciples. He selected 500 of these, and then 100 from these. Finally, he selected ten as being the best suited for teaching his horrible doctrines. He had chosen them as intimate counselors and associates in his crimes. Lest his doctrines be called in question by anyone, when dying, he decreed that the Pythagorean epithet be placed in his books. This phrase is, "He himself said," or, "So our books teach us." This means that it is evil to question the truth or the infallibility of these absurd fables, which are horrible and execrable. These are not tenets, but crimes. They are not doctrines, but abominations. They are not histories, but fables.[58]

•

Again, this is obviously not a flattering portrait. Kircher begins by saying that the Buddha believed in Pythagoreanism. For the church, this did not mean that he was a student of geometry but that he believed in the transmigration of souls. Also known as metempsychosis, this view had since antiquity been attributed to Pythagoras, who is said to have heard the voice of a dead friend in the yelps of a puppy. For the church, the doctrine of reincarnation was a heresy. Kircher recognizes that the Buddha (a term he does not use) is known by a number of names, mistakenly adding in the Hindu god Rama; according to later Hindu mythology, the Buddha was the ninth avatar, or incarnation, of the god Vishnu, with Rama being the seventh and Krishna the eighth. However, Kircher correctly identifies India as the Buddha's place of birth, using the Vietnamese name for India, "Tien Truc Gnoc" (that is, Thiên Trúc Ngọc). Calling the Buddha by the Japanese name Xaca (that is, Shaka), he correctly notes that before his birth the Buddha's mother dreamed that a white elephant had entered her womb. And when he was born, he is said to have taken seven steps, pointed to the sky and the earth, and announced that he was superior to both. The Buddha's mother died seven days later, but nowhere does it say that he murdered her, as Kircher claims.

The claim that the Buddha killed his mother did not originate with Kircher, nor would it end with him. It was something of a commonplace in European biographies of the Buddha. We recall that Saint Jerome wrote, "To come to the Gymnosophists of India, the opinion is authoritatively handed down that Budda, the founder of their religion, had his birth through the side of a virgin. And we need not wonder at this in the case of Barbarians when cultured Greece supposed that Minerva at her birth sprang from the head of Jove, and Father Bacchus from his thigh." In other words, like the gods of other pagans, the Buddha sprang from a body part of another god. But this was not enough for the Jesuits. Although they did not require an anatomical explanation in the case of Athena springing full-blown from the brow of Zeus, they did in the case of the Buddha. As good classicists, they knew that Julius Caesar was said to have been born when his mother's womb was cut open (hence our term *caesarean*). Still, for the Buddha they arrived at a far more grisly explanation: the baby Buddha developed teeth in the womb and then gnawed his way out through his mother's right side. As one might expect, she died in childbirth.[59]

Next, Kircher describes the Buddha as instituting the practice of idolatry (with the help of Satan) and then spreading the practice all over Asia. It is his work, therefore, that the Christian missions must undo, the task made all the more difficult, apparently, by the fact that Buddhist texts begin with the phrase "So our books teach us"—presumably an allusion to the phrase that begins Buddhist sutras, "Thus did I hear" (*evaṃ mayā śrutam*). The Belgian Jesuit Philippe Couplet (1623–1693) was another who explained that the Buddha's discourses begin with that phrase, which he rendered in Latin as *sic ego accepi*.[60] For reasons that remain unclear, the phrase (as they understood it) proved particularly loathsome to European antagonists of the Buddha. In his 1671 *Atlas Chinensis*, Arnoldus Montanus writes, "He taught these Diabolical Perswasions forty nine Years publickly through all *India*, and Commanded one of his most beloved Disciples to maintain this first Rule in any Argument or Dispute, *viz., It stands thus in the Books*; which was almost after the same manner amongst Scholars of Pythagoras, who to shun private Disputations, concluded their Differences with these words, *viz., Ipse dixit, He said it himself*."[61]

Nonetheless, by the early decades of the eighteenth century, Europeans had gathered a great store of knowledge about Asia, with much of the knowledge about Buddhism gathered by Roman Catholic missionaries. One even finds discussions of the Buddha's meditation posture:

•

SIAKA was the Son of one of the King's of *Ceylan*. When he was but nine-teen Years of Age, he not only abandoned all the Pomps and Vanities of the World, but his Wife too and only Son, to become the Disciple of a celebrated Anchoret. Under this great Master he made a very consider-able Progress in the State of Contemplation; and the more effectually to wean his Thoughts from all external Objects, he habituated himself to sit in such a Posture, as, according to the Disciples of *Siaka*, engages the Mind so intensively, that a Man thereby descends, as it were, into himself, and is wholly wrapped up in his own Ideas. We are obliged to make use of these formal Terms, to give you the Energy and full Force of their enthusiastic Expressions. *Siaka's* Posture abovementioned, was this. He sat with his Legs a-cross directly under him, and his Hands laid one over another, in such a Manner as that the Tip of his Thumbs met close together. The Reader might reasonably expect to have seen him in a more painful Attitude; 'twas in this Situation, however, that the Divine Truths were revealed to this Enthusiast; that he penetrated into the most hidden Mysteries of Religion, and discovered the Existence both of Heaven and of Hell; that he entertained an adequate Idea of the State of Souls after their Separation from the Bodies which they ani-mated, and all their various Transmigrations; that he was fully appris'd of their Rewards and Punishments in another Life; together with the Omnipotence of the gods, and their Divine Providence, &c. On this Rev-elation he grounded his System, and in Process of Time confirmed his Disciples in the stedfast Belief of it.[62]

•

During this golden age of scholarship, knowledge of the world be-gan to be compiled in French in works such as *Histoire générale des voyages* (*General History of Travel*), in fifteen volumes by Abbé Prévost (himself a former Jesuit), and in English in works such as *The Mod-ern Part of the Universal History from the Earliest Account of Time Com-piled from Original Writers*. The most famous such contribution dur-ing the Enlightenment, however, was Denis Diderot and Jean le Rond d'Alembert's *Encyclopédie, ou dictionnaire raisonné des sciences, des arts et des métiers* (*Encyclopedia, or Systematic Dictionary of the Sciences, Arts, and Trades*), published in 1765. For the study of religion, a landmark work, noted earlier, was *Cérémonies et coutumes religieuses de tous les peuples du monde*, published in Amsterdam between 1723 and 1743, a collaboration of the editor, Jean-Frederic Bernard, and the great engraver Bernard Picart. In order to close this chapter and summarize the state of European knowledge about the Buddha in the early eighteenth century, an article about the Buddha from Picart is provided here (for a translation of the corresponding Diderot and d'Alembert *Encyclopédie* entry, see appendix 2). Bernard and Picart's debt to the Jesuits is clear from the opening sentence:

•

BUT the *Jesuits* who have oblig'd us with the History of *China*, assure us, that the most fatal Blow Religion ever felt, was given her by *Fo* and his Disciples. This *Fo* began to flourish and meet with universal Approbation amongst the *Chinese*, about two and thirty Years after the Death of *Jesus Christ*. His Idol, they say, was brought thither from *India*. The Minds of the People were perfectly dispos'd to give it a favourable Reception, and at that Juncture Superstition and Idolatry gain'd Ground apace. Some have asserted, that this *Fo* was a *Ghost* who broke loose from the infernal Regions; but not to dwell on such a chimerical Suggestion, what follows is the best and most rational Account, in our Opinion, that can be given of him. Others, therefore, inform us, that he was born in *India*, about one thousand Years before Christ, and that he was of Royal Extraction; that at first his Name was *Che-kia*, or *Xe-quia*; but when he had attain'd the Age of thirty Years, he chang'd it into *Fo*. As *Laokun* sprang from his Mother's Left Side, so *He* miraculously issued from his Mother's Right, who died in her Labour. Some Time before his Birth, she dreamt that she had swallowed (others say that she was brought to the Bed of) an Elephant, and this awful Dream is the original Cause of that Reverence and Respect which the Kings of *India* pay to their white Elephants. This *Fo* was blest with uncommon Strength, and could stand alone as soon as ever he was born. He took seven Steps, pointing with one Hand to the Heavens, and with the other to the Earth. His Tongue likewise was immediately loosen'd; he spoke at his very Birth, and gave all about him a surprising Characteristick of his Mission. *I am*, said he, *the only Being to whom Honour is due, upon Earth, or in the Heavens*. When he was seventeen Years of Age, he married, and had a Son, whom he soon after abandon'd, as he did all the rest of Mankind. He withdrew

into a solitary Desart, with three or four favourite Philosophers, whom
he made choice of for the Direction of his future Conduct. At thirty
two he began to be inspir'd; he was then posses'd with, and full of the
Deity, and at once became omniscient. From that Moment he was constituted a god, and establish'd the Veneration and Respect which the
People had for him by innumerable *Miracles*, or rather, (not to profane
that sacred Term, the true and genuine Signification whereof a great
Part of those who profess themselves Christians are perfect Strangers
too,) by Impostures and Delusions. In a very short Time he had a prodigious Train of Admirers and Disciples, who, in Imitation of their new
God, chang'd their Names according to the various Countries where
they propagated their Doctrine. But this Deity himself at last was convinced, that he was but a Man, like those who ador'd him; for he died
in the seventy ninth Year of his Age; and when he found himself at the
Point of Expiration, that the Measure of his Iniquities might be full,
he endeavour'd to inspire and poison his Followers with his atheistical
Principles. He told them ingenuously, *That till that Time he had talk'd
to them in obscure and unintelligible Terms; but don't deceive yourselves,*
said he, *and vainly imagine to find out of* Nothing *the first Principle of all
Things; for from* Nothing *all Things deriv'd their Beings, and to* Nothing *will
they all return. This is the dark Abyss of all our Hopes.* This Doctrine, perhaps, notwithstanding the Horror and Detestation which it naturally
creates at first View, might appear less shocking and insupportable,
if we would reconcile it with the Principles of the *Siamese*, by substi-
tuting the Idea of their *Nireupan* in Lieu of that abominable *Nothing*.
But be that as it will, by this Recantation, he divided his Disciples into
two Sects, one of which follow'd literally the Doctrines which *Fo* taught
in his Life-Time; that is to say, Idolatry; the other embrac'd the dying
Words of their great Master, as fundamental Articles of their Faith, and
openly declare themselves profest Atheists. This Sect, if we may credit
Father *Gobien*, is strenuously oppos'd by that of the *Philosophers*, whose
Doctrine favours another kind of Libertinism. Some have attempted
to reconcile these direct Contradictions of *Fo*, by the Supposition that
he laid down a double Law; that is, in their Terms, an *external* and an
internal Law. The former is preparatory to, and directs us to the latter, and is afterwards of no Manner of Importance; no more than the
Props which support an Arch-Roof, when the Work is completed. But
after all, it must be acknowledg'd, that amidst these various Opinions,

and those which we shall treat of in the Sequel of this Discourse, some are very dark and obscure, and others seem very loose and licentious, either on Account of their having been injudiciously related, or from the dangerous Consequences that may actually be drawn from them. Father *Kircher* has given us a farther Account of this *Fo*, which shall be inserted hereafter in its proper Place.[63]

•

This is a significant passage in many ways, and one that merits more consideration than can be provided here. From the outset, the Buddha and his disciples are charged with introducing idolatry into China; although unstated, the dream of Emperor Ming is clearly the referent here. It is the idol of the Buddha that is worshipped by the Chinese, and it is due to its influence that superstition spread across the land.

Picart immediately takes up the question of the Buddha's identity: was he a demon (as Francis Xavier had suggested) or a man? Dismissing the suggestion of some that he was a ghost who had escaped from hell, the Buddha's human, and at times all-too-human, life is recounted next. He was born in India of royal blood about a thousand years (in fact, about five hundred) before Christ. His name was Che-kia (that is, Śākya, his clan name), but when he was thirty, he changed it to Fo (Buddha; in fact, he achieved buddhahood at age thirty-five). Before his birth, his mother had the horrible dream that she swallowed an elephant or, even more horribly, mated with one (his mother dreamed that an elephant had entered her womb). An unusually strong child, he could walk and talk from birth, declaring his supremacy (as Buddhist sources also state). He married at age seventeen and had a son, whom he abandoned, "as he did the rest of Mankind" (the Buddha's son, Rāhula, whom he left behind when he went out in search of enlightenment, is usually said to have been born when his father was twenty-nine). He retired from the world with three or four of his favorite philosophers (according to traditional sources, he left alone, eventually joining five other ascetics).

At the age of thirty-two (traditionally, thirty-five), the Buddha "began to be inspir'd; he was then posses'd with, and full of the Deity, and at once became omniscient" (meaning that he became a buddha, who is said to be omniscient). Because he performed miracles, which were in fact impostures and delusions, he came to be regarded as a god, and he gathered a large following of disciples. But as the end of his life approached, he realized that he, too, was human. Here, in a variation of the Buddha's death provided by Borri, he denounces on his deathbed everything that he had taught and introduces a new and pernicious doctrine of atheism—everything comes from nothing and returns to nothing. Picart finds this doctrine less abominable if it can be understood as a version of the Siamese doctrine of Nireupan (nirvana). As a consequence, the Buddha's followers divided into two groups: the first, who followed the idolatry that he taught during his lifetime, and the second, who followed his final teaching of nothingness. Picart cites Father Gobien—the Jesuit writer Charles le Gobien (1653–1708), founder of the thirty-six-volume series *Lettres édifiantes et curieuses écrites des missions étrangères par quelques missionnaires de la Compagnie de Jésus* (*Edifying and curious letters written from the foreign missions by some missionaries of the Society of Jesus*)—that this latter sect was opposed by "the Philosophers," meaning the Confucians. Picart notes that some have attempted to reconcile the earlier and later teachings of the Buddha, with the former seen as a preparation for the latter. Yet he seems reluctant to speculate further: "But after all, it must be acknowledg'd, that amidst these various Opinions, and those which we shall treat of in the Sequel of this Discourse, some are very dark and obscure, and others seem very loose and licentious, either on Account of their having been injudiciously related, or from the dangerous Consequences that may actually be drawn from them."

Thus, in conclusion we can note that by the end of the seventeenth century, the idol observed across Asia, an idol known by many names, had acquired a biography. The biography was with rare exceptions (such as that of Borri) unflattering. We feel a certain indignation, even a righteous indignation, at the way the story of the Buddha was distorted by Europeans, especially the missionaries. Sometimes it seems maddeningly muddled, at others willfully misread in an effort to portray the Buddha in a negative light. We know better now, and can only feel embarrassed at the folly of our forbears.

But our indignation rests, at least in part, on the notion that there is a single life story of the Buddha to be distorted, a story that is somehow historical, somehow factual. Yet the story of the Buddha that we read today in textbooks is the product of centuries of accretion, with legends interpolated into legends, and with various Buddhist cultures adding their own elements to make the story their own.

Christian missionaries also attempted to make the story their own by telling it in their own way, in their own language, for their own purposes. What disquiets us, however, is that their portrayal of the Buddha is largely negative. Or at least, it seems so to us, we who have become so deeply conditioned to see the Buddha not as the Jesuits saw him, and not so much even as Buddhists have, but as a later generation of Europeans saw him.

In general, and not particularly surprisingly, the most accurate and detailed information about the Buddha and his life would come from those who had visited a Buddhist land, learned to speak (if not always read) the language, and then spoke with local Buddhists, often monks, about their master. This was not possible in India, where there were no Buddhists. The information thus came from China, Japan, and Tibet, from Sri Lanka, Thailand, and Burma. In India, the British would instead ponder statues of the Buddha.

The most outlandish speculation about the Buddha came from those who had never visited Asia, such as George Stanley Faber, whom we will meet in the next chapter. Yet what would come to be regarded as the greatest advances in understanding the identity of the Buddha would be made by those who never journeyed to Asia, who never spoke with a Buddhist, who never stood before a statue of a Buddha in a cave temple. These contributions would come from those who had only books.

But that would not occur until the beginning of the nineteenth century. Still, by the end of the seventeenth century, progress had been made. The many names of the Buddha had been reduced to a more manageable number; it was generally understood that Sommona-Codom and Fo and Xaca were the same person. He was a historical figure, a man and not a god, although there was evidence of the work of Satan in his life and teaching. It was also understood that he had been born in India. But in the next century, this last and seemingly most mundane fact would be called into question.

CHAPTER THREE. The Man

BOUDHOU is superior to all the gods; he is, however, not what we mean by a god, being inferior to them in some things, and above them in others. He is not purely a spirit, as he has a body: he over-runs the different worlds with rapidity, in the same manner as the geniuses in the Arabian Tales, well beloved by VISHNOU, and aided by his power. He governs the bad spirits, who have withdrawn their allegiance from the gods, and who are hurtful to men: yet he is the son of a king, a husband, a father, and a pilgrim. He is eighteen cubits in height, eats rice and vegetables, and has several of the attributes of humanity. He is called SAMAN the Saint by Excellence. I have made every inquiry, and have been informed that there is no etymology for the word BOUDHOU in the ancient languages of Ceylon. Whatever may be the opinion of the Singhalese respecting him, we shall consider him as a man.

JOSEPH ENDELIN DE JOINVILLE, 1801

The Buddha was born in northeast India (now southern Nepal) sometime in the sixth or fifth century BCE. The religion that he founded flourished there for almost two millennia, extending, at different moments in its long history, from Kashmir in the north to the Coromandel Coast in the south, from Sind in the west to Assam in the east. But it was gone by the time that the Portuguese explorer Vasco da Gama's fleet landed in Calicut on the southwest coast in 1498. In 1510, the Portuguese established a permanent settlement at Goa. The Dutch followed, eventually displacing the Portuguese, with trading posts on both the southeast and southwest coasts. In 1617, the Mughal emperor Jahangir granted the British East India Company permission to trade in India. In 1757, the company's troops, under the command of Lord Clive, defeated the Nawab of Bengal at the Battle of Plassey. A century later, the year of the Sepoy Rebellion, the British East India Company controlled most of the Indian subcontinent. Its charter was canceled by Parliament in 1858, and India was placed under the direct control of the British Crown.

Thus far, we have traced the story of Europe's encounter with the Buddha through accounts left by travelers such as Marco Polo and missionaries such as Matteo Ricci. Over the course of the sixteenth and seventeenth centuries, the Buddha, at first one of many Oriental idols, known by many names, came to develop some specificity. As the number of names by which the idol was known began to shrink, a variety of myths about his life and teachings began to converge. This knowledge about the Buddha was gained for the most part in lands that are today called China, Vietnam, Japan, Burma, Thailand, and Sri Lanka, but not in India. And the men who gathered it came for the most part from lands that are today called Portugal, Spain, Italy, the Netherlands, and France, but not from Great Britain.

In this chapter, our focus shifts, generally to India and to the British. By the eighteenth century, most but not all scholars thought that the Buddha was a historical figure. However, no one was sure exactly when he had lived or where he was from. Once the Europeans were well established in India (in the form of the East India Company)—the land that was both the cradle of Buddhism and the only place in Asia where Buddhism was absent—the British, and others, started seeking him elsewhere. They would conclude that the Buddha was not *from* India, but instead had come *to* India. But when, and why? Among the many theories set forth, two of the most influential came from Engelbert Kaempfer, a Westphalian physician in the employ of a different trade empire, the Dutch East India Company.

A Moor from Memphis

Kaempfer was born in 1651 in the town of Lemgo in Westphalia. His father was the minister of Saint Nicolai, a large Lutheran church; his mother was a daughter of a former minister there. He studied at a number of universities in northern Europe, excelling both in academic subjects and as a musician. In Cracow, where he studied philosophy and foreign languages, Kaempfer earned a doctorate in philosophy and then went on to Königsberg, where he studied medicine ("physick") and natural history. He next traveled to Sweden, where

King Charles XI appointed him secretary to a delegation about to depart for Persia, with the aim of establishing trade relations and persuading Persia to sever its ties with the Ottoman Empire. The Turks were threatening Europe; 150,000 of their troops would besiege Vienna on July 14, 1683.

The Swedish delegation embarked on its journey on March 20 of that year. In order to proceed to Persia, it needed the permission of the Russian czar, and so traveled to Moscow. On July 11, it had an audience with the famous "double czars," the physically infirm and mentally weak Ivan V and his half-brother, the eleven-year-old (and not yet "Great") Peter. The group then continued its journey by boat, sailing down the Volga to the Caspian Sea, where the craft was almost lost in a storm; the delegation's safety was further threatened by being on a boat with two rudders and two pilots who did not understand each other's language. Eventually, the group arrived in Persia and proceeded to the capital of Isfahan in January 1684. However, the court astrologers had determined that it would be dangerous for the king, Suleiman I, to appear in public until July 30.

During the long wait, and indeed throughout the journey, Kaempfer made good use of his time by "herborizing"—identifying new plant forms especially for their medicinal qualities, knowledge eventually published in his important Latin work *Amoenitatum Exoticarum* (*Exotic Pleasures*). Yet his interests were not confined to botany; they encompassed all elements of Persian life and history.

The Swedish delegation would spend two years in Persia. When it was time to return home, Kaempfer decided to leave the group and travel east alone. He proceeded south to the Persian Gulf, making detailed descriptions of the flora and fauna he encountered along the way. He suffered a near-fatal case of malaria in Gamron. In late June, he boarded a Dutch ship in the Persian Gulf, taking the position of surgeon to the fleet of the Dutch East India Company. Kaempfer wrote of the company, "This off-spring of Japhet [son of Noah, considered the progenitor of the European race] enjoys, more than any other European nation, the blessing of Noah, to live in the tents of Shem, and to have Canaan for their servant. God hath so blessed their valour and conduct, that they have enlarged their trade, conquests and possessions throughout Asia, to the very extremities of the East."[1]

And Kaempfer would travel to the "extremities of the East" in the employ of the Dutch, stopping in Arabia, the Malabar Coast in southwest India (where he spent six months), then Sri Lanka, Bengal, and Sumatra, before reaching Batavia (Jakarta) in Indonesia, head-quarters of the Dutch East India Company, in September 1689. Eight months later, he again put to sea, having been appointed physician to the Dutch embassy to Japan. Before proceeding north, the ship first sailed to Siam, eventually reaching Japan in September 1690. Kaemp-fer would spend the next two years there. At that time, the Dutch were restricted to Dejima, an island with a specific purpose.

As noted in chapter 2, Francis Xavier began the Roman Catholic mission to Japan in 1549, and over the next decades Christian mis-sionaries (mostly Portuguese) enjoyed considerable success there. Then during the first decades of the seventeenth century, Christian-ity was brutally suppressed by the shogun in a series of persecutions, although European trade missions were initially allowed to continue. However, the shogunate wished to strictly limit the European pres-ence in Japan, and thus in 1634 an artificial island, called Dejima, was constructed in Nagasaki Bay, to which all Portuguese traders were confined. After a Christian uprising in 1637, all Europeans were ex-pelled from Japan except for the Dutch, with the Dutch East India Company granted permission to establish a trading center on Dejima. The Dutch were favored in part because they expressed no interest in missionary activity. From 1639 until the arrival of Commodore Matthew Perry's black ships in 1853, they were the only Europeans allowed on Japanese territory.

On Dejima, the Dutch were kept under strict watch and were re-garded with suspicion. Kaempfer writes of the interpreters assigned to them, "But as we are only merchants, whom they place in the low-est class of mankind, . . . there is no other way to gain their friendship, and to win them over, to our interest, but a willingness to comply with their desire, a liberality to please their avaricious inclinations, and a submissive conduct to flatter their vanity."[2] Given his training, he could provide medical advice as well as information on mathemat-ics and astronomy, which were of great interest to the Japanese. In addition, "with a cordial and plentiful supply of European liquors, I could also, in my turn, freely put to them what questions I pleased, about the affairs of their Country, whether relating to the govern-ment in Civil or Ecclesiastical affairs, to the customs of the natives, to the natural and political history, and there was none that ever refused to give me all the information he could, even when we were alone, in such things, which they are otherwise strictly charged to keep secret."[3]

Kaempfer received invaluable service from a young Japanese, Imamura Gen'emon Eisei, who was appointed his servant. Kaempfer taught him anatomy and medicine as well as how to read and write Dutch, and paid him a handsome salary. In turn, his servant provided him with a great deal of information, and also procured books and explained their contents to him. In the course of his two-year stay, Kaempfer was twice allowed to make the long journey from Nagasaki to Edo (Tokyo), where he met the Tokugawa shogun, seeing a great deal of the country along the way. He left Japan in November 1692.[4]

Engelbert Kaempfer died in his home city of Lemgo on November 2, 1716, with his extensive writings left unpublished. His history of Japan, written in High Dutch, was translated into English and published in London in 1727 as *The History of Japan, giving an Account of the ancient and present State and Government of that Empire; of Its Temples, Palaces, Castles and other Buildings; of its Metals, Minerals, Trees, Plants, Animals, Birds and Fishes; of The Chronology and Succession of the Emperors, Ecclesiastical and Secular; of The Original Descent, Religions, Customs, and Manufactures of the Natives, and of their Trade and Commerce with the Dutch and Chinese. Together with a Description of the Kingdom of Siam.* The book contains a great deal of information about Buddhism that would be repeated in other works over the course of the eighteenth century. Kaempfer's work was a major source for Bernard Picart's *Cérémonies et coutumes religieuses de tous les peuples du monde* as well as Denis Diderot and Jean le Rond d'Alembert's *Encyclopédie.* For the European encounter with the Buddha, Kaempfer is a figure of particular importance; he put forth two of the most influential theories about the Buddha, theories that we might call "the African hypothesis" and "the two-buddha theory." He sets out both in the passage below. It is a long passage, but worth reading and pondering at some length:

•

The Religion of these People is the Pagan Doctrine of the Brahmans, which ever since many Centuries hath been profess'd amongst all the

Nations from the River Indus to the extremity of the East, except that
at the Court of the Grand Mogul, and in his great Cities, as also in Sum-
matra, Java, Celebes, and other neighbouring Islands the Mahometism
[Islam] has gain'd so much ground, that it seems to prevail above it. This
general Paganism, (which is to be distinguish'd from the Religion of the
old Persians worshipping the Sun, now almost extinct) tho' branch'd
out into several Sects and Opinions, according to the various Customs,
Languages, and Interpretations, yet is of one and the same Origine. The
Siamites represent the first Teacher of their Paganism in their Temples, in the figure of a Negro sitting, of a prodigious size, his hair curl'd,
the skin black, but as it were out of respect gilt over, accompanied on
each side by one of his chief Companions, as also before and round him
by the rest of his Apostles and Disciples, all of the same colour and most
in the same posture. They believe according to the Brahmans, that the
Deity dwelt in him, which he prov'd by his Doctrine, Way of Life, and
Revelation. For Wistnu, by which they mean the Deity, having already
many hundred thousands of years before assum'd different forms, and
visited the World eight different times, appear'd the ninth in the person of this Negro, whom for this reason they stile Prahpuditsau, that is
to say, the Saint of high descent; Sammana Khutama, the Man without
Passions: Prah bin Tsjau, the Saint who is the Lord; or plainly Prah, the
Saint, or Budha' (or Phutha' in one syllable, according to their guttural
pronunciation, like that of the Hottentots). The Ceylanese call him Budhum, the Chinese and Japanese Sacka, or Siaka, or plainly Fotoge, that
is, the Idol, and with an honourable Epithet Si Tsun, the great Saint.

About his origine and native Country, I find the account of those
Heathens do not agree. The Siamites call the Country of his nativity
Lanca, which is the Island of Ceylon, from whence they say, their Religion was first brought over to them, and afterwards further propagated through the neighbouring Countries as far as China and Japan.
Accordingly there are still to be seen some foot steps of their Religion,
as well as that which they exercis'd before, as of the other sprung up in
the room of it, on the top of a high mountain in the Island of Ceylon,
by the Europeans call'd Pico d'Adam, which they look upon as holy, and
in their Maps place it in the Centre of the World. The Ceylonese themselves call the Country of his nativity Macca desia, meaning by it the
Kingdom of Siam, for which they make use of the Pali, or the Bible of
the Siamites, which the Peguans call Maccatapasa, in their Khom, or

Language of the Khomuts, owning that they had it from the Siamites. The Chinese and Japanese pretend that this Saint, and the Doctrine he reveal'd, had their origine in the Country of Magatta, or as the Japanese call it, Tensik Magatta Kokf, that is the Heavenlandish Magatta, which according to their description and opinion is the Continent of India, including Pegu and Siam, adding withal, that Siaka was the Son of the King of those Countries, the Inhabitants of which ascribe to each other the origin of their Teacher, a Prophet, as it seems, being always thought the greater for being of a foreign Country. The Benjans and learned Brahmans believe that Budha had neither Father nor Mother, and consequently own, they know nothing of his birth and native Country. They represent him in the figure of a man with four arms, and as for the rest have no other Legends concerning his miracles and actions, besides a tradition of his adorable piety having now for 26430 years been sitting on a Tarate flower, and praising the supreme God even since 21639 years (reckoning from the present 1690 year of Christ,) when he first appear'd and reveal'd himself to the world. But the Siamites, and other Nations lying further East, have whole Books full of the birth, life and miracles of this God Prah, or Siaka. I am at a loss how to reconcile these various and opposite accounts, which I have gather'd in the abovesaid Countries, unless by supposing, what I really think to be the true opinion, *viz.* that the Siamites and other Nations lying more Easterly have confounded a younger Teacher with Budha' and mistaken the former for the latter, which confusion of the Gods and their names is very frequent in the Histories of the Greeks and Egyptians; so that Prah or Siaka, is not the same with Budha, much less with Ram, or Rama, as he is call'd by Father Kircher in his Sina Illustrata, the latter having appear'd many hundred thousand years before, but that he was some new Impostor who set up but about five hundred years before Christ's nativity. Besides this, many circumstances make it probable, that the Prah, or Siaka, was no Asiatick, or Indian, but some Egyptian Priest of note, probably of Memphis, and a Moor, who with his Brethren being expell'd their native Country, brought the Egyptian Religion into the Indies, and propagated it there, and this for the following Reasons.

1. There appears in several material Points a conformity between this Eastern, and the Ancient Egyptian Paganism; for the Egyptians represented their Gods, as these Heathens now do, in the form of different sorts of Animals and human Monsters; whereas their Neighbours

in *Asia*, as for example, the Persians, Chaldeans, and other Nations professing the same Religion, worship'd rather the Luminaries of the Heavens, particularly the Sun, and the Fire, as being its Image; and it is probable, that before the introduction of the present Paganism among the Indians, they had the same sort of worship with the neighbouring Chaldeans and Persians. For as it cannot be suppos'd, that these sensible Nations liv'd without any Religion at all, like the brutal Hottentots, it is highly probable, that they rever'd the divine Omnipotence by worshiping, according to the Custom of the Chaldeans, the Sun, and other Luminaries of the Firmament, as such parts of the Creation, which most strike the outward senses, and fill the understanding with the admiration of their unconceivable proprieties. And there are still to this day among those Heathens some remains of the Chaldean Religion, consisting in a worship paid to the Sun and the Stars, which however is not taught by their Priests, but only tolerated like some supererogatory worship, just as there remain even in Christian Governments, certain ancient pagan customs and superstitions, especially the Bachanals. Two Articles in the Egyptian Religion, which were most religiously maintain'd, were, the Transmigration of Souls, and a Veneration for Cows, particularly for the holy Cow at Memphis, call'd Apis, or Serapis, which had divine honours paid her, and was serv'd by Priests. Both these Articles are still observ'd among the Asiatick Heathens, particularly those that inhabit the West-side of the Ganges; for no body there dares to kill the least and most noxious Insects, as being animated by some transmigrated human Soul; and the Cows, whose Souls they think are by frequent transmigrations, as it were, deified, are serv'd and attended with great veneration, their Dung being burnt to ashes is turn'd into holy Salve, their Urine serves for holy Water, the Image of a Cow possesses a peculiar Chapel before their Temples, is every day honour'd with fresh flowers, and hath sweet-scented oyl poured upon her. It is also remarkable, that the nearer those Heathens are to *Egypt*, the greater Zeal appears among them with relation to these two Articles, and the more remote they are from it, the more they abate in it, so that in *Siam* and the more Eastern Kingdoms, even the Priests themselves make no scruple of eating Cows Flesh, provided they have not given occasion, nor consented to their killing; nor doth the opinion of the transmigration of the Souls prevail there so much, as it does among the Benjans in Hindostan, for the Inhabitants of the East-side of the

Ganges grant no quarters to Fleas or Flies, that attack their Skin. I shall barely mention, that among these Asiatick Heathens we meet not only with the greater Deities of the Egyptians, but also with the lesser, tho' they are disguised by other names, and fabulous circumstances, which however might be easily clear'd up and reconcil'd.

2. It is observable, that twenty three Centuries ago, or according to the most exact computation in the five hundred and thirty sixth year before Christ's nativity, Cambyses, the Persian Tyrant, subverted the Religion of the Egyptians, kill'd their Apis, or holy Cow, the Palladium of their Worship, and murder'd, or exil'd their Priests. Now if one considers that the Siamites, reckoning, their Soncarad, or Ecclesiastical Epocha from the death of their great Saint, their 2233-4th year falls in with our present 1690th year after Christ's nativity, it will appear, that the said *Epocha* agreed with that time, and that it may be concluded from thence, that then a notable Priest of *Memphis*, to whom they gave the name of Budha, Siaka, or the great Saint, fled with his Brethren into India, where he publish'd his Doctrine, which was so well receiv'd, that it spread to the extremity of the Orient.

3. This Saint being represented with curled Hairs, like a Negro, there is room to conclude, that he was no native of India, but was born under the hot Climate of Africa, considering that the Air in India produces on its black Inhabitants none of that curl'd Wool, but long and black Hair, quite lank, and very little curl'd: And tho' the Siamites crop theirs, so as to leave it only of the length of a Finger; yet as it stands on end like bristles, it is easily distinguish'd from the woolly Curls of a Negro, and consequently it is more probable, that Budha was of African, than of Siamite extraction.[5]

•

For Dr. Kaempfer, the religion of the Japanese, the religion that would eventually come to be known as Buddhism, was a pagan doctrine among the four categories of religion of the day: Christianity, Judaism, Mahometism (Islam), and Paganism or Idolatry. He translated *Butsudō*, the Japanese word for "Buddhism," as "The Way of the Idol." It was, in addition, the pagan doctrine of the brahmans, a religion found also in India and practiced there. Together with his contemporary in India, Father Queyroz (whom we met in chapter 2), Kaempfer was among the first to recognize that this religion was practiced across Asia. Queyroz mentions Ceylon, Arracan and Pegu (both in Burma), Siam, Tartary (Tibet), China, and Japan.[6] Dr. Kaempfer speaks instead of its geographical sweep, from the Indus River in modern Pakistan to "the extremity of the East," Japan; but he carefully excepts Muslim regions: the "Court of the Great Mogul," that is, the Mughal Emperor in Delhi; other cities in India; and the Muslim regions of what is now Indonesia—the islands of Sumatra, Java, and Celebes (Sulawesi). He understands that all paganisms are not the same, and he distinguishes this one from the sun-worshipping variety that had existed in pre-Muslim Persia—presumably referring to the Roman cult of Mithraism or perhaps to Zoroastrianism—something he had likely learned about from a French Capuchin missionary at the court of Isfahan, Father Raphael du Mans (1613-1696), whom Kaempfer had befriended during his time in Persia.

Dr. Kaempfer declares that the paganism he has encountered in Japan, and which is found across Asia, has a single origin, despite its various branches and sects in different regions. Its founder, or first teacher, is depicted in Siam as "a Negro sitting, of a prodigious size, his hair curl'd, the skin black, but as it were out of respect gilt over." The primary evidence of his race seems to have been his curly hair. As Kaempfer notes at the end of this long passage, the people of India, the land of the Buddha's origin, have hair that is long and straight. Since he is describing Siamese statues of the Buddha, perhaps the Siamese are representing the Buddha with hair like theirs. But he notes that when they allow their closely cropped hair to grow out, it is straight and bristly; neither Indians nor Thais have "the wooly Curls of a Negro." The claim that the Buddha was a Negro would be repeated many times over the next century and a half. It was only in the middle of the nineteenth century that ancient Indian statues of the Buddha would be discovered by the British in Gandhara in India (what is now Pakistan). From that point on, the Buddha's curls would look Greek rather than African to the European eye.

As we shall see below, in his "Third Anniversary Discourse" delivered in Calcutta to the Asiatick Society of Bengal on February 2, 1786, the British philologist and jurist Sir William Jones would argue that the mountain people of the Indian states of Bengal and Bihar were of African origin. They had noses and lips like Abyssinians. They differed only in their hair, but this seemed to be an effect of climate; the "crisp and wooly" hair of the Africans was the natural state. As proof, he pointed to statues of the Buddha: "We frequently see figures of Buddha with curled hair, apparently designed for a representation of it in its natural state."[7] And in 1810, the British army veteran Edward Moor (1771–1848) would write, "Some statues of BUDDHA certainly exhibit thick *Ethiopian* lips; but all, with wooly hair: there is something mysterious, and still unexplained, connected with the hair of this, and only of this, *Indian* deity. The fact of so many different tales having been invented to account for his crisped woolly head, is alone sufficient to excite suspicion that there is something to conceal— something to be ashamed of; more exists than meets the eye."[8]

The British jurist J. H. Harington, on a visit to the "Temple at Oogulbodda" in Sri Lanka on March 10, 1797, took the opportunity to ask the monks there about the Buddha's hair. They were insulted by his suggestion of African origins:

•

There are several other images of BUDDHA in this temple, which, having no peculiar characteristic, do not call for distinct notice. It may be of use to observe, however, that on my pointing out the uniformity of the head-dress, in respect to the crisped hair; and asking whether it was meant to represent the hair of an *Abysinnian*; the priests, of whom four were present, answered in the negative, with apparent abhorrence; and the priest who had before attended me, repeating his previous information of BUDDHA's being the son of SUDODHANA rajah, and born in *Muggud deish* (*Bahar*) added, in explanation of the hair being short and crisped, that BUDDHA had on a certain occasion cut his hair with a golden sword, and its appearance in consequence was meant to be represented on his images.[9]

•

And the monks were correct. During his first twenty-nine years, the future Buddha, Prince Siddhārtha, lived the life of a prince, sequestered in a palace of delights. As a prince, he wore his hair long and uncut, piled on top of his head, sometimes wrapped in a turban. But when he was twenty-nine—after encountering old age, sickness, and death on chariot rides beyond the walls that had shielded him for so long—he famously left the palace, leaving behind his wife and newborn son, in search of a state beyond birth and death. The story of his departure is often told in Buddhist texts. One of the most famous accounts occurs in a work, perhaps from as late as the fifth century CE, entitled the *Account of Origins* (*Nidānakathā*), an introduction to a collection of stories about the Buddha's former lives. Here, from Henry Clarke Warren's 1896 translation, is what happened after the prince left the palace and found himself in the forest:

•

Next he thought, "These locks of mine are not suited to a monk; but there is no one fit to cut the hair of a Future Buddha. Therefore I will cut them off myself with my sword." And grasping a scimitar with his right hand, he seized his top-knot with his left hand, and cut it off, together with the diadem. His hair thus became two finger-breadths in length, and curling to the right, lay close to his head. As long as he lived it remained of that length, and the beard was proportionate. And never again did he have to cut either hair or beard.

Then the Future Buddha seized hold of his top-knot and diadem, and threw them into the air, saying,—

"If I am to become a Buddha, let them stay in the sky; but if not, let them fall to the ground."

The top-knot and jewelled turban mounted a distance of a league in the air, and there came to a stop. And Sakka, the king of the gods, perceiving them with his divine eye, received them in an appropriate jewelled casket, and established it in the Heaven of the Thirty-three as the "Shrine of the Diadem."[10]

•

And so, although Buddhist monks shaved their heads, the Buddha never shaved his. His hair never grew from that moment, but remained tightly curled on his head. Among the famous eighty "secondary marks" (*anuvyañjana*) of the Buddha's body, six deal with his hair: black as a bee, thick, soft, not disheveled, not rough, and fragrant. In statues of the Buddha, especially those made in Southeast Asia, the Buddha's curls are often depicted as individual rings, tightly coiled into tiny cones arrayed across his head. Some European travelers mistook them for snails, others for spikes. But to many, they looked like the "crisped" hair of a Negro, a sense confirmed for many by what they regarded as the statues' broad noses and thick lips. To Kaempfer and many after him, these apparent features indicated that the Buddha came not from India but from Africa, and elaborate theories were developed to support this claim. The Buddhists themselves either did not know this or had hidden it—Kaempfer describes the Siamese statues of the Buddha as "black, but as it were out of respect gilt over." But he puts forth this theory only after reporting what the natives themselves say about the identity of the Buddha.

He reports that "they" (presumably the Siamese) believe, like the brahmans of India, that the deity dwelt within this Negro, that he was the ninth incarnation of "Wistnu" (Vishnu). Kaempfer is mistaken here, because he failed to distinguish Hindu from Buddhist doctrine; Buddhists do not consider the Buddha an incarnation of the Hindu deity. However, Hindus do, and by Kaempfer's day the nine incarnations were known to Europeans.

According to its most famous enumeration, the great god Vishnu is said to have had nine avatars (Anglicized from the Sanskrit *avatāra*, or "descent"), appearing in the world at crucial moments to restore righteousness. These incarnations follow an apparently evolutionary order, from fish, to tortoise, to boar, to half-lion half-man, to dwarf, to human. The most famous of the avatars of Vishnu are the seventh and eighth, Rama and Krishna. The tenth avatar, Kalki, is yet to appear.

Long after his death, the Buddha was incorporated into the Hindu pantheon as the ninth incarnation of Vishnu. The specific purpose of Vishnu's incarnation as the Buddha is variously portrayed in the Hindu *purāṇas* (stories about the gods). In one well-known narrative, demons gain power through the recitation of the Vedas and the practice of asceticism, thus challenging the supremacy of the gods. In order to deprive the demons of their power, Vishnu appears as a sage who condemns the practice of Vedic sacrifice, ignores caste distinction, and denies the existence of a creator deity. The demons become disciples of this new teacher and embrace his teachings. As a consequence, they not only lose their power but are reborn in hell. The purpose of Vishnu appearing as the Buddha was therefore one of deception: to convince the demons that things that are true and efficacious—Vedic sacrifice, caste distinction, and a creator god—are in fact false. These are three things that, according to the Buddhist tradition, the Buddha did in fact reject (although his attitude toward caste was more nuanced than is often portrayed in European scholarship), and that he rejected because they are false.

Not surprisingly, the story of the Buddha's incarnation as Vishnu is not accepted by any of the Buddhist schools or reported (at least approvingly) in any Buddhist text, although Vishnu's future tenth incarnation, Kalki, would find his way into the apocalyptic myth of the *Kālacakra Tantra* in the eleventh century. However, two elements of the Hindu myth (which is hardly an instantiation of the ecumenical spirit, as it has so often been portrayed in neo-Hinduism) would attach themselves to the person of the Buddha, both in post-Buddhist India and in the West: his condemnation of animal sacrifice (especially of the beloved Indian cow) and his rejection of the caste system. The caste system is something that Europeans would also come to condemn, and the Buddha's condemnation of it two millennia earlier would prove to be an important element in his subsequent appeal in the West, where he was presented as a "reformer."

Dr. Kaempfer next turns to the various names by which the Buddha is known in various Asian languages: "Sammana Khutama" (the Thai pronunciation of the Pāli Samaṇa Gotama, "the ascetic Gautama"), Prahpuditsau (that is, *phra phuttha chao*, or Lord Buddha), and Prah bin Tsjau (*phra pen chao*, or Supreme Buddha) in Siam, Budhum in Ceylon, Sacca or Siaka in China and Japan (in fact, Shijia and Shaka, respectively, abbreviations of Śākyamuni), Fotoge (that is, *hotoke*, a Japanese word for "Buddha"), which Kaempfer translates simply as "the Idol," and Si Tsun (that is, Shizun, Chinese for "World Honored One").

Having enumerated the variety of names by which this Negro is known in Asia, Kaempfer addresses the question of where he came from. He is clearly exasperated by what he has learned from his informants: "I find the account of those Heathens do not agree." He then illustrates this, explaining that the Siamese think that the Buddha came from Ceylon, leaving his footprints on Adam's Peak. Yet according to Kaempfer, the Sinhalese believe the Buddha came from Siam, which, he says, they call "Macca desia," a variant of which, Maccatapasa, is found among the "Peguans," the inhabitants of Lower Burma, in the language of "Khom," the Thai word for the Khmer language (a word that likely derives from Kambojadeśa, the Sanskrit term for Cambodia). The Chinese and Japanese pretend that he came from Magatta. But where Kaempfer sees disagreement about the place of the Buddha's birth, there is in fact considerable consistency, with Macca desia, Maccatapasa, and Magatta Kokf all being local variations of Magadha, the name of a region in ancient India where the Buddha achieved enlightenment and spent most of his life. Kaempfer is perhaps correct, however, when he observes that a prophet is "always thought the greater for being of a foreign country."

He notes that the Japanese place their Magatta Kokf in India, but explains that the Indians themselves, the brahmans and "Benjans" (presumably Bengalis), have no knowledge of the Buddha's birthplace because he had no parents. They describe him as a four-armed man who has been sitting on a Tarate flower for 24,470 years. Elsewhere, Kaempfer identifies this flower as a *nymphaea magna incarnata*, a kind of water lily known to the ancients as an Egyptian flower, the *faba aegyptia*. Yet despite the Indians' ignorance concerning the origins of a man supposedly born among them, "the Siamites, and other Nations lying further East, have whole Books full of the birth, life, and miracles of the God Prah, or Siaka." Kaempfer declares himself at a loss for making any sense of these conflicting accounts of the origin of this god worshipped throughout Asia. And so, rather than trying to do so, he presents his own theory.

We see, then, in Dr. Kaempfer's account a process whereby the various idols that the Europeans encountered across Asia in the previous centuries began to coalesce, by fits and starts, into one. From our perspective, this appears simply as a frustratingly slow movement from one error to another, with an accurate portrait of the Buddha yet to be painted. But from another perspective this process was essential to our modern notion of Buddhism as a single world religion. At first, for the missionaries and scholars of the day, Buddhism was various forms of idolatry across Asia, each with its own idol. Next, it was a single religion with a single founder. At first, that religion was idolatry and its founder was the accursed idol Fo. Later, the religion was called Buddhism and its founder was the compassionate Buddha. But whether idol or savior, before the Buddha could become one, he became two.

Kaempfer argues that two figures—one very ancient, one relatively recent—had been confused by Siam and the other nations of Asia. The ancient figure, named Budha, had lived hundreds of thousands of years ago. The recent figure, called Prah by the Siamese and Siaka by the Chinese and Japanese, lived about five hundred years before Christ. He was an impostor, declaring himself to be Budha. Furthermore, although this Prah or Siaka taught in India, he was not from there. He was an Egyptian, a priest of Memphis, the royal city of the pharaohs, and he was a Moor. He and his followers had been driven from Egypt, eventually making their way to India. Kaempfer offers several pieces of evidence supporting this theory of the Egyptian origin of the Negro god.

He first notes what he perceives as the similarity between the religion of Egypt and the religion of India and points east; in both, gods are represented in the form of animals or human monsters. This is quite different from the religion of the Persians and the Chaldeans (Babylonians), who worship the sun, other luminaries of the heavens, and fire. Since Persia is closer to India than Egypt, it would seem logical that the Persians and the Indians would share the same religion, the worship of the sun. Kaempfer thus speculates that because all sensible nations (in the sense of peoples) have religion, the original religion of India and the eastern lands was similar to that of Persia. It was this religion that was displaced by the teachings of the priest of Memphis, although remnants of solar worship remain among the Asians.

Two important elements of Egyptian religion are found among the Asian heathens: the belief in the transmigration of souls and the veneration of cows. These, Kaempfer observes, are held more strongly on the western side of the Ganges River, the side closer to Egypt, than on the eastern side. He even reports that those in western India dare not kill the most noxious insects, while those in the east "grant no quarter to Fleas or Flies." He also notes, correctly, that whereas in India the cow is worshipped, in Siam, farther from Egypt, even Buddhist monks eat beef as long as the animal has not been slaughtered specifically for them. He notes, incorrectly, that the belief in reincarnation is weaker in Siam than it is in Hindostan. Moreover, Dr. Kaempfer mentions in passing, without providing any examples, that both the major and minor deities of Egyptian religion are to be found among the Asian heathens, although they are disguised. All of this suggests to him that the religion found in India—stronger in the west, weaker in the east—had been transported from Egypt, displacing the solar worship that existed upon the arrival of the priest of Memphis.

Dr. Kaempfer is specific about why and when this priest left Egypt.

Relating a history he likely learned from reading Herodotus, he reminds the reader that in 536 BCE, the Persian tyrant Cambyses defeated the Egyptians, killed their sacred cow, and murdered or exiled their priests. In fact, in 525 BCE, Cambyses II, the son of Cyrus the Great, defeated the Egyptians at the Battle of Pelusium and proceeded to Memphis, where he captured the pharaoh and slaughtered thousands of Egyptians; it is said that the Persian soldiers advanced into battle carrying cats, knowing that the Egyptians would not shoot their arrows for fear of harming their sacred animal. Kaempfer notes that the Siamese measure time from the death of their founder; indeed, many Buddhist calendars divide time into the period before and after the Buddha's passage into nirvana. During his time in Siam, Kaempfer learned that the Christian year 1690 corresponded to the Siamese year of 2234, thus placing the death of the god that they call Budha or Siaka in 544 BCE. These two dates—536 BCE and 544 BCE— are sufficiently close to suggest that this Budha was in fact a priest of Memphis exiled by Cambyses. Further proof, if needed, is found in his curly hair; "consequently it is more probable, that Budha was of African, than of Siamite extraction."

One of the chief proponents of the theory that Egypt was the source of pagan idolatry was one of the most famous scholars of the seventeenth century, the great Jesuit savant Athanasius Kircher (1602–1680), described as "the last man who knew everything." We encountered his vitriolic biography of the Buddha in the previous chapter. Kircher wrote some forty works on a remarkable range of topics, including biblical studies, geology, biology, and engineering. The most famous of these was his *Oedipus Aegyptiacus*, a three-volume study of ancient Egypt published between 1652 and 1654, so named because Kircher believed that he had solved the riddle of Egyptian hieroglyphics. Kircher was, sadly, wrong; the solution would not come until the discovery of the Rosetta Stone almost two centuries later. Yet he produced elaborate translations of Egyptian texts, and he believed that Egypt was the source of human civilization; Adam and Eve, he argued, spoke Egyptian. Perhaps his second most famous work was *China Illustrata*, published in 1667. Kircher wrote it without leaving Rome, drawing on the considerable corpus of reports and letters that his fellow Jesuits had by that time sent from China.

Kircher discerned a direct connection between Egypt and China.

After the flood, Noah's son Ham (Cham) went to Egypt and then to Persia, eventually establishing colonies in Bactria. From there, his progeny spread to China, "the last place on earth to be colonized."[11] The Chinese were thus descendants of the Egyptians and derived their writing system from hieroglyphics. They also received their religion from Egypt, many centuries later. Kircher tells the same story of Cambyses and the exodus of Egyptian priests by sea to India, where they discovered ancient monuments to Hermes, Bacchus, and Osiris and revived the worship of these gods. From there, Egyptian religion, including the doctrine of the transmigration of souls, spread to Indochina, China, and Japan, "bringing along its fanatic crowd of innumerable gods and goddesses."[12] For Kircher, "there is no cult of the ancient Egyptians and their descendants which isn't followed today by our modern barbarians, who have changed the worship of sun and moon, or Isis and Osiris, into that of Foto [the Buddha] and Chamis [Japanese *kami*]. . . . All the old mysteries, rites, and superstitious ceremonies have been borrowed for the new pagan religions, just as if reflected in a mirror."[13] This is specifically the case for Buddhism, which he calls the sect of Siequa (that is, Śākyamuni Buddha) or Omyto (Amitābha):

•

When we investigate this sect, its doctrines show that it came from the naked philosophers of the brahmins, Persians, and Bactrians, who formerly inhabited all Indostan. They believe in a multitude of worlds and in metempsychosis, which is the entrance of human souls into animals, and in all the Pythagorean teachings. . . .

They live apart on hills and in caves for the sake of meditation. Their temples are full of huge idols of bronze, marble, wood, and clay. You would think these are Egyptian shrines. [14]

•

The two-Buddha theory next appears in 1762, in a work entitled *Alphabetum Tibetanum*, a summary in Latin of the records of the Capuchin mission to Lhasa (1708–1745) by the Augustinian friar Antonio Agostino Giorgi (1711–1797). It is a huge and vexing text, filled with some accurate information and much fantastical theorizing, appearing all the more authoritative with words in Greek, Hebrew, Arabic,

Devanagari, and Tibetan script on many of its more than nine hundred pages. In a lecture to the Asiatic Society of Bengal in 1832, the eminent Orientalist (and assistant surgeon of the British East India Company) H. H. Wilson (1786–1860) described a Tibetan passage cited by Father Giorgi: "He prints them therefore without any translation, but nevertheless, pretends to explain their purpose in his notes on the text, in which he assembles a crude mass of extravagancies from Hebrew, Chaldaic, Coptic, and Syriac, and compares these Tibetan characters to the mystic numbers and letters of the ancient Scythians and Egyptians, and some of the early Sectarians and Heretics of the Christian Church. This display of unprofitable erudition is in fact only a shelter for his ignorance."[15] Nonetheless, Giorgi's tome remained an influential source on Tibet into the nineteenth century; it was cited favorably by Kant himself.

For Giorgi, as for Kaempfer, there were two Buddhas, both separated by long periods of time. The first was of Egyptian origin and associated with the Egyptian god Osiris. But whereas for Kaempfer the second Buddha came to India some five centuries before the birth of Christ, for Giorgi he came after Christ's resurrection. This figure, whom Giorgi calls Butta, impersonated Christ. So taken were the Tibetans with this Butta that they named their country for him; the Tibetan word for "Tibet" is *Bod*. Giorgi writes:

·

We have exposed him as twins, namely as *Butta* and *Xaca*: a first one, whose arrival was nearly a thousand years before Christ and a second one, who has become known to the Tibetans only after [Christ's] ascension. We have seen both as similar, with the same name homonymous and fabulous. However, the first one was fabricated by heathen myths, the second one was invented by Gnostic, Basilidian, Manichean, and sacrilegious legends of the Pseudo-Christians. This new *Butta*, who was excogitated by the Gnostics at the end of the first century of the Christian calendar, became known to the Scyths, Indians, Chinese, and Tibetans. We have said that he [claimed to be] God's son Jesus Christ himself, born of a virgin mother, conceived by the Holy Spirit, filled with the Holy Spirit. . . . However, the ancients and the pagans have with utmost irreverence dressed him in the filthy and horrible rags of the virgin born *Butta*. We have also demonstrated, how *Mani's* tricks were so advanced that he strived to be regarded by the Tibetans as the *Butta* himself and as the heavenly spirit.[16]

•

The next figure to propound the two-Buddha theory is far more renowned today than Kaempfer or Giorgi. He is Sir William Jones (1746-1794), the distinguished British philologist and jurist. Already skilled in both Persian and Arabic, in 1783 he was knighted and appointed judge to the Supreme Court of Bengal; he would spend the remainder of his life in India, devoting much of his efforts to the study and translation of Sanskrit poetry, drama, and law books. In 1784, he founded the Asiatick Society of Bengal in Calcutta, and in his "Third Anniversary Discourse" to the society on February 2, 1786, he famously declared, "The *Sanscrit* language, whatever be its antiquity, is of a wonderful structure; more perfect than the *Greek*, more copious than the *Latin*, and more exquisitely refined than either, yet bearing to both of them a stronger affinity, both in the roots of verbs and in the forms of grammar, than could possibly have been produced by accident; so strong indeed that no philologer could examine them all three, without believing them to have sprung from some common sources, which, perhaps, no longer exists."[17]

Like Dr. Kaempfer and Father Giorgi (and so many scholars of the day), Jones was fixated on ancient Egypt and Ethiopia. Also like them, he subscribed to the two-Buddha theory. Yet unlike Kaempfer and Giorgi, Jones spent much of his life in India, where the two-Buddha theory allowed him to resolve a problem that arose from his conversations with brahman priests. The scholars of the East India Company were not yet aware of the Sanskrit Buddhist texts that their own Brian Hodgson would discover in Kathmandu in the early 1820s, and thus relied on Hindu sources for their knowledge of the Buddha. As discussed above, in the Hindu *purāṇas*, the Buddha is listed as one of the incarnations of Vishnu. However, Jones encountered two conflicting views of the Buddha among his Hindu informants. For some, he was indeed an incarnation of Vishnu and was revered for condemning the sacrifice of cattle, as the Vedas had enjoined. For others, the Buddha was a heretic, whose followers had been rightfully driven from India.

This latter view had been noted by Europeans for more than a century before Jones. For example, on October 4, 1667, François Bernier (1620–1688) wrote a letter entitled "Describing the Superstitions, strange customs, and Doctrines of the Indous or Gentiles of Hindoustan; from which it will be seen that there is no Doctrine too strange or too improbable for the Soul of man to conceive," in which he noted:

•

Among the philosophers who have flourished in *Hindoustan*, six bear a great name; and from these have sprung the six sects, which cause much jealousy and dispute, the *Pendets* [pundits] of each pretending that the doctrines of their particular sect are the soundest, and most in conformity to the *Beths* [Vedas]. A seventh sect has arisen, called *Bauté*, which again is the parent of twelve others; but this sect is not so considerable as the former: its adherents are despised and hated, censured as irreligious and atheistical, and lead a life peculiar to themselves.[18]

•

In a period closer to that of Jones, the attitude of these brahmans was described in 1810 by Edward Moor (1771–1848) in *The Hindu Pantheon*:

•

SUCH *Hindus* as admit BUDDHA to be an incarnation of VISHNU, agree in his being the last important appearance of the deity on earth; but many among the *Brahmans*, and other tribes, deny their identity; and the *Buddhists*, countenanced by the *Rahans*, their priests, do, in general, likewise assert the independent existence, and of course paramount character, of the deity of their exclusive worship. As most of VISHNU's *Avataras* were apparently destined for the accomplishment of some especial object, so this BUDDHA seems to have been for the purpose of reclaiming the *Hindus* from their proneness to animal sacrifice, and their prodigality even of human blood. A people having once satisfied themselves, that the fat of bulls, and kids and goats, is acceptable to their deities, and a priesthood having gained such a triumph as to persuade their deluded flock into a belief of the meritorious immolation of their brethren or themselves, cannot but with great difficulty be diverted from practices, and divested of feelings, so repugnant to humanity; their continued existence evincing their strength and tenacity. The mild heresy preached by BUDDHA, a leading tenet of which is the *sin of depriving any animal of life,* would naturally alarm the orthodox priesthood, whose coffers overflowed from the donations of affrighted sinners, and whose hierarchy was threated by the dawn of reason and the diffusion of philosophy. It cannot therefore be supposed, that such an innovation, condemning the prescribed doctrines of their most sacred books, and the practices founded on them of the most sacred sect, in its consequences deeply involving the supposed sanctity of both, could be contemplated by the *Brahmans* without considerable jealousy, or its progress witnessed without opposition. And we are accordingly informed, the *Buddhism* having in time so encroached on the respect antecedently shown to the *Brahmans,* and caused a great diminution of their flock, that latter were roused, not only to the exercise of legitimate and reasonable means of resistance, but at length to the excesses of invective, and the terrible resource of civil and religious persecution. Whatever rivalrous enmity might anciently have been excited, it seems now happily extinct: rivalry is no longer, and enmity died with it. The orthodox supremacy of the *Brahmans,* in almost all parts of the hither peninsula, views with piety, and perhaps with contempt, the heretical insignificance of the fallen *Rahans,* or priests of BUDDHA.[19]

•

Thus, although the brahmans granted grudging respect to the Buddha for saving the sacred cow from the sacrificial altar, their general attitude to the Buddha and Buddhism, according to Moor, was one of contempt.

In the Hindu *purāṇas,* Sir William Jones also found a story of a great flood: the first incarnation of Vishnu warns the world of the coming deluge. Jones saw this as a confirmation of the account in the book of Genesis, which for scholars of his day was regarded as a historical event that could be dated using biblical genealogies. In this case, at least some of the nine incarnations of Vishnu were likely historical figures, and the more recent of the nine, including the Buddha, could be dated. Thus, in an address to the Asiatic Society of Bengal in Calcutta on February 2, 1786, Jones stated that "we may fix the time of *Buddha,* or the *ninth* great incarnation of Vishnu, in the year *one thousand* and *fourteen* before the birth of Christ."[20] For Jones, this was the first of the two buddhas, who lived 1,014 (or 1,027) years before Christ and who was revered by the Hindus as the ninth incarnation of Vishnu. The second buddha lived a millennium later. He stole the name of the first Buddha and denounced the brahmans, earning their ire. According to Jones:

•

The Brahmans universally speak of the Bauddhas [Buddhists] with all the malignity of an intolerant spirit; yet the most orthodox among them consider Buddha himself as an incarnation of Vishnu: this is a contradiction hard to be reconciled; unless we cut the knot, instead of untying it, by supposing with Giorgi, that there were two Buddhas, the younger of whom established the new religion, which gave so great offence in India, and was introduced into China in the first century of our era. . . . It seems highly probable, on the whole, that the Buddha . . . though he forbad the sacrifices of cattle, which the *Vedas* enjoin, was believed to be Vishnu himself in a human form, and that another Buddha, one perhaps of his followers in a later age, assuming his name and character, attempted to overset the whole system of the Brahmans, and was the cause of that persecution, from which the Bauddhas [Buddhists] are known to have fled into very distant regions. May we not reconcile the singular difference of opinion among the Hindus as to the time of Buddha's appearance, by supposing that they have confounded the two Buddhas, the first of whom was born a few years before the close of the last age, and the second, when above a thousand years of the present age had elapsed?[21]

•

Thus, the first Buddha, the one worshipped by the Hindus as an incarnation of their god, simply sought to prevent the slaughter of cattle. The second Buddha made a more thoroughgoing attack on brahmanical authority. As a consequence, his followers were eventually driven from India. This would explain the apparent contradiction in the brahmans' attitude toward the Buddha. There were in fact two, and brahmans respected the first and condemned the second.

Although Jones believed, like others, that the first Buddha and his teachings did not originate in India and had been imported there, he did not immediately accept the African hypothesis. At one point, he speculated that the Buddha was identical to Odin, and that a foreign race had imported the rites of these gods into Scandinavia and India.[22] However, he eventually abandoned this theory in favor of another: "that *Sacya* or *Sisak* [the Buddha], about two hundred years after *Vyasa*, either in person or by a colony from *Egypt*, imported into this country the mild heresy of the ancient *Bauddhas*."[23] Jones believed that Ethiopia and India (or Hindustan, as he called it) were colonized by the same race. Describing the Hindu and Buddhist monuments being excavated in India by the British, he wrote:

The letters on many of those monuments appear, as I have before intimated, partly of Indian, and partly of Abyssinian or Ethiopick, origin; and all these indubitable facts may induce no ill-grounded opinion, that Ethiopia and Hindustan were peopled or colonized by the same extraordinary race; in confirmation of which, it may be added, that the mountaineers of Bengal and Bahar can hardly be distinguished in some of their features, particularly their lips and noses, from the modern Abyssinians, whom the Arabs call the children of Cush: and the ancient Hindus, according to Strabo, differed in nothing from the Africans, but in the straitness and smoothness of their hair, while that of the others was crisp or wooly; a difference proceeding chiefly, if not entirely, from the respective humidity or dryness of their atmospheres; hence the people who received the first light of the rising sun, according to the limited knowledge of the ancients, are said by Apuleius to be the *Aru* and Ethiopians, by which he clearly meant certain nations of India; where we frequently see figures of Buddha with curled hair apparently designed for a representation of it in its natural state.[24]

We must note, however, that not all scholars of the day were swept up in this Egypto-mania. An important resister was the Abbé Mignot, Alexandre-Jean des Aunais (circa 1730-1791, also known as Vincent Mignot), the nephew of Voltaire, remembered today for his efforts to secure a Christian burial for his less than pious uncle. On February 27, 1761, he presented a paper in which he carefully considered the chronologies presented in the ancient Greek histories and concluded, "The *Budda* or the *Siamese* Fo thus could not have been an Egyptian priest who came to India to escape the persecution of Cambyse."[25] Yet on the African hypothesis (and by extension, the two-Buddha theory), the Abbé Mignot would remain a voice in the wilderness.

As the East India Company extended its control over India, all manner of British military officers, physicians, surveyors, and botanists wrote about Buddhism. A particularly well-traveled scholar was the Scottish surgeon and botanist Francis Hamilton (1762–1829). A member of the Buchanan clan of Scotland, in 1818 he changed his surname to Buchanan; earlier works of his are thus under the name of Francis Hamilton, and later works under the name of Francis Buchanan. After spending ten years at sea as a ship's surgeon, in 1795 he was assigned to the first British mission to the kingdom of Ava (in modern Burma), during which he assembled a substantial herbarium of Burmese flora. It was during his time there that Hamilton met the Italian missionary Vincenzo Sangermano (from whom we will hear below). Using materials provided to him by the Catholic priest, in 1801 Hamilton published a long article in *Asiatick Researches* entitled "On the Religion and Literature of the Burmas," which provided one of the most extensive descriptions of Buddhism to date. In 1802, Hamilton was posted to Kathmandu, where he collected Nepalese plants. However, he did not desist from his study of religion. In 1819, after his return to Scotland (and after changing his surname), he published *An Account of the Kingdom of Nepal: And of the Territories Annexed to This Dominion by the House of Gorkha*, in which he compared the Buddhism he observed in Burma with that of the Newar and Tibetan communities in Kathmandu. Throughout his travels, Dr. Hamilton seems to have kept abreast of the growing scholarship on Buddhism, which he surveys in the passage below. As will be clear, despite his extended contact with Buddhist communities in Burma and Nepal, he also held fast to the African hypothesis, although he parted company with Sir William Jones on the two-Buddha theory:

•

DIFFERENT learned men have supposed BOUDDHA to have been the same with NOAH, MOSES, or SIPHOAS, thirty-fifth king of *Egypt*: but as I have not at present access to the works of HUET, VOSSIUS, of TOURMONT, I do not know on what reasons such suppositions have been formed. Sir W. Jones supposed BOUDDHA to have been the same with SESAC or SESOSTRIS, king of *Egypt*, "Who by conquest spread a new system of religion and philosophy, from the *Nile* to the *Ganges*, about 1,000 years before CHRIST." The affinity of the religion of *Egypt* with the present superstition of the *Hindustan*, and the fatal resemblance of the words SESAC and SAKYA, one of the names of GODAMA, seem to have given rise to this supposition. In my opinion, however, no two religions can be well more different, than that of the *Egyptian* polytheist, and that of the *Burma* unitarian. SESAC or SESOSTRIS is indeed placed by antiquarians at the time to which the learned judge alludes: but I shall hereafter have occasion to show, that, according to the most probable accounts, the origin of the religion of GODAMA ought to be referred to a much later period. That the religion of the *Brahmens* was introduced from *Egypt*, I have already mentioned as an opinion highly probable: but I suspect that this happened by no means so early as the time of SESOSTRIS, whose object in his military expeditions appears rather to have been plunder, and the captures of slaves, than the propagation of religion or philosophy. The persecution of the *Egyptian* priests by CAMBYSES is a more likely period for any very extensive emigration into *India*; at the same time it is not improbable, that the *Egyptians*, who before this traded to *India*, had previously communicated some knowledge of their science to the *Hindus*.[26]

•

Over the subsequent decades, the African origins of the Buddha were debated by scholars, with those favoring the hypothesis consistently noting the flat nose and thick lips of the Buddha images, and especially the hair, described as "wooly," "frizzled," and "crisped." In 1819, the great French Sinologist Jean-Pierre Abel-Rémusat (1788–1832) published an article in the *Journal des Savants* entitled "Note sur quelques epithets descriptives de Bouddha" ("On Some Descriptive Epithets of Buddha"), in which he reputed the African origins of the Buddha. The persistence of the claim might be measured by the fact that when Abel-Rémusat published the same article six years later in his *Mélanges Asiatiques*, he felt it necessary to rename it "Sur quelques epithets descriptives de Bouddha, qui font voir que Bouddha n'appartenait pas a la race négre" ("On Some Descriptive Epithets of Buddha Showing that Buddha Did Not Belong to the Negro Race").

The British physician John Davy (1790–1868) was the younger

brother of the famous chemist Sir Humphry Davy, inventor of the miners' lamp that bears his name. Davy served as inspector general of hospitals for the British army, and in this capacity was posted throughout the empire, including at the colony of Ceylon. Based on his time there, in 1821 he published *An Account of the Interior of Ceylon, and of Its Inhabitants: With Travels in That Island*, which included a chapter entitled "Doubtful Points of the Religion of Boodhoo." Here Dr. Davy, a good scientist, uses his powers of observation to address the question of the origins of Buddhism:

•

The question in what part of the world this religion first appeared is still involved in considerable obscurity. The majority of oriental scholars are in favour of its western origin, and maintain that it is derived from some part of Africa,—probably Ethiopia. A very few hold the contrary opinion, that the north of Asia was its birth-place and cradle.

The principal argument of those who maintain the first opinion, is derived from the appearance of some of the images of Boodhoo. It is said, they show that Boodhoo was an African, having marked on them the short woolly hair, the flat dilated nostrils, the thick fleshy lip, and indeed every feature of the African countenance. If this be generally so, it certainly is strong evidence. I have paid particular attention to innumerable figures of Boodhoo, made in Ceylon; I have seen several from Ava and Siam; two or three of Foh, from China; one of Mahamoonie, and of a Lama, and a Dalai Lama, from Tibet; and the result of my observations is the persuasion, that the asserted resemblance is either accidental or fanciful. The features of the Tibetian, Burman, and Chinese images, are more or less Tartar; and those of the Ceylon figures, Singalese:—and, it is worthy of remark, that the more carefully and ably the figures are made, the more complete is the copying of the national features. The argument, therefore, from the African countenance, appears to me untenable; and I know no other of force in favour of African origin, which the Boodhists themselves will not patiently listen to, considering even the supposition a species of insult,—their ideas of the African (of the Kaffer) being very low, and full of contempt, as is evident, from their giving him the office of tormentor in the infernal regions, in common with dogs and crows. If questioned respecting the hair of Boodhoo, they say it was like their own, and that the object of artists is not to represent curly, woolly hair, but hair cut short, as Boodhoo's was when he became priest; and, to prove this, they observe, that one long hair or lock was left uncut on his forehead, which is represented as a circle or curl, in all images that are correctly executed.[27]

•

Yet five years later, and a year after Abel-Rémusat thought it necessary to rename his essay, we find the African hypothesis once again in the work of another British physician, George Finlayson, who served as assistant surgeon of His Majesty's Eighth Light Dragoons. Unlike Davy, Finlayson argues in favor. We read in his *The Mission to Siam, and Hue, the Capital of Cochin China, in the Years 1821–2*:

•

Several circumstances and ceremonies in the religion of Buddha would seem to identify its origin, in a great measure, with that of ancient Egypt. The physiognomy, the form, and the stature of Buddha are as distinctly Ethiopic as they are different from those which characterize the various tribes which inhabit either the western or eastern parts of the Asiatic continent. That it is a religion foreign to Asia, the uncertainty which still exists with regard to the country or district which gave it birth would seem to render probable. The proofs which have been brought forward in favour of Ceylon, and of Magadha, would seem to rest upon very slender foundations.[28]

•

Thus, the African hypothesis remained persistent, so much so that it was addressed by such giants of nineteenth-century scholarship as James Cowles Prichard. In his five-volume *Researches into the Physical History of Mankind* (1844), Prichard devotes six pages to "the hypothesis that the Aborigines of India and of the Himálaya were a race of Negroes," concluding that the hypothesis is false and saying of the images of the Buddha, "It is very probable that the countenance imitated in these figures is the broad face of the Siamese and other Indo-Chinese nations, and not the physiognomy of the African."[29] Eugène Burnouf, the protagonist of chapter 4, in an appendix to his translation of the *Lotus Sutra* (1852), reports and dismisses the view that the Buddha was an African, citing Abel-Rémusat and Prichard for support, and explaining that the Buddha's hair was not frizzy (*crépus*) but curly (*bouclés*).[30]

Regardless of whether or not they subscribed to the African hypothesis, we discern in the words of these various authors a strikingly different tone in their discussions of the Buddha. Their interest is more historical—we might even say scientific. They differ from the authors we have encountered in previous chapters in at least three important ways. First, they are not missionaries; second, they are not Catholics; third, they are writing for the most part about India. The British East India Company did not allow Christian missionaries into India until 1815. Before that time, and extending to the time that India became a British colony, many officers of the company would express a profound interest in and respect for what they regarded as the classical civilization of India. However, although they made extensive use of brahman pundits in making their translations, they often condemned the caste system and the elaborate rituals that the brahmans performed, seeing in it reflections of Papism. In 1815, as the Church Missionary Society (composed primarily of German and English Protestants, soon followed by the Church of Scotland) began sending missionaries to India, there were no Buddhists left to convert. This is not to say that British missionaries elsewhere in Asia, such as those in the British colony of Sri Lanka, would not condemn the Buddha. But by that time, the science of philology had begun to play its part.

L'âge des faux amis

The discovery of Sanskrit and the rise of philology would eventually transform European knowledge of the religions of India. However, it also spawned, or at least invigorated, the pseudoscience of false etymology—the late eighteenth century could be called *L'âge des faux amis*, the Age of False Cognates. As a consequence, after many gods with many names had finally been identified as one god, the Buddha, he would again become many gods with many names. Louis-Mathieu Langlès (1763–1824), professor of Persian at the Collège de France and conservator of Oriental manuscripts at the Bibliothèque Nationale under Napoleon, begins in the passage below by correctly identifying the various Asian versions of the names and epithets of the Buddha as referring to a single person, but then takes wing on a flight of fancy:

•

Without wishing to engage ourselves in chronological discussions, as uncertain as they are superfluous, we allow ourselves to believe, following the original fragments preserved in several ancient languages, that we have identified the same legislator in the *Boutta* of the ancient Gymnosophists, the *Sammana-Kantama* of the Peguans, the *Sammana-Coudom* of the Siamese, the *Foé* of the Chinese, the ancient *Boudso* or *Chaca* of the Japanese, the *Vichnou* of the Hindus in one of his incarnations, the *Lama* of the Tibetans, the *Baouth* of the Singhalese, the *Thic-Ca* of the Tonquinese, the *Thoth* of the Egyptians, the *Boa* of the Tungus, the *Torus* of the Laplanders, the *Ouden* or *Woden* of the gothic nations, to whom Wednesday is further dedicated in the name *Woden-tag*, Wednesday in English (*Boud-Var* in Sanskrit), *Mercurii dies*; Mercury, Hermes, Toth and Boudh are but the same person.[31]

•

The unsurpassed master of such identifications, however, was the remarkable Anglican cleric and biblical scholar George Stanley Faber (1773–1854). He had first gained notoriety in 1799, when he preached sermons at Oxford in which he connected five of the seven vials of wrath mentioned in Revelation 16 — "And I heard a great voice out of the temple saying to the seven angels, Go your ways, and pour out the vials of the wrath of God upon the earth" — with recent events. Faber would later identify the pouring of the fifth vial ("And the fifth angel poured out his vial upon the seat of the beast; and his kingdom was full of darkness") with Napoleon's escape from Elba in 1815. The following year, he published *The Origin of Pagan Idolatry Ascertained from Historical Testimony and Circumstantial Evidence*, a marvelous and vexing three-volume work. An unacknowledged ancestor of Frazer's *The Golden Bough* a century later, it carries an epigraph on the title page that can only be read ironically today: "Every reasonable Hypothesis should be supported on a fact." In the preface, Reverend Faber sets forth his hypothesis:

•

The various systems of Pagan Idolatry in different parts of the world correspond so closely, both in their evident purport and in numerous points of arbitrary resemblance, that they cannot have been struck out independently in the several countries where they have been established, but must have all originated from some common source. But, if they all originated from a common source, then either one nation must have communicated its peculiar theology to every other people in the way of peaceful and voluntary imitation; or that same nation must have communicated it to every other people through the medium of conquest and violence; or lastly all nations must in the infancy of the world have been assembled together in a single region and in a single community, must at that period and in that state of society have agreed to adopt the theology in question, and must thence as from a common centre have carried it to all quarters of the globe.

These are the only three modes, in which the universal accordance of the Gentiles [pagans] in their religious speculations can possibly be accounted for. But, as the incredibility of the first, and as the equal incredibility and impossibility of the second, may be shewn without much difficulty; the third alone remains to be adopted. Now this third mode both perfectly harmonizes with the general purport of Heathen Idolatry, and minutely accords with an historical fact which is declared to us on the very highest authority. An examination of the theology of the Gentiles forces us to conclude, that all mankind were once assembled together in a single community, and that they afterwards spread themselves in detached bodies over the face of the whole earth: Holy Scripture asserts, that such was actually the fact.[32]

•

Like Sir William Jones before him, Faber placed great stock in the existence of flood stories in the myths of many nations, seeing them as confirmation of the flood account in Genesis. All of humanity were thus the descendants of the three sons of Noah: Ham, Shem, and Japeth. According to Genesis 11, their offspring, that is, all mankind, assembled into a single community that spoke a single language. They gathered on a plain in the land of Shinar and began building a tower—what would come to be known as the Tower of Babel—that would reach up to heaven. God, fearing that they would be able to do whatever they imagined, "confounded their language," and scattered them across the face of the earth.

Reading extensively in *Asiatick Researches* and other scholarly journals of the day, Faber discerned sets of three in the various forms of idolatry of the world, and ascribed this pattern to the origin of humanity from the three sons of Noah. Because all of humanity once spoke a single language before God's intervention, he also placed great stock in cognates. Thus he accepted, for example, Sir William Jones's identification of the Buddha with Woden: "We are compelled therefore to believe even *a priori*, that Buddha and Woden are the same deity, and consequently that the theology of the Gothic and Saxon tribes was a modification of Buddhism. . . . With respect to the name, *Wod* or *Vod* is a mere variation of *Bod*; and *Woden* is simply the Tamulic mode of pronouncing *Buddha*: for, in that mode of enunciation, *Buddha* is expressed *Pooden* or *Poden*: and *Poden* is undoubtedly the same word as *Voden* or *Woden*."[33]

But Faber went much further than Jones, finding the Buddha literally everywhere:

•

The identity of Thoth and Buddha cannot be doubted: and, when their history is inquired into, it can be as little doubted, that they are severally the great father, who is primarily Adam and secondarily Noah. But the character of these deities runs into that of Idris and Edris: and as they appear no less than he to be the patriarch Enoch, so he no less than they will prove also to be the great father who was manifested at the commencement of both worlds.

In allusion to the triple offspring of Adam and Noah, the oriental Buddha was believed to have triplicated himself, and is pronounced to be the same as the triad springing from unity. Much the same idea seems to have been entertained of Thoth or Hermes, as we may collect from the title of *Thrice-greatest* which was bestowed upon him: for, as his identity with Buddha may be distinctly proved from other considerations, and as Buddha was esteemed as a triple deity, the descriptive title of Thoth must obviously be understood as relating to his supposed triplication.[34]

•

Elsewhere, the Buddha is identified with the Roman god Terminus, and with Mercury, Janus, and Hercules. We also learn that "the very name indeed of *Colossus* points out the deity, who was represented from Hindostan in the east to Britain in the west. One of the Buddha's titles is *Coll* or *Cala*, and another is *Esa*: from *Col-Esa*, the compound of these two, was probably derived the word *Colossus*. These remarks will serve as a clue to the real history of the Cyclopes."[35]

Meanwhile, as scholars in Europe (and in India) continued to develop fanciful theories about the Buddha's origins and identities, Roman Catholic missionaries continued to talk with Buddhist monks and translate contemporary Buddhist works. Father Vincenzo (Vincentius) Sangermano (died 1819) was a Catholic priest of the Barnabite Order who spent the years from 1783 to 1806 as a missionary in Burma. His account was published in 1833 as *A Description of the Burmese Empire*. In it, Father Sangermano notes that in order to explain the religion of the Burmese, or "The Laws of Godama," as he calls it, he translated a short treatise that a celebrated Burmese monk, the tutor to the king, had written in 1763 at the request of a Catholic bishop. We thus have a brief account of the life of the Buddha, in all of its mythologized glory, as it was understood by a leading Burmese monk of the eighteenth century, as paraphrased by Father Sangermano:

•

This treatise may give some idea of the laws of Godama regarding seculars; of those respecting the Talapoins, I shall speak further on. The sermons of Godoma, as they are called, are all contained in a great book called Sout [sutras], and it must be confessed that they inculcate some fine morality, of which I will give some specimens in the next chapter.

11. The books which contain the history of Godama represent him as a king who, having laid aside the ensigns of royalty, withdrew himself into a solitary place, put on the habit of a Talapoin, and gave himself up to the study and practice of virtue. But Godama had even before this acquired great merits. For he had already lived in 400,100,000 worlds, having begun as a little bird, and passed through 550 transmigrations, some happy, some unhappy, so as once even to have been an elephant. These former merits, united to his present generous abdication, procured for him at the age of thirty-five the gift of divine wisdom. This consists in seeing into the thoughts of all living beings; in the foreknowledge of all future events, however distant they may be: in the knowledge of the merits and demerits of all men; in the power of working miracles, particularly by causing fire and water to issue from his eyes at the same time, or fire from one eye and water from the other;

and finally in a tender love towards all things living. Among other prodigies related of him, we may notice the one said to have happened at his birth; for he was no sooner born than he walked seven paces towards the north, exclaiming: "I am the noblest and greatest among men. This is the last time that I shall be born; never again shall I be conceived in the womb." In his stature also and the properties of his body there was something extraordinary. His height was more than nine cubits, his ears hung down to his shoulders, his tongue being thrust out of his mouth reached even to his nose, and his hands, when he stood upright, touched his knees. In walking he always appeared elevated at least a cubit from the ground; his clothes did not touch his body, but were always a palm distant from it; and in the same manner, anything he took up remained always at a distance of a palm from his hands. During the forty-five years that he spent on earth after becoming a God, he was continually employed in the promulgation of his laws, and it was said that through his preaching 2,400,000,000 persons obtained the Niban [nirvana]. In the eightieth year of his age he died of dysentery, brought on by an excess in eating pork. Previous to his death he recommended that his statue and relics should be preserved and adored. . . .

12. Godama, upon his death, was immediately transported to the Niban, where he remains in a sort of ecstasy, without hearing, or seeing, or feeling, or having any sense of what goes on in the world, and in this state he will remain for eternity; and such will be the lot of all who have the good fortune to obtain this reward. But the laws of Godama will be observed upon earth for the space of 5000 years, reckoning from the day of his death, from which year, therefore, the Burmese begin their era. Of this period 2352 years have already elapsed. As soon as it is at an end, the laws of Godama will cease to be binding, another God must appear to promulgate a new code for the government of mankind.[36]

•

That other God is the future Buddha, Maitreya, who will appear in our world when the teachings of the previous Buddha, Gautama Buddha, have been entirely forgotten. Sangermano's book, in which this quite typical Buddhist account of the Buddha appears, was published in English in 1833. A very different Buddha would appear in a book published in French just eleven years later, and the Buddhist Buddha would begin to pass into oblivion.

Officers of the Company

During the early decades of the nineteenth century, scholarship on India spiked, almost entirely because of the growing presence of the British East India Company. It was scholarship, but it was not the work of professional scholars in the modern sense of the term. It was carried out by officers of the company. A perusal of the tables of contents of the leading journals of the day, such as *Asiatick Researches, Transactions of the Royal Asiatic Society of Great Britain and Ireland*, and *Transactions of the Literary Society of Bombay* (see appendix 3), reveals articles by majors, captains, generals, physicians, and attorneys, who composed essays on Indian art, architecture, and religion as an avocation. These men read the work of other members of the East India Company, but also remained abreast of theories circulating in Europe, theories that they were not hesitant to dispute.

A particularly learned officer was the Irish major Michael Symes (1761–1809). He went to India at the age of nineteen as a cadet in the Bengal army of the East India Company. Rising through the ranks, in 1788 he transferred into the Seventy-Sixth Regiment of the British army as a lieutenant, and was promoted to captain in 1793. In 1795, the Governor-General of India, Sir John Shore, had him lead an embassy to the court of King Bodawpaya of Burma in an effort to establish trade relations. Based on his seven months in Burma, in 1800 he published *An Account of an Embassy to the Kingdom of Ava, Sent by the Governor-General of India, in the Year 1795*. Here, he demonstrates an impressive familiarity with the various positions of the day on the identity of the Buddha, drawing on works we have encountered in previous chapters, such as those of Simon de la Loubère, who had been sent by Louis XIV to the court of Siam, and that of Guillaume Joseph le Gentil, the French astronomer. And he cogently disputes some of the more fanciful theories, politely expressing his disagreement with Sir William Jones's view that the Buddha was the Norse god Odin:

•

Whatever may be the antiquity of the worship of Boodh, the wide extent of its reception cannot be doubted. The most authentic writer[37] on the eastern peninsula calls the image of Gaudma, as worshipped by the Siamese, Somona-codom: being unacquainted with the language of

Siam, which, from so short a residence as four months, it was impossible he could have acquired, he confounds two distinct words, Somona, and Codom, signifying Codom, or Gaudma, in his incarnate state; the difference between the letters C and G may easily have arisen from the mode of pronunciation in different countries; even in the Birman manner of uttering the word, the distinction between these letters is not very clear. The Boodh of the Indians and the Birmans, is pronounced by the Siamese Pooth, or Pood, by the vulgar, Poo; which, without any violence to probability, might be converted by the Chinese into Foe;[38] the Tamulic termination *en*, as Mr. Chambers remarks, creates a striking resemblance between Pooden and the Woden of the Goths; every person who has conversed with the natives of India knows that Boodh is the Dies Mercurii, the Wednesday, or Woden's day, of all Hindoos. Chronology, however, which must always be accepted as a surer guide to truth, than inferences drawn from the resemblance of words, and etymological reasoning, does not, to my mind, sufficiently establish that Boodh and Woden were the same. The period of the ninth incarnation of Vishnu was long antecedent to the existence of the deified hero of Scandinavia. Sir William Jones determines the period when Boodh appeared on the earth to be 1014 years before the birth of Christ. Odin, or Woden, flourished at a period not very distant from our Saviour, and was, according to some, a contemporary of Pompey and of Julius Caesar. The author of the Northern Antiquities places him 70 years after the Christian era. Even the Birman Gaudma, conformably to their account, must have lived above 500 years before Woden. So immense a space can hardly be supposed to have been overlooked: but if the supposition refers, not to the warrior of the north, but to the original deity Odin, the attributes of the latter are as widely opposed to those of Boodh, who was himself only an incarnation of Vishnu, as the dates are incongruous. The deity, whose doctrines were introduced into Scandinavia, was a god of terror, and his votaries carried desolation and the sword throughout whole regions; but the Ninth Avatar[39] brought the peaceful olive, and came into the world for the sole purpose of preventing sanguinary acts. These apparent inconsistencies will naturally lead us to hesitate in acknowledging Boodh and Woden to be the same person: their doctrines are opposite, and their eras are widely remote.

Had that distinguished genius,[40] whose learning so lately illumined the East, been spared for the instruction and delight of mankind, he would probably have elucidated this obscurity, and have removed the dusky veil that still hangs over the religious legends of antiquity. The subject,[41] as it now stands, affords an ample field for indulging in pleasing theories, and fanciful speculations; and as the probability increases of being able to trace all forms of divine worship to one sacred and primeval source, the inquiry in proportion becomes more interesting, and awakens a train of serious ideas in a reflecting mind.[42]

•

The army surgeon John Davy, who served in Sri Lanka, also dismissed the identification of the Buddha with Odin along with the notion that the ancestors of the British were Buddhists. He made these arguments in "Doubtful Points of the Religion of Boodhoo," a chapter from his *An Account of the Interior of Ceylon, and of Its Inhabitants: With Travels in That Island*, published in 1821.

Yet British scholarship on Buddhism was not limited to officers who made excursions to the Buddhist lands of Sri Lanka and Southeast Asia. The absence of Buddhists in India by the time of the British arrival there did not prevent them from writing about it. Indeed, the absence of living Buddhists and the presence of their remains may have encouraged this writing.

William Erskine (1773–1852) traveled to India in 1804 at the invitation of his fellow Scotsman, Sir James Mackintosh, and eventually secured a position as clerk to the small-cause court in Bombay. An amateur scholar, he assisted Mackintosh in founding the Literary Society of Bombay that same year. Erskine taught himself Persian and devoted great efforts to translating the memoirs of Babur (1483–1531), the first Mughal emperor of India. He also developed an interest in the Buddhist, Jain, and Hindu temples in the region, including a famous group of caves, filled with Hindu and Buddhist statues, located on Elephanta Island in Bombay Harbor. On November 2, 1813, he read a paper to the Literary Society of Bombay entitled "Account of the Cave-Temple of Elephanta, with a Plan of the Drawings of the Principal Figures," which includes the following:

•

When the Brahmins are taxed with [accused of] idolatry, they always excuse themselves, as has been already remarked, by alleging the necessity of making an impression on rude minds by means of some intelligible symbols, on which the ignorant may fix their thoughts, and to which they may look for reward and punishment.

As in many of their incarnations the gods are supposed to have appeared with several heads, with the heads of animals, with a number of hands, and other singularities; their images in the temples correctly represent all these peculiarities. . . .

The religion of the Bouddhists differs very greatly from that of the Brahmins; as in the latter, God is introduced everywhere,—in the former, he is introduced no where. The gods of the Brahmins pervade and animate all nature; the god of the Bouddhists, like the god of the Epicureans, remains in repose, quite unconcerned about human affairs, and therefore is not the object of worship. With them there is no intelligent divine being who judges of human actions as good or bad, and rewards or punishes that as such;—this indeed is practically the same as having no God. Good and ill, according to their creed, are however supposed to spring invariably from virtue and vice; there being as they believe an inseparable and necessary connexion between virtue and prosperity, vice and misfortune. Yet, as the mind of man must have some object of confidence on which to rest its hopes and to which to direct its supplication and prayer, they teach that from time to time men of surpassing piety and self-denial have appeared on the earth, and from their singular worth have after death been transferred to a state of superior bliss; which state, however, they say that we can only intimate by describing it as an absence of all pain, as we can only define health as an absence of all disease. These saints or prophets, after reforming the world in their lifetime, and by their superior sanctity attaining the power of performing miracles, are still imagined after death to have certain powers of influencing us. It is these men transferred by death to bliss who are the object of Bouddhist worship. This worship assumes different forms in different countries, and is by some supposed to be more widely diffused than any other religion. In Siam it is chiefly paid to Godoma or Sommona-Codom: but it is worthy of remark, that wherever this form of religion prevails in its original state, the relics of these holy men or saints are the object of worship. The largest temples are often in the form of a pyramid or of the section of a globe, and are supposed to contain a tooth, hair, or other relic of a saint. The forms of these holy places have been adopted from the custom prevalent in these countries of depositing the ashes of the deceased under a pyramid or globular mound: the pyramids are often of great size, and on their summits are umbrellas which are frequently adorned with bells; sometimes this pyramid is gilded over. Other temples of nearly similar construction, but hollow within, contain images to which adoration is directed. The images of these saints have different attitudes, sometimes sitting cross-legged in a meditative posture, sometimes standing upright.

As all the ideas of this religion relate to men, and as no incarnations or transformations of superior beings are recorded, it is obvious that in their temples we can expect to find no unnatural images, no figures compounded of man and beast, no monsters with many hands or many heads.[43]

•

We note here that despite so many centuries of condemnation, Erskine does not apply the term *idolatry* to the Buddhists. He reserves it for the brahmans, and implies that the brahmans themselves concede the point when they are "taxed with" (that is, accused of) idolatry. The god of the Buddhists—no longer Pythagorean but now Epicurean—is not an object of worship; indeed, the Buddhists have no God. Instead, there is the law of karma, although Erskine does not use that term. His central point, supported by the statues that he saw, is that the religion of the brahmans differs from the religion of the Buddhists because the Buddhists worship not monsters but men, men who have achieved a certain sanctity. A positive view of the Buddha and his Buddhism was thus beginning to develop in India: it is anticaste, its art portrays humans rather than demons, it has philosophy in the place of ritual. As Erskine writes elsewhere, philosophy and ritual exist in a religion in inverse proportion: "Perhaps the Bouddhist is not only a simpler but a more intellectual religion. The use of numerous external symbols has a natural tendency to call off the attention from dogmas or opinions to forms and ceremonies. The religions in Europe that have the simplest ceremonial are the most metaphysical."[44]

The simplicity of the Buddha's image compared to those of Hindu deities soon came to extend to the perceived simplicity of something less visible: the Buddha's teaching. This was repeatedly mentioned in one of the persistent debates of the first decades of the nineteenth century: Which came first, Buddhism or Brahmanism (known today as Hinduism)? We read in Robert Tytler's 1817 *Inquiry into the Origin, and Principles of Budaic Sabism*, "The *simplicity* discernible in Buddhism, the genuine principles of disinterested humanity, and piety which pervade the whole of the system, clearly demonstrate the originality of this admirable and unadorned fabric over the *complicated* structure, decorated with false notions of embellishment with meretricious ornaments of all kinds which are visible in the multifarious tenets peculiar to modern Hindus."[45]

Thus by the beginning of the nineteenth century, a discernible shift had begun to take place in the European valuation of the Buddha, a valuation that seems to arise largely from comparison, where the ancient Buddha is judged superior to the modern brahmans and their gods. We read in Michel Jean François Ozeray's *Recherches sur Budduo ou Bouddou*, published in 1817: "It is an undeniable fact; Boudou is a famous personage; he was not wrested from oblivion through the pains of a hardworking annalist or a skilful antiquarian. It is neither to an inscription nor to a medallion that he owes a new existence; he is known by his life and his morals. Descended from the altar where blindness and superstition had placed him, Boudou is a distinguished philosopher, a sage born for the happiness of his fellow creatures and for the good of humanity."[46]

Even with such praise, the negative valuation of Buddhism that had been consistent since the first Roman Catholic missionaries came to Asia remained firmly in place into the nineteenth century. For example, we find Karl Friedrich Neumann, author of *History of the Pirates Who Infested the China Sea from 1807-1810*, decrying the negative effect that Buddhism had had on the peoples of Asia:

•

It has for some time past been the fashion of learned men to praise greatly the doctrine of Shakiamuny; but it seems that this praise is very much overrated. It is true that Buddhism blunted the edge of the barbarian ferocity of the Mongolians; but what positive advantages have resulted from this doctrine in Tartary? Is the state of society much better than it was in the time of Chingize [Genghis Khan]? There are thousands of idle people whose business it is to do *Nothing*, to think on *Nothing*, and to live as much as possible upon *Nothing*. . . . But this we know, man is born to act and to suffer, and not to spend his life in worthless speculations and monkish idleness; he is not born to thwart all his affections, but to enjoy the world. The low state of half the human kind, the mean oppression of the weaker sex in every country where Buddhism prevails, would alone speak volumes against this doctrine.[47]

·

Yet despite this negative view of Buddhism, condemnation did not necessarily extend to its founder. Finding statues of the Buddha in India, but no Buddhists to worship them, Europeans began to distinguish between the ancient founder and his modern followers, as if the Buddha bore no responsibility for Buddhism. How could he be responsible for what happened to his teachings, once they had been driven from India? The Buddha could be separated from Buddhism.

With no Asian devotees left in India, the Buddha began to attract those of a different race. Europeans condemned the superstition and sacerdotalism they observed in Hinduism. They also knew, from the Hindus' own sources, that the Buddha had opposed two of the foundations of that tradition which they, too, condemned: the caste system and animal sacrifice. The Buddha's opposition to each struck Europeans of the Enlightenment as particularly enlightened, upholding a different variety of the Rights of Man, one that included the right of anyone from any social class to win liberation from rebirth. His opposition to sacrifice, and the rituals that surrounded it, appealed particularly to the anti-Papist sentiments of Anglican Englishmen and Presbyterian Scots. And so the Buddha elicited a certain sympathy, because, at least as the Europeans understood the story, the Buddha was persecuted, and his followers were eventually expelled from India. As Charles Coleman explained in 1831, the Buddha "is said to have appeared to reclaim the Hindus from numerous abominations into which they had fallen, and to teach them more benevolent forms of worship than those which, through the means of human and animal sacrifices, they then practised. These mild doctrines were too simple, and interfered too strongly with the privileges of the Brahminical priests to be long tolerated by them. A religious war, in consequence, ensued between the old and the new sects, and that of Buddha was ultimately expelled from the hither peninsula of India."[48]

This expulsion of the Buddhists by the brahmans (a historical fiction) elicited a certain sympathy but also a certain regret on the part of British writers: how different might India be today if the gentle philosophy of the Buddha had prevailed over the superstitions of the brahmans? And there was also a sense of loss. After Buddhism spread beyond the borders of India into China, Japan, Tibet, Siam, and Burma, it inevitably became corrupted, mixing with the primitive cultures it encountered there. As John Crawfurd (1783–1868), who arrived in India as an army surgeon and later became one of the British East India Company's leading diplomats, wrote in 1820, "We shall be compelled to consider the religion of the Burmans, Siamese, and Cingalese, as corruptions of genuine Buddhism, most probably superinduced by local causes and superstitions, which, operating upon the original system, produced, in the course of ages, a form of worship differing essentially from its purest form."[49]

For other British writers, the expulsion of Buddhism from India was also to be lamented because the original teachings of the Buddha had been lost. We thus close this chapter with a lament and a question raised by Edward Upham (1776–1834), the eccentric mayor of Exeter, yet another of the amateur Orientalists who never set foot in Asia. Among his many works is the first English-language book with *Buddhism* in its title: *The History and Doctrine of Budhism, Popularly Illustrated: With Notices of the Kappooism or Demon Worship and of the Bali or Planetary Incantations of Ceylon, Embellished with 43 Lithographic prints from the Original Singalese Designs* (1829). Four years later, he published unreliable translations (by others) of three important Sri Lankan chronicles, including the *Great Chronicle* (*Mahāvaṃsa*). In the preface, he writes:

•

While these volumes principally unfold the historic annals of Budhism, together with the faith and doctrines of Guadma as established in Ceylon, their earlier records excite in numerous passages the deepest regret, as they impress upon us the conviction that we have in them but the relics and fragments of a far more refined and intellectual code, which passages manifest a system of ethics so much superior to the modern dogmata of the Buddha Guadma, that we cannot help lamenting the cause which has annihilated the evidences of their more intimate connexion, and only allowed us to surmise, from very insufficient guides, what that more ancient and purer doctrine really was. Where, indeed, can we at present look for the solution of this interesting problem?[50]

·

Upham was unaware that his question would soon be answered—not in India but in Paris.

CHAPTER 4. The Text

It is true, that the various accounts of GODAMA, said to be given in the legends of the different nations following his religion, agree so little together, that they can hardly be made matter of historical evidence. But many of these differences may have arisen from the mistakes of travellers; and it is only by procuring faithful translations of the different legends, that we can be enabled to determine what credit is due to their contents. In the mean time I must say, that I know of no plausible reason for believing that GODAMA did not exist, and was not an Indian *prince, as his followers universally allege.*

FRANCIS BUCHANAN, 1801

On July 7, 1834, a young French scholar living in Paris sent a letter to Kathmandu. It was addressed to an official of the British East India Company who was serving as Resident to the Court of Nepal. In it, he explains that he "would be happy if, by your protection, I could acquire some of the most important Buddhist books in Sanskrit, of which I hope to be able to translate some portions, and which moreover would remain in my country after me." He goes on to express his willingness to pay for the books (at the rate of one rupee for five hundred stanzas of text), offering "250 rupees, a sum that I commit beforehand to pay immediately to the person whom you designate, and in the manner that will be most pleasing to you, forthwith upon receiving the volumes, which should not be less than twelve or fifteen. I also commit myself to pay all costs of transportation, etc. . . . I would be most obliged to you to have written on the first page 'Volume belonging to M. Eug. Burnouf.' This measure is necessary so that the book is not sent by mistake to other people or to some learned body."[1] The British official sent the books to Paris, and the French scholar began to read. The story of the Buddha was about to change forever. This chapter will explain how that happened.

"This Almost Unknown Subject"

The British official was Brian Houghton Hodgson, a largely forgotten figure in the history of the British Empire—remembered, when he is remembered at all, for his contributions to the ornithology of the Himalayas. He was born in 1801 into a well-connected but impoverished Derbyshire family, the second of seven children. At age fifteen, with the help of family connections, he gained admission to Haileybury, the college established by the East India Company in 1806 to train its future officers. He excelled at Bengali, Persian, Hindi, political economy—which he studied with Thomas "Pop" (for "Population") Malthus—and classics, graduating first in his class. After two years at Haileybury he traveled to the College of Fort William in Calcutta to continue his studies, arriving in early 1818. Once in India, he began to suffer liver problems and was told by a physician that his options were three: "six feet under, resign the service, or get a hill appointment," that is, an appointment to a posting in the north at a higher elevation, away from Calcutta's heat and humidity. This diagnosis would have a lasting impact on the European understanding of the Buddha.

Rather than resign from the East India Company and return to England, Hodgson opted for a hill appointment. In 1814, the company had gone to war with Nepal, which had expanded its territory considerably under the Shah dynasty in the late eighteenth century. By 1816, the Gurkhas of Nepal had been defeated by the British, and Nepal had lost a third of its territory. Under the terms of the Treaty of Sugauli, ratified on March 4 of that year, much of that territory was ceded to the East India Company, including Kumaon, a region in the Himalayan foothills. In 1819, Hodgson was appointed assistant commissioner there. Another condition of the treaty was that the British appoint a representative in Kathmandu, called Resident to the Court of Nepal. After only a year in Kumaon, Hodgson was assigned to Kathmandu as Assistant Resident, returning to Calcutta in 1822 as acting deputy secretary in the Persian Department of the Foreign Office. However, his return to the lowlands caused his liver ailment to recur, so he was again forced north. During his time in Calcutta, his position in Kathmandu had been filled, so in 1824 he returned there as postmaster, before again being appointed Assistant Resident the following year. He would be named Resident in 1833.

The Nepalese court had been forced to accept the presence of the British Resident under duress, and did so reluctantly. In order to limit the influence of the British legation, the court restricted its movements to the Kathmandu valley. With nothing better to do, Hodgson, twenty years old when he first arrived, began to study the local culture. In a letter of August 11, 1827, to Dr. Nathaniel Wallich, a Danish botanist in the employ of the East India Company, he described how he came to undertake his studies of Buddhism:

•

Soon after my arrival in Nipál (now six years ago), I began to devise means of procuring some accurate information relative to Buddhism: for, though the regular investigation of such a subject was foreign to my pursuits, my respect for science in general led me cheerfully to avail myself of the opportunity afforded, by my residence in a *Bauddha* country, for collecting and transmitting to Calcutta the materials for such investigation. There were, however, serious obstacles in my way, arising out of the jealousy of the people in regard to any profanation of their sacred things by an European, and yet more, resulting from Chinese notions of policy adopted by this government. I nevertheless persevered; and time, patience, and dexterous applications to the superior intelligence of the chief minister, at length rewarded my toils.

My first object was to ascertain the existence or otherwise of *Bauddha* Scriptures in Nipál; and to this end I privately instituted inquiries in various directions, in the course of which the reputation for knowledge of an old *Bauddha* residing in the city of *Pátan*, drew one of my people to his abode. This old man assured me that Nipál contained many large works relating to Buddhism; and of some of these he gave me a list. Subsequently, when better acquainted, he volunteered to procure me copies of them. His list gradually enlarged as his confidence increased; and at length, chiefly through his kindness, and his influence with his brethren in the *Bauddha* faith, I was enabled to procure and transmit to Calcutta a large collection of important *Bauddha* scriptures.

Meanwhile, as the *Pátan Bauddha* seemed very intelligent, and my curiosity was excited, I proposed to him (about four years ago) a set of questions, which I desired he would answer from his books. He did so; and these questions and answers form the text of the paper which I herewith forward. . . . Having in his answers quoted sundry *slókas* in proof of his statements; and many of the scriptures whence these were taken being now in my possession, I was tempted to try the truth of his quotations. Of that, my research gave me in general satisfactory proof. But the possession of the books led to questions respecting their relative age and authority; and, tried by this test, the *Bauddha's* quotations were not always so satisfactory. Thus one step led to another, until I conceived the idea of drawing up, with the aid of my old friend and his books, a sketch of the terminology and general disposition of the external parts of Buddhism, in the belief that such a sketch, though but imperfectly executed, would be of some assistance to such of my countrymen as, with the books only before them, might be disposed to enter into a full and accurate investigation of this almost unknown subject.[2]

•

Hodgson used this portion of his letter for the opening paragraphs of the published version of his first essay on Buddhism, "Sketch of Buddhism, derived from the Bauddha Scriptures of Nipál," appearing in 1830 in the *Transactions of the Royal Asiatic Society of Great Britain and Ireland*.

Hodgson begins with an attitude of ambivalence toward the very topic of Buddhism. He explains that since he was already living in Nepal and under restricted conditions imposed by the Nepalese court (hence his reference to the "Chinese notions of policy adopted by this government"), he concluded that in the interests of science, he should find out what he could about the local religion. Like so many officials of the British East India Company, he pursued this study as an avocation. He does not seem motivated by any particular interest in Buddhism, nor is he captivated by a particular problem posed by it. Instead, his motivation derives from his "respect for science in general"; any more formal investigation of Buddhism would have been something "foreign to my pursuits." Yet Hodgson feels a sense of responsibility to gather the materials that would make it possible for others, specifically members of the Asiatic Society in Calcutta, to conduct such an investigation.

Hodgson is remembered today for the specimens he collected; he would eventually send over ten thousand zoological specimens from the Himalayas to the British Museum. He would be praised by Joseph Hooker and Charles Darwin, and a flower (the *Rhododendron hodgsonii*) and a bird (the *Prinia hodgsonii*) were named for him. But the first specimens he collected were Buddhist scriptures.

His purpose was to "devise means of procuring some accurate information relative to Buddhism." That is, in keeping with his respect for science, he was concerned first with method. His work was initially impeded by the suspicions of the Nepalese, who feared the pollution of their tradition by a foreigner, but this problem was eventually overcome (although Hodgson does not explain how). Now free to begin his investigations, he does not set out to record the pilgrims' activities around the great stupas of Kathmandu or to observe the Newars' ceremonies (which he also eventually would do). Instead, "My first object was to ascertain the existence or otherwise of *Bauddha* Scriptures in Nipál."

In this respect, Hodgson was very much in keeping with the spirit of his age: a concern with ancient texts, especially Sanskrit texts. In 1784, Charles Wilkins, a member of the East India Company and a founder of the Asiatic Society, published *The Bhagvat-Geetâ, or Dialogues of Kreeshna and Arjoon*. In Paris in 1786, A. H. Anquetil-Duperron produced his translation of four *Oupnek'hat* (*Upaniṣad*) from the Persian. Sir William Jones published *Sacontalá; or, the fatal ring: an Indian drama*, his translation of the poet and dramatist Kālidāsa's Sanskrit play *Śakuntalā*, in 1792 and, two years later, *Institutes of Hindu law: or, the ordinances of Menu, according to the gloss of Cullúca*, his translation of the *Laws of Manu* (*Manavadharmaśāstra*). But these were all Hindu, or, as they were termed at the time, "Brahmanical," texts. Buddhism was largely unknown in Sanskrit, apart from the Hindu representations of the Buddha as the ninth avatar of Vishnu.

Although Nepal was a predominantly Hindu kingdom, the Kathmandu valley was home to the Newar community, which had continued to practice Buddhism, based on Sanskrit texts, after the demise of the religion in India. With the aid of the distinguished Newar pundit Amṛtānanda ("the old *Bauddha*," or old Buddhist, of Hodgson's letter), Hodgson began to collect Sanskrit manuscripts of Buddhist sutras (as well as Tibetan block prints), which he would eventually send around the world, beginning in 1827 with 66 manuscripts to the library of the East India Company's College of Fort William in Calcutta. These gifts would continue until 1845: 94 manuscripts to the Library of the Asiatic Society of Bengal, 79 to the Royal Asiatic Society, 36 to the India Office Library, 7 to the Bodleian, 88 to the Société Asiatique, 59 to Eugène Burnouf—a total of 423 works.

With one important exception, these manuscripts went largely unread. Before turning to that exception, it is important to note that Buddhist scriptures were being read, in canonical languages other than Sanskrit, by Europeans to the north, south, and west of India: to the north, by a Moravian missionary to the Mongols and by a Transylvanian in search of the Hungarian homeland; to the south, by yet another British civil servant; to the west, by two remarkable savants in Paris.

Five Readers of Buddhist Texts

The first of the Parisian savants was a German, Julius Heinrich Klaproth (1783–1835).[3] Born in Berlin, he was the son of the famous chemist (and discoverer of uranium) Martin Heinrich Klaproth (1743–1817). As a young man, he became fascinated with Chinese, teaching himself the language from a Spanish-Chinese dictionary in the Berlin Royal Library that had been compiled by a Roman Catholic missionary. Eventually, Klaproth would also learn Manchu, Mongolian, Sanskrit, Turkish, Arabic, and Persian. He attracted the attention of Count Jan Potocki, a Polish nobleman, who invited him to join a Russian embassy to China in 1805. When the embassy was unable to reach Beijing, he returned to St. Petersburg, where he continued his studies of Chinese and Manchu at the Academy of Sciences before returning to Berlin. By 1816, he had concluded that the leading center in Europe for Oriental studies was Paris. Supported by a stipend from the Prussian government, Klaproth would spend the rest of his life there, making important contributions to lexicography and writing scathing reviews of works by those whose linguistic skills did not match his own.

In 1824, Klaproth published a life of the Buddha, drawn from Mongolian sources, in *Journal Asiatique*, a publication he had helped to found.[4] He begins:

•

No other religion, other than that of Jesus Christ, has contributed as much to the betterment of men than that of *Bouddha*. Originating in Hindustan, it is spread throughout most of Asia. Its domination extends from the sources of the Indus to the Pacific Ocean and even to Japan. The fierce nomads of Central Asia were changed by it into soft and virtuous men, and its beneficent influence is felt as far as southern Siberia.

Like all the beliefs that originate from India, Bouddhisme is founded on a great principle, "that the universe is animated by the same spirit, individualized under innumerable forms by matter, which is only an illusion."

The Buddha appeared as a reformer of the dominant religion of India. He rejected the Vedas, blood sacrifice, and the distinction of castes. Otherwise, the philosophical principles of his doctrine are the same as those found in the other branches of the religion of the Hindus.[5]

•

We see here a very different tone from the descriptions of the Buddha in previous centuries. Klaproth writes in the wake of the French Enlightenment and the French Revolution, a time when the church was attacked and when liberty, fraternity, and equality were extolled. As we shall see, that fraternity would be extended to an ancient Indian sage.

This statement is followed by Klaproth's translation of a Mongolian biography of the Buddha. At the end of it, he explains that he has published the biography so that people who are not prejudiced by the "fad for systems" could compare it with the traditions about Odin. He does not see the slightest resemblance between the two, calling such claims an "unsupportable hypothesis." In Paris in 1824, decades after it had been proposed by Sir William Jones, it appears that this point still needed to be made.

The other savant in Paris was the great French Sinologist Jean-Pierre Abel-Rémusat (1788–1832), appointed in 1814 to the newly established chair in Chinese at the Collège de France. Like Klaproth, he was self-taught, having been trained as a physician. When a French cleric showed him a Chinese text on the medicinal qualities of various plants, he taught himself Chinese in order to read it. Over the next decade, Abel-Rémusat would become one of the founding figures of Sinology in the West. His most important contribution to European views of the Buddha was the *Foe koue ki*, whose full title is *Foĕ Kouĕ Ki ou Relation des royaumes bouddhiques: Voyage dans la Tartarie, dans l'Afghanistan et dans l'Inde, exécuté à la fin du IVᵉ siècle, par Chỹ Fă Hian* (*Foĕ Kouĕ Ki or Record of Buddhist Kingdoms: Travels in Tartary, in Afghanistan and in India, executed at the end of the fourth century by Chỹ Fă Hian*), published in Paris in 1836. This was Abel-Rémusat's translation of the *Fo guo ji* (*Record of Buddhist Kingdoms*), the travel journals of the Chinese monk Faxian (337–circa 424), which provides an invaluable description of Buddhism in India and Sri Lanka at the beginning of the fifth century. The Chinese text is relatively short, only about fifty pages in translation; but Abel-Rémusat wrote detailed notes in which he sought to identify and explain the many Buddhist persons, places, and doctrines that occur in Faxian's work, making use of other Chinese sources as well as the available scholarship of the day.

Abel-Rémusat died in the cholera epidemic of 1832, when the *Foe koue ki* was only half finished. Klaproth took over the project until his own death three years later, whereupon it was completed by Ernest Augustin Xavier Clerc de Landresse (1800–1862) and published in 1836. Until 1844, the *Foe koue ki* was the most detailed study of Buddhism to be produced in Europe, and it remains a lasting testimony to how much of the Indian Buddhist tradition can be accurately understood from Chinese sources. For the European view of the life of the Buddha, it was the first concerted attempt to identify the places in the Buddha's biography with actual locations in India. Because Faxian's text is organized according to his itinerary, the events of the life of the Buddha are recounted out of sequence. However, if those elements were extracted and placed in biographical order, Abel-Rémusat's work would represent the most detailed life of the Buddha to appear in Europe to that time, consisting of extracts from Chinese Buddhist texts. For Abel-Rémusat, there was no question about the Buddha's place of origin. He was Indian, and the arena of his teaching could be identified with the help of an account by a Chinese pilgrim.

Buddhist texts were also being read beyond Paris. Isaak Jakob Schmidt (1779–1847), a German Russian born in Amsterdam, served as a Moravian missionary in the Kalmyk region of Russia between the Black and the Caspian Seas, whose Mongol population practiced Tibetan Buddhism. He learned both Tibetan and Mongolian, and went on to establish Tibetan studies and Mongolian studies in Russia. In 1837, he published a translation from Tibetan into German of the *Diamond Sutra*, the first Mahāyāna sutra to be translated into a European language. It had been originally composed in Sanskrit; Schmidt translated its Tibetan translation. He also translated the Gospels into Mongolian and Kalmyk.

Another European from the north was more remarkable. Jones's discovery that Sanskrit, Greek, and Latin are linguistically related set off a search for the origin of what would be known as the Aryan languages. But the early nineteenth century also saw quests for the origins of other languages and language families of Europe that were not part of the Aryan family, such as Finnish, Estonian, and Basque. One of these quests would play an unexpected role in the development of Buddhist studies in Europe. In 1819, a young Transylvanian scholar named Alexander Csoma de Kőrös (1784–1842) set out to "discover the obscure origins of our homeland," that is, of the Hungarians and the Hungarian language, which was neither Germanic, Slavic, or Romance. Hungarian scholars of the day speculated that the Hungarian people and their language came from the East among the Huns and the Avars, perhaps even the Turks. And so Csoma made his way to Constantinople, but fled when the city was struck by an epidemic. He then journeyed to Alexandria in order to study Arabic, but the epidemic followed him there. He sailed to Syria and continued east by caravan to Baghdad, then to Tehran, then Kabul. From his studies of Arabic sources, he became convinced that the ancient homeland of his ancestors was to be found among the Uighurs in the Tarim basin of the modern Xinjiang region of China, an area then called Bokhara.

Csoma arrived in Kashmir in 1822. Searching in vain for a caravan that he could join for the journey to Yarkand, he spent the next year traveling back and forth—between Srinagar, the capital of Kashmir, and Leh, the capital of Ladakh, the westernmost region of the Tibetan cultural domain—hoping to encounter one. On such a trip, he instead encountered an Englishman, traveling alone in the opposite direction. This was Dr. William Moorcroft (1767–1825), author of *Cursory Account of the Methods of Shoeing Horses* and a veterinarian serving as

"Superintendent of Stud" for the British East India Company. Moor-croft had traveled extensively through northern India since leaving England in 1808, even leading an expedition through southern Tibet in 1812. He persuaded Csoma to postpone his search for the source of the Hungarian language until he learned Tibetan.

In June 1823, Csoma settled in Ladakh, where he arranged to study Tibetan language and literature under the tutelage of a lama recom-mended by Moorcroft. He studied diligently for the next seven years in a variety of locations along the southwestern borders of Tibet, sometimes with a British stipend, sometimes without resources. A British physician who visited him in 1828 described the scene:

•

At that spot he, the Lama, and an attendant, were circumscribed in an apartment nine feet square for three or four months; they durst not stir out, the ground being covered with snow, and the temperature below the zero of the scale. There he sat, enveloped in a sheepskin cloak, with his arms folded, and in this situation he read from morning till evening without fire, or light after dusk, the ground to sleep upon, and the bare walls of the building for protection against the rigours of the climate. The cold was so intense as to make it a task of severity to extricate the hands from their fleecy resort to turn the pages.[6]

•

During this time, Csoma produced a Tibetan-English dictionary, a grammar of the Tibetan language, and an English translation of the great ninth-century compendium of Buddhist terminology, the *Mahāvyutpatti*. In 1830, he departed the Tibetan borderlands for Cal-cutta, the headquarters of the East India Company, where he worked in the library of the Asiatic Society. In 1842, he set off from Calcutta to travel to Sikkim, planning then to proceed through Lhasa to his long-postponed destination, the Tarim basin. But disease, which he had successfully outrun years before, caught him in Darjeeling, where he died of malaria. In recognition of his role in the discovery of Tibetan Buddhism, in 1933 Csoma was officially recognized as a bodhisattva by Taishō University in Japan.

While in Calcutta, Csoma published numerous articles on Tibetan Buddhist literature under the auspices of the Asiatic Society of Bengal. Among these was an article in its journal, *Asiatic Researches*, which appeared in 1839. Thirty-two pages in length, including extensive notes, "Notices on the Life of Shakya, Extracted from the Tibetan Authorities" was one of the most detailed and accurate (in terms of its representation of the tradition) accounts of the life of the Buddha to appear in a Western language. Rather than translating a single text, Csoma produced a synthetic biography, drawing on two famous Sanskrit lives of the Buddha, which he read in Tibetan translation: the *Lalitavistara* and the *Abhiniṣkramaṇa*. He also notes, again correctly, the presence of many biographical elements in the *vinaya*, or monastic code. The biography is supplemented by numerous translations of relevant passages, including a lengthy extract on the funeral of the Buddha.

Csoma organized "Notices on the Life of Shakya" around the famous "twelve deeds" that all buddhas are said to perform. They are as follows, in his rendition:

I.   He descended from among the gods.
II.   He entered into the womb.
III.   He was born.
IV.   He displayed all sorts of arts.
V.   He was married, or enjoyed the pleasures of the conjugal state.
VI.   He left his house and took the religious character.
VII.   He performed penances.
VIII.   He overcame the devil, or the god of pleasures (*Káma Déva*).
IX.   He arrived at supreme perfection, or became *Buddha*.
X.   He turned the wheel of the law or published his doctrine.
XI.   He was delivered from pain, or died.
XII.   His relics were deposited.

Under "He turned the wheel of the law or published his doctrine," Csoma provides a list of the four noble truths, or "the four excellent truths," as he calls them: "(1) There is sorrow or misery in life. (2) It will be so with every birth. (3) But it may be stopped. (4) The way or mode of making an end to all miseries."[7] In the same section, he notes, "Both in the *Dulva* [or *vinaya*, the section of the canon devoted to the monastic code] and in the *Do* [or *sūtra*, the section of the canon containing discourses of the Buddha] class, there are many stories concerning SHÁKYA's peregrination; and how several individuals either singly or in the company turn *Buddhists*: but, it seems, many of the stories are fanciful."[8]

In describing the Buddha's final hours, Csoma writes, "The substance of his doctrine is repeated in these volumes, with respect to some metaphysical subtleties. There are many discussions on the nature or essence and the qualities of *Tathagata* or *Buddha* (God), as also on that of the human soul. On the state of being under bondage and liberated. On the means of obtaining final emancipation. On the six transcendent virtues, especially on charity. On causal concatenation, and on several other articles."[9]

While Csoma was toiling in the cold of the Himalayas, George Turnour (1799–1843) was laboring in the heat of Sri Lanka. He was born in Sri Lanka, the son of a British civil servant, and after being educated in England, he returned to spend most of his brief career there, studying Sinhala and Pāli literature. In the *Ceylon Almanack* of 1833 and 1834, he published "Epitome of the History of Ceylon, and the Historical Inscriptions," republished in 1836 in a single volume as *The First Twenty Chapters of the Mahawanso and a Preparatory Essay on Pali Buddhistical Literature*. The latter work contains a translation of "the first twenty chapters of the Mahawanso and a prefatory essay on Pali Buddhistical literature." The *Mahāvaṃsa* (*Great Chronicle*) of Sri Lanka recounts the (legendary) visits of the Buddha there and the history of the subsequent transmission of the dharma from India to the island. Turnour did not complete his study of the text before his untimely death.

His introduction to the translation, itself over one hundred pages, provides a fascinating insight into the state of the study of Buddhism in the years before Eugène Burnouf. Never hesitant to politely identify shortcomings in the work of other scholars, Turnour's own contributions were as self-effacing as they were learned. He wrote, "The sole object I have in view at present is to collect and arrange matter for the subsequent consideration of competent parties; and if in the progress of this humble task, I occasionally enter upon a critical examination of those materials, I wish those observations to be regarded rather as indexes to the repositories from whence collateral information has been drawn, or indications of the points which demand further inquiry, than as opinions in themselves entitled to

weight, and advanced with the view to invite criticism."[10] The focus
of Turnour's endeavors was not so much the life and teachings of the
Buddha but the role of Buddhism in chronicling its own history and
hence the history of South Asia—countering the charge, current at
the time, that India had no historical literature. He was particularly
interested in the three councils (or convocations, as he calls them) of
monks called to establish the contents of the canon in the first centuries after the Buddha's passage into nirvana. The first of these is said
to have occurred shortly after the Buddha's death, which Turnour
placed in 543 BCE.

In the course of his project, Turnour produced the most detailed
life of the Buddha, or Gotamo Buddho, as he called him, to appear
in a European language to that point. In 1837 and 1838, he published
the four-part "An Examination of the Páli Buddhistical Annals" in the
Journal of the Asiatic Society of Bengal.[11] As with other works on Buddhism of the day, Turnour's essays appeared among articles address-
ing the most disparate subjects. The first part of his study, from July
1837, is preceded in the journal by "Meteorological Register" for the
month of June and is followed by "On the Indian Boa, Python Tigris"
by Lieutenant T. Hutton.

The "Annals" of Turnour's title are the Pāli canon, the famous
"three baskets" (*tipiṭaka; Piṭakattayan* for Turnour) and their traditional commentaries, the *Aṭṭhakathā*. Turnour saw considerable
historical value in the accounts of the three councils for establishing
an accurate chronology of Buddhism in India and Sri Lanka. He was
dismissive of the events that typically preceded the life of the Buddha
in the chronicles: a description of the creation of the world and of
the twenty-four buddhas who came before Gautama Buddha. As he
explains, "Both the chronology and the historical narrative prior to
the advent of GOTOMÓ BUDDHO, are involved in intentional perversion and mystification; a perversion evidently had recourse to for the
purpose of working out the scheme on which he based that wonderful
dispensation, which was promulgated over Central India, during his
pretended divine mission on earth of forty-five years, between 588
and 543 before the birth of Christ; and was subsequently recognized,
almost throughout the whole of Asia, within two and half centuries
from that period."[12]

Turnour is wrong about the speed with which Buddhism spread

throughout Asia. We shall note, however, that for him the presence of "intentional perversion and mystification" in some of the Buddhist historical narratives does not extend to all of them. He believed that the narrative of the life of the Buddha marks the point at which myth becomes history. Yet the transition is not complete when passing from the story of the buddha of the previous historical age, Kāssapa, to the buddha of the current age, Gotama; Turnour placed little stock in the story of the Buddha's life. But he found reasons to find historical facts in the story of the Buddha's death:

•

The fame of SĀKYA had, at the period of his death, been to a certain extent established; and the creed of that wonderful impostor had been recognized in the central regions, at least, of India. It is justifiable therefore to infer, that a considerable portion of the incidents recorded, as far as they could be produced by human imposture, practised among a superstitious and credulous Asiatic population, actually took place. Whereas at the period of his birth, and even up to the time of his secession from a secular and domestic existence, the circle must have been restricted almost to his own family, within which alone the delusion of his predicted Buddhohood could have been fostered, and its pretended realization been recognized. No external co-operation, therefore, of a deluded populace could have been enlisted on an extended scale, till a more advanced stage of his pilgrimage. The account of the birth of BUDDHO given in the paper No. 3, must consequently, as it regards its narrative of the superstitious enthusiasm then prevalent, partake more largely of a fictitious character, than this narrative of his death does.[13]

•

Turnour next provides his translation of large portions of the *Great Discourse on the Final Nirvana* (*Mahāparinibbāna Sutta*), the account of the Buddha's final days, his death, his funeral, and the distribution of his relics—a text that Turnour calls "perhaps the most interesting section in the *Piṭakattayan*," that is, the entire Pāli canon. This would be his last contribution to the study of Buddhism. In 1838, he was transferred from Kandy, site of the sacred tooth relic of the Buddha, to the capital, Colombo. He fell ill in 1841 and returned to Europe; he died in Naples in 1843.

We note that Turnour's attitude toward the Buddha, despite his extensive knowledge of Buddhist scriptures, did not differ markedly from that of earlier generations of European travelers and missionaries to Asia: the Buddha is a "wonderful impostor"; Buddhists are "credulous" and "superstitious." The difference for Turnour lay in the specificity of his analysis: the Buddha is not merely a historical figure whose origins are lost in the mists of time. He is a historical figure whose death can be dated, with a life story in which historical fact can be distinguished from mythological fiction. The quest for the historical Buddha had begun.

Sanskrit Comes to Paris

And so this was the state of knowledge about the Buddha, as Brian Hodgson's gift of Sanskrit manuscripts was making its way across the seas to Europe from Kathmandu. Accurate translations of Buddhist texts were being made from Pāli, Chinese, Mongolian, and Tibetan. Reflecting on this period in 1862, Max Müller wrote, with some hyperbole, "It never rains but it pours. Whereas for years, nay, for centuries, not a single original document of the Buddhist religion had been accessible to the scholars of Europe, we witness, in the small space of ten years, the recovery of four complete Buddhist literatures. In addition to the discoveries of Hodgson in Nepal, of Csoma de Körös in Thibet, and of Schmidt in Mongolia, the Honorable George Turnour suddenly presented to the world the Buddhist literature of Ceylon, composed in the sacred language of that island, the ancient Pâli."[14]

Still, there was nothing yet available in Sanskrit, the ancient language that European scholars treasured above all others, the language that Sir Williams Jones had linked to Greek and Latin. Indeed, knowledge of Sanskrit came rather slowly to Paris. As noted above, Charles Wilkins published *The Bhagvat-Geetâ, or Dialogues of Kreeshna and Arjoon* in 1784, and Jones produced *Sacontalá; or, the fatal ring: an Indian drama*, his translation of Kālidāsa's Sanskrit play *Śakuntalā*, in 1792. Both of these works had been translated into French shortly after they appeared. However, instruction in Sanskrit did not begin in Paris until 1803.

On March 25, 1802, Great Britain and the French Republic signed the Treaty of Amiens, putting a temporary end to hostilities between the two nations that had begun in 1793. The treaty would have two important effects on the history of Buddhism. First, under the terms of the treaty, control of the coastal regions of Sri Lanka, which the British East India Company had wrested from the Dutch some years earlier, was formally ceded to Britain as a Crown colony; in 1815, the Kingdom of Kandy fell to the British, and the entire island soon came under their control.

The treaty also allowed various members of the British upper classes to visit Paris. J. M. W. Turner and William Hazlitt each filled sketchbooks while visiting the Louvre. (Travel was reciprocal; Marie Tussaud of waxworks fame took her skills to London.) Also among the British visitors was Alexander Hamilton (1762–1824), a Scot and former lieutenant in the Bengal army. Hamilton had gone to India in 1783 and soon developed an interest in "Sungscrit." In fact, in 1790 he wrote a letter to the Governor-General of India, Lord Cornwallis (who had surrendered to George Washington at Yorktown nine years before), asking that he be relieved of his daily duties at the garrison in order to be able to devote his time to the study of the language: "The liberal and enlightened policy of the Honble Court could not fail to suggest to them the difficulty of governing a nation, without an intimate acquaintance with its language, religion, laws, manners and customs: and that with respect to the Hindûs, who constitute the great body of the people, and who for their superiority in mental endowments as well as in industry and number, merit first consideration, that knowledge is chiefly to be expected from the development of science contained in their Sacred Language."[15]

In 1795, Hamilton, who had resigned from the army in 1790, returned to Britain after twelve years in India. He remained an active member of the Asiatic Society, and was a contributor to the newly founded *Edinburgh Review* and the *Asiatic Annual Register*. His enthusiasm for the language was such that upon his return to Scotland he became known as "Sanscrit" Hamilton. In late 1802 or early 1803, he traveled to Paris to examine the Indian manuscripts held by the Bibliothèque Nationale.

The Peace of Amiens lasted a little more than a year. Britain declared war on France on May 18, 1803. Four days later, Napoleon ordered the detention of all British males between the ages of eighteen and sixty then traveling in France. Among the 1,181 arrested was Hamilton. However, two important figures in Paris recognized his value: at that moment, he was the only person in continental Europe with a knowledge of Sanskrit. Through the efforts of Count Constantine de Volney (1757–1820), an Orientalist and member of the Senate, and Louis-Mathieu Langlès (1763–1824), director of the École des langues orientales vivantes, Hamilton was able to remain in Paris rather than be sequestered with his countrymen in Verdun.[16] As a token of his gratitude, he catalogued the Sanskrit manuscripts in the Bibliothèque Nationale, and he offered private Sanskrit lessons to a small group in Paris. His students included the Count de Volney himself as well as a visitor from Germany, Friedrich von Schlegel. Hamilton lived in Schlegel's house in Paris, and their study of Sanskrit together is said to have inspired Schlegel's 1808 *Über die Sprache und Weisheit der Indier* (*On the Language and Wisdom of the Indians*), in which he famously declared, "The Renaissance of antiquity promptly rejuvenated all the sciences; we might add that it rejuvenated and transformed the world. We could even say that the effects of Indic studies, if these enterprises were taken up and introduced into learned circles with the same energy today, would be no less great and far-reaching."[17]

In 1806, after Hamilton's departure, Antoine Leonard de Chézy (1773–1832), a student of Persian working as assistant librarian in the Department of Manuscripts at the Bibliothèque Nationale, set out to teach himself Sanskrit, making use of various materials in the library's collections and the translations into English coming from Calcutta. He succeeded in his task, but paid a high personal price: his wife and children left him in the process.

Julius Klaproth's sense that Paris was the place for Oriental studies would be confirmed. Already in 1795, the chair of Oriental Languages at the Collège de France had been divided into chairs of Persian and Turkish. Then, in 1814, chairs in Indology (Langues et littératures sanscrites) and Sinology (Langues et littératures chinoises et tartares mandchoues) were established at the Collège de France, with Chézy appointed to the first and Jean-Pierre Abel-Rémusat to the second. Some years later, a chair in Egyptology would be established for Jean-François Champollion (1790–1832), brilliant decoder of the Rosetta Stone. Among Chézy's Sanskrit pupils was Eugène Burnouf.

Born in Paris on April 8, 1801, Burnouf was the son of the distinguished classicist (and translator of Tacitus) Jean-Louis Burnouf

(1775–1844). As a child, he learned Greek and Latin from his father and studied at the Lycée Louis-le-grand. In 1822, he entered the École des Chartes, receiving degrees in both letters and law two years later. He also studied Sanskrit, with his father and then with Chézy, who had been the senior Burnouf's Sanskrit teacher. Burnouf was twenty-two when he published his first translation from the Sanskrit in the *Journal Asiatique* in 1823; it was a translation of a fable about the snake and the frogs from the *Hitopadeśa*, a famous collection of animal tales. The following year, he published "Sur un usage remarquable de l'infinitif sanscrit" ("On a Remarkable Usage of the Sanskrit Infinitive") in the same journal. If, as the title of that article might suggest, Burnouf's life seems less colorful than the other figures in this chapter, it was. He devoted most of the waking moments of his short life to reading books. His life story has little drama, but the impact of his reading would be dramatic.

The year 1826 was consequential for Burnouf. He published, in collaboration with the young Norwegian-German scholar Christian Lassen (1800–1876), *Essai sur le pâli*[18] (on the canonical language of the Theravāda Buddhist traditions of Sri Lanka and Southeast Asia, or, as it was called at the time, "Southern Buddhism"). A short book by Burnouf's subsequent standards (222 pages, with some examples of Pāli alphabets), it was devoted largely to grammar and orthography. Buddhism is often mentioned, however, especially for its role in the spread of Pāli in Southeast Asia. Burnouf and Lassen include a discussion of the topic that was so important to George Turnour: the various Buddhist traditions on the date of the death of Shakya Mouni Bouddha, as Burnouf called him, a topic to which he would return.

Also in 1826, Burnouf was appointed adjunct secretary of the Société Asiatique, which had been founded in 1822; he would become secretary in 1832. And in that same year, he married Reine Victoire Angélique Poiret; they would have four daughters. In 1829, Burnouf was named professor in general and comparative grammar at the École Normale. While there, he received an award from the Count de Volney for his work in "the transcription of Asiatic scriptures in Latin letters."

As the award suggests, Burnouf had mastered many languages. He was an accomplished scholar of Avestan, the sacred language of Zoroastrianism, still practiced by the Parsis in India. Between 1829 and

1833 (with a final volume in 1843), he published, at his own expense and with fonts of his own design, a 562-page lithograph of the *Vendidad Sadé* (or *Videvdat*) from a manuscript in the Bibliothèque Royale that had been brought to Paris by Orientalist Abraham Hyacinthe Anquetil Duperron (1731–1805). This collection contains works on myth, doctrine, and law, in the form of dialogues between the god Ahura Mazda and the prophet Zoroaster. Between 1833 and 1835, Burnouf published *Commentaire sur le Yaçna, l'un des livres liturgiques des Parses*, a translation of a commentary on the *Yasna* (a word meaning "worship" or "oblations"), the main liturgical section of the Avestan canon.

A cholera epidemic swept through Paris in 1832, claiming the lives of both Chézy and Abel-Rémusat, the holders of the chairs in Sanskrit and in Sinology at the Collège de France. Burnouf was appointed to succeed his teacher in the chair of Sanskrit. His friend Stanislas Julien (1797–1873) was selected to succeed Abel-Rémusat in the chair of Sinology; he would go on to make important contributions to Buddhist studies, Daoist studies (he translated the *Dao de jing* in 1842), and Chinese grammar; he also wrote treatises on porcelain and silkworms.

When a scholar is appointed to a chair, he is expected to deliver an inaugural lecture. In his, on February 1, 1833, Burnouf made no mention of Buddhism. Yet he expressed the enthusiasm of his age, describing ancient India as possessing "perhaps the richest literary history that a people can offer to the curiosity and admiration of Europe."[19] He declared, "It is India, with its philosophy and myths, its literature and laws, that we will study in its language. It is more than India, gentlemen, it is a page from the origins of the world, of the primitive history of the human spirit, that we shall try to decipher together. . . . There is no philology without philosophy and history. The analysis of the operations of language is also a science of observation; and if it is not the very science of the human spirit, it is at least one of the most astonishing faculties with whose aid the human spirit manifests itself."[20]

Burnouf continued to publish studies of Avestan language and literature, but as holder of the chair in Sanskrit, he turned his attention to India and launched a major project, which he called *Le Bhagavata Purana ou histoire poétique de Krîchna* (*The Bhagavata Purana or Poetic Story of Krishna*). In it, Burnouf provided his edition of the *Bhagavata*

Purāṇa, his translation, and his typically learned comments on the Sanskrit text, the famous Hindu compendium of the legends of Lord Krishna. He published three large volumes (of 768, 725, and 681 pages, respectively) between 1840 and 1847, and planned as many as three more in order to present all twelve cantos of the text.

Burnouf soon attracted a devoted circle of students from France and elsewhere in Europe, many of whom would go on to become some of the greatest scholars of the day. At least one was from America— Edward Eldridge Salisbury (1814–1901), a Congregationalist deacon who brought the study of Sanskrit from Paris to Yale in 1841. On May 28, 1844, Salisbury delivered a lecture entitled "Memoir on the History of Buddhism" at the first meeting of the American Oriental Society. This fifty-page report, based largely on Burnouf's work (and eventually published in the *Journal of the American Oriental Society* in 1849) was the first scholarly article on Buddhism to be written by an American. In his diary entry of March 20, 1845, Max Müller describes his first meeting with his future teacher: "Went to see Burnouf. Spiritual, amiable, thoroughly French. He received me in the most friendly way, talked a great deal, and all he said was valuable, not on ordinary topics but on special. I managed better in French than I expected. 'I am a Brahman, a Buddhist, a Zoroastrian. I hate the Jesuits'—that is the sort of man. I am looking forward to his lectures."[21]

The Sutras Arrive

It was shortly after Burnouf's appointment to the chair of Sanskrit at the Collège de France that the Société Asiatique, of which he was secretary, received a communication from Brian Houghton Hodgson in Kathmandu. Hodgson was offering to send Sanskrit manuscripts of Buddhist texts to Paris. The receipt of these texts would change the direction of Burnouf's scholarship for the last fifteen years of his life. It would also change our view of the Buddha.

When word of Hodgson's offer reached the Société Asiatique, Burnouf wrote to him directly on July 7, 1834, initiating what would become a long correspondence. This first letter begins with "Monsieur." Eventually, Burnouf would address Hodgson as "mon cher savant ami" (my dear learned friend). In the letter, Burnouf expresses his "great satisfaction in learning that the books of Buddha (Sâkya) existed in Sanskrit." He then asks, "Would I not be guilty of an in-discretion and take up your valuable time to beseech you to acquire for me some of the books that you judge the most valuable and the most appropriate for understanding pure Buddhism, that is to say, the part of the system that is not tainted with any modification by Brahmanism?"[22]

On or around April 20, 1837, twenty-four Sanskrit manuscripts of Buddhist texts arrived in Paris, sent by Hodgson seven months be-fore. On July 14, another sixty-four texts arrived, which Hodgson had had copied in Kathmandu and then sent to the Société Asiatique. He would eventually provide Burnouf with another fifty-nine manu-scripts. Suddenly, Burnouf had before him more Buddhist Sanskrit manuscripts than any previous European scholar, with the obvious exception of Brian Hodgson in Kathmandu. But unlike Hodgson, Burnouf was able to read them. These texts included sutras and tan-tras of Sanskrit Buddhism, composed for the most part during the first six centuries of the Common Era. Largely lost in India but preserved in Nepal, these Indian works, and their translations into Chinese and Tibetan, were among the most important in the history of Bud-dhism. They included the *Perfection of Wisdom in Eight Thousand Verses* (*Aṣṭasāhasrikāprajñāpāramitā*) and the *Sukhāvatīvyūha*, which tells of Sukhāvatī, the "Land of Bliss" and abode of Amitābha, the Buddha of Infinite Light; it was the fundamental sutra for the Pure Land tradi-tions of East Asia. Hodgson also sent the *Laṅkāvatāra*, a central text for the Yogācāra school in India and the Chan and Zen traditions of East Asia, and the *Guhyasamāja*, among the most influential of Bud-dhist tantras and particularly important in Tibet. There was the *Bud-dhacarita*, Aśvaghoṣa's beautiful verse biography of the Buddha. And there was the *Saddharmapuṇḍarīka*, the famous *Lotus Sutra*.

On June 5, 1837, Burnouf wrote to Hodgson to report that the So-ciété Asiatique had instructed him and Eugène Jacquet (1811–1838) to examine the twenty-four volumes that had arrived in April. The two young scholars divided the texts between them and began to read. Burnouf first chose, perhaps at random, a very important text, the *Perfection of Wisdom in Eight Thousand Verses* (*Aṣṭasāhasrikāprajñāpāra-mitā*), considered by scholars as the earliest of the many "perfection of wisdom" texts. But he was put off by it, as he explained to Hodg-son, "because I saw only perpetual repetitions of the advantages and merits promised to those who obtain *prajñapāramitā*. But what is this *prajñā* itself? This is what I did not see anywhere, and what I wished to learn."[23] He set it aside and picked up another:

•

I turned to a new book, one of the nine *dharmas* [the sacred texts of Nepal], the *Saddharmapuṇḍarīka*, and I can promise you that I have not repented my choice. Since about April 25, I have without reserve devoted every moment that I could steal from my occupations as professor of Sanskrit and academician to this work, of which I have already read rather considerable portions. You will not be astonished that I did not understand everything; the material is very new for me, the style as well as the content. But I intend to reread, with pen in hand, your excellent memoirs of the *Asiatic Researches* of London and Calcutta, as well as the *Journal* of Prinsep. Though many things are still obscure to my eyes, I nevertheless comprehend the progression of the book, the mode of exposition of the author, and I have even already translated two chapters in their entirety, omitting nothing. These are two parables, not lacking in interest, but which are especially curious specimens of the manner in which the teaching of the Buddhists is imparted and of the discursive and very Socratic method of exposition. . . . I confess to you that I am passionate about this reading, and that I would like to have more time and health to attend to it day and night. I will not, however, set aside the *Saddharma* without extracting and translating substantial fragments, convinced that there is nothing I could better do to recognize your liberality than to communicate to the scholars of Europe part of the riches that you have so liberally placed at our disposal. I will exert myself in that until this winter, and I will try to dig up some printer in Germany to bring out an *Analysis* or *Observations on the Saddharmapundarika*.[24]

•

This "Analysis" or "Observations" would evolve over the next seven years. In a letter of October 28, 1841, Burnouf tells Hodgson that he has finished printing his translation of the *Lotus Sutra*, "but I would like to give an introduction to this bizarre work."[25] Three years later, he would publish it: *Introduction à l'histoire du Buddhisme indien* (*Introduction to the History of Indian Buddhism*).[26]

By October 27, 1837, Burnouf had finished all but the final fifteen folios of his translation of the *Lotus Sutra*. On November 3, he began translating the *Kāraṇḍavyūha*, an important sutra about Avalokiteś- vara, the bodhisattva of compassion, that contains the famous mantra *oṃ maṇi padme hūṃ*. He completed the translation of this rather dif- ficult text ten days later. After taking a day off, on November 14, 1837, apparently finally able to overcome his initial aversion, he returned to the *Perfection of Wisdom in Eight Thousand Verses*, eventually complet- ing a translation of ninety percent of the text. An incomplete listing of Burnouf's translations of Buddhist texts found among his papers at the time of his death would include the *Great Chronicle* (*Mahāvaṃsa*) of Sri Lanka (the same text studied by George Turnour) from Pāli into Latin; the monastic code (*patimokka*) translated from Pāli and Bur- mese; large portions of the *Divyāvadāna* and the *Avadānaśataka*, two important Sanskrit collections of Buddhist legends; and hundreds of pages of translations from the Pāli and Burmese of *jātaka* stories, the stories of the Buddha's previous lives.[27] Only one of these would be published, and then only after Burnouf's death: the *Lotus Sutra*.

The Story of the *Histoire*

As the son of a classicist, Burnouf seems to have been trained almost from birth to decipher dead languages. When he received eighty- eight manuscripts in a dead language, composed long ago in a land where Buddhism was long dead, he could set to work, shielded from the sensations of a Buddhist setting—never leaving Europe, rarely leaving Paris, never seeing a Buddhist, much less conversing with one—sitting instead in his study, surrounded by ancient texts that he was well trained to read. He notes in passing, "I can assert that there is nothing in all the Sanskrit literature as easy to understand as the texts of Nepal, apart from some terms the Buddhists used in a very special way; I will not give any proof of this other than the considerable number of texts that it was possible for me to read in a rather limited time."[28] The "considerable number of texts" included many lengthy and (at least in the estimation of lesser mortals) dif- ficult sutras in the history of Buddhism.[29]

Of the Sanskrit manuscripts he received from Hodgson, Burnouf somehow decided that he should translate and publish the *Lotus Sutra*

first. He did so without knowing that it is arguably the most influential of all Buddhist texts, with particular importance in East Asia.
He seems to have chosen it because he was captivated by its content,
especially its famous parables, including the burning house and the
prodigal son. Burnouf completed the translation of the sutra in November 1839, and then had it printed by 1841. The translation itself
required 283 pages, with an additional 149 pages of notes—certainly
more than enough for a book. But he did not publish it.

Burnouf delayed the publication of his *Lotus Sutra* for two reasons.
The first was that he wanted to provide a number of appendices on
various terms and concepts that appear in the sutra. He completed
twenty-one of these before he died. They were then edited by his
student Julius von Mohl and published in 1852, the year of Burnouf's
death, as *Le Lotus de la bonne loi traduit du Sanscrit accompagné d'un
commentaire et de vingt et un mémoires relatifs au Buddhisme* (*The Lotus
of the True Law Translated from the Sanskrit Accompanied by a Commentary and Twenty-One Memoranda Related to Buddhism*). It is a massive
work, 897 pages long.

The second reason for Burnouf's delay would have profound consequences for the Buddha, or at least for our understanding of him.
Burnouf felt that his translation of the *Lotus Sutra* would not be com-
prehensible to European readers unless he wrote an introduction;
that introduction grew to 647 large pages with tiny notes. According
to his plan, this work would be only the first volume of the introduction to his translation of the *Lotus Sutra*. He intended at least one, and
perhaps as many as three, additional volumes (depending on what he
meant by *memoire*, or memorandum). The first, the only one that was
published, is devoted to what Burnouf calls the Buddhist literature
of Nepal, preserved in Sanskrit. The second volume, which he said
would have five sections, would be devoted to the Buddhist literature
of Sri Lanka, preserved in Pāli. This study would be followed by another memorandum comparing the Sanskrit collection of Nepal with
the Pāli collection of Sri Lanka. Finally, he would compose another
memorandum, in six sections, that would analyze various Buddhist
traditions on the date of the Buddha's death. From there, he would go
on to examine the fate of Buddhism in India after the Buddha's death,
identifying the various periods of Buddhism's departure from India
to other regions of Asia.

Throughout *Introduction to the History of Indian Buddhism*, Burnouf alludes to these various subsequent volumes, suggesting that he fully intended to complete them all. And we learn from a letter to his student Max Müller dated October 7, 1848, that he was hard at work on the second volume, because his research on cuneiform inscriptions had been interrupted by the sound of gunfire from the battles at the barricades on the streets of Paris. Apparently, it became too distracting for him to work on the inscriptions, and so he was writing the second volume on Buddhism: "I am now working at the second volume of my Introduction to Buddhism, having been obliged to set aside the work I had begun on the Nineveh inscriptions. These researches cannot be carried out on usefully in a time of political disturbance, such as the present; the tempest in the streets distracts the mind. . . . Under these circumstances, I am devoting myself to Buddhism, to occupy my mind."[30]

The task that Burnouf set for himself in *Introduction to the History of Indian Buddhism* was unlike anything he or any other European had attempted to do: write a monograph about Buddhism based on his own translations of canonical Buddhist scriptures. Up to this point in his work, apart from writing scholarly articles and the brief coauthored work on Pāli, Burnouf had edited or translated individual texts. For this project, he went further. He first translated a substantial number of Buddhist texts (and read many more), and then synthesized what he had read into his own introduction to Buddhism. He did so with very few resources (such as dictionaries and grammars) available to him, and without an established and reliable tradition of scholarship to serve as his foundation. Here is how Burnouf described the task he faced. The state of the scholarship that preceded him will be familiar from our previous chapters:

•

The task I impose on myself, although different, is equally arduous. It is necessary to browse through almost one hundred volumes, all manuscripts, written in four languages still little known, for whose study we have only lexicons, I could say of imperfect vocabularies, one of which has given birth to popular dialects even whose names are almost unknown. To these difficulties of form, add those of content: an entirely new subject, innumerable schools, an immense metaphysical apparatus, a mythology without boundaries; everywhere disorder and a dispiriting vagueness on questions of time and place; then, outside and among the small number of scholars whom a laudable curiosity attracts towards the results promised to this research, ready-made solutions, opinions that are immovable and ready to resist the authority of the texts, because they pride themselves in resting on an authority superior to all others, that of common sense. Do I need to recall that, for some people, all the questions related to Buddhism were already decided, when no one had read a single line of the books I shall analyze shortly, when the existence of these books was not even suspected by anyone? For some, Buddhism was a venerable cult born in Central Asia, and whose origin was lost in the mists of time; for others it was a miserable counterfeit of Nestorianism; the Buddha has been made a Negro, because he had frizzy hair; a Mongol, because he had slanted eyes; a Scythe, because he was called Śākya. He has even been made a planet; and I do not know whether some scholars do not still delight today in recognizing this peaceful sage in the traits of the bellicose Odin. Certainly, it is permissible to hesitate, when to such vast solutions one promises only to substitute doubts, or only explanations that are simple and almost vulgar. The hesitation can even lead to discouragement, when one retraces one's steps and compares the results obtained to the time they have cost. I would like, nevertheless, to rely upon the indulgence of serious persons to whom these studies are addressed; and while they leave me with the feeling of my insufficiency, with which I am affected more than ever, the hope for their benevolent consideration has given me the courage to produce these rough drafts, destined to open the way to research, which, while still not having a numerous public, is nonetheless in itself of incontestable value for the history of the human spirit.[31]

•

The challenges Burnouf faced, then, were both practical and philosophical, logistical and ideological, located both in the manuscripts on his desk and in the minds of his colleagues. The texts he had were in four languages—Sanskrit, Tibetan, Chinese, and Mongolian—for which the available dictionaries were unreliable. One of those languages, Sanskrit, had "given birth to many popular dialects," including Pāli. The texts composed in these languages were not systematic, instead presenting vast and baffling worlds with few markers in his-

torical time and geographical space. The number of European scholars who were qualified to read these texts was few, but that had not
prevented others lacking such credentials from holding forth on Buddhism "when the existence of these books was not even suspected by
anyone."

This is a key phrase. Up until this time, knowledge of Buddhism
had been gathered from sources that were somehow alien to its origin. This knowledge had come from outside India, from China, Japan,
Tibet, Sri Lanka, or Southeast Asia. Or it had come from outside Buddhism, from the Hindu priests whose ancestors, according to the theories of the day, had driven Buddhism from its homeland. No one had
suspected that the original texts of Buddhism survived, not in translation but in their original language, Sanskrit. These texts, Burnouf
would argue, contained the original teachings of the Buddha himself,
untainted by translation. Yet, unaware of the existence of these texts,
others had put forward all manner of outlandish theories about the
Buddha, relying only on their "common sense," theories we have encountered in the previous chapters. The planet with which the Buddha was identified is Mercury; we will meet the chief proponent of
this view, Paulinus a S. Bartholomaeo (1748–1806), in the conclusion.
But rather than adding his own grand theories, Burnouf admits that
he can only offer solutions that are tentative and "almost vulgar," in
the sense of ordinary. He concludes by saying that he has undertaken
this great task because of the value the Buddhist texts hold for the
history of the human spirit. The key word here is *human*.

We might recall that after condemning the Buddha as a demon and
devil, Christian missionaries would later condemn him for being a
mere mortal. An anti-Christian text from Japan, the *Kirishitan Mo-
nogatari* (*Tale of the Christians*), probably compiled in 1639, presents
the Christian view: "Shaka, if you'd really like to know, was the son of
King Jōbon of India. He was disinherited by his father and lived withdrawn on Dandoku Mountain, and there, giving his mouth free rein,
he worked his deception upon all sentient beings. . . . To be deluded by
the teachings of Shaka (who was just an everyday person) is just like
falling under the spell of a fox. But it seems that by his clever tongue
Shaka arranged to trick the fools of the Three Countries [India, China,
and Japan]."[32]

Two centuries later in Paris, the humanity of the Buddha would take on an entirely different meaning. Perhaps the most important sentence in the entire 647 pages of Burnouf's *Introduction to the History of Indian Buddhism* occurs on the first page of the foreword, where he declares that the belief called Buddhism is completely Indian, literally "a completely Indian fact" (*un fait complétement indien*). His choice of the term *fact* is telling. It points to his conviction that the Buddha and Buddhism are matters of history rather than matters of myth; that the true Buddhism, as he declares repeatedly, is a human Buddhism that arose not in an imagined heaven but on the contested soil of ancient India. Burnouf is convinced that much about the history and social milieu of Buddhism, both its history and the chronology of its subsequent development, can be gleaned from reading its scriptures.

Like other scholars of the day, Burnouf believed that Buddhism had been driven from India by the brahman priests of Hinduism; once in exile, it had inevitably become tainted by the foreign cultures it encountered, whether in China, Tibet, or Siam. The Buddhism found in those nations, therefore, had been abstracted by time and language, resulting, inevitably in his view, in significant loss: "It is clear, indeed, that as Buddhism moved away from its cradle, it lost a portion of the life that it drew from its long abode in the country where it had flourished for so many centuries, and, obliged to use, in order to propagate among new peoples, diverse idioms sometimes little amenable to the expression of its own conceptions, little by little it hid its original forms under borrowed cloth."[33]

Thus, in the first chapter he demonstrates what at the time was only suspected by a few: that the most important Buddhist texts preserved in the languages of Tibetan, Mongolian, and Chinese are in fact translations of works originally composed in Sanskrit. He devotes the remainder of the chapter to a detailed argument—an argument that remains frustratingly compelling over a century and a half later—for the importance of reading Buddhist texts in the language in which they were originally composed. Burnouf does not dismiss the usefulness of translations into other languages. However, he provides several examples of what can be lost in translation. He writes, "The genius of India has marked all its products with a character so special that whatever the superiority of mind and whatever freedom in the use of their methods one grants to the Oriental translators, one cannot prevent oneself from recognizing that they must necessarily have brought to their versions certain features of the original that often will remain unintelligible to the reader who does not have the means to resort to the Indian text itself."[34]

Burnouf then goes on to consider the various traditional categories for classifying Buddhist texts. Throughout, he intersperses his descriptions and analyses with extended passages from the various Buddhist texts he had been translating since the arrival of Hodgson's dispatch; almost forty percent of the entire volume is composed of Burnouf's translations and his copious notes. He chose to organize the book around the most famous of the categories of Buddhist texts: the division into the *tripiṭaka*, or "three baskets." These are the *sūtras*, or discourses of the Buddha; the *vinaya*, or works on monastic discipline; and the *abhidharma*, or works on philosophy (Burnouf renders that term as "metaphysics").

For his vision of the Buddha, Burnouf's most important point in his discussion of the sutras he received from Hodgson is the distinction he draws between what he calls the "simple sutras" and the "developed sutras." The former term is his own coinage; he derives the latter from an epithet found in the titles of some Mahāyāna sutras, *vaipulya*, which means "broad" or "extensive." Burnouf considers the simple sutras to be the older and the more authentic, originating from the Buddha himself or his immediate disciples. As such, they provide the clearest sense of the Buddha's true teachings as well as the most valuable information on the early history of Buddhism. For Burnouf, the developed sutras clearly come from a later period, perhaps composed abroad after Buddhism's expulsion from India, and are filled with mythological elements.

Burnouf divides the sutras into these two groups based on both their form and their content. The simple sutras are written in proper Sanskrit and are in prose with occasional stanzas. In contrast, the developed sutras are a mixture of prose and verse, with the verse sometimes written in various dialects of Sanskrit, what he calls "barbaric Sanskrit," perhaps by those who no longer remembered the proper grammatical forms:

•

The style of these portions is an unspeakable mixture in which an incorrect Sanskrit is bristling with forms, some of which are entirely

Pāli and others that are popular in the most general sense of this term. There is no geographical name to give to such a language; but one understands at the same time that such a mixture could be produced in places where Sanskrit was not studied in a scholarly manner, and among populations who had never spoken it or who only knew dialects derived at degrees more or less distant from the primitive root. I am thus inclined to believe that this part of the great sūtras must have been written outside of India or, to express myself in a more precise manner, in the countries situated beyond the Indus or in Kashmir, for example, a country where the scholarly language of Brahmanism and Buddhism must have been cultivated with less success than in central India. It seems to me rather difficult, not to say impossible, that the gibberish of this poetry could have occurred in an epoch when Buddhism flourished in Hindustan.[35]

●

Even more important, the simple sutras differ from the developed sutras in their content. The simple sutras depict the Buddha above all as a teacher of ethics and morality, speaking directly to a human society, one in which his teachings are opposed by brahman priests. The developed sutras are entirely different. Their abstruse metaphysics derives not from the Buddha and his circle but from the subsequent musings of monks safely cloistered from the society where the Buddha fought the vested interests of the brahmans. "The ordinary sūtras show us Śākyamuni Buddha preaching his doctrine in the midst of a society that, judging from the legends in which he plays a role, was profoundly corrupt. His teaching is above all moral; and although metaphysics are not forgotten, it certainly occupies a less grand position than the theory of virtues imposed by the law of the Buddha, virtues among which charity, patience, and chastity are without objection at the first rank."[36] Burnouf does not hesitate to express his preference for the simple sutras:

●

The scene of the first is India, the actors are humans and some inferior divinities; and save for the power to make miracles that Śākya and his foremost disciples possess, what occurs there seems natural and plausible. On the contrary, everything that the imagination can con-

ceive as immense in space and time is still too confining for the scene of
the developed sūtras. The actors there are these imaginary bodhisattvas, with infinite virtues, with endless names one cannot pronounce,
with bizarre and almost ridiculous titles, where the oceans, the rivers,
the waves, the rays, the suns are coupled with qualities of unmerited
perfection in a manner most puerile and least instructive, because it
is without effort there. No one is left to convert; everyone believes,
and each is quite sure to become a buddha one day, in a world of diamonds or lapis lazuli. The consequence of all this is that the more developed the sūtras are, the poorer they are in historical details; and
the farther they penetrate into metaphysical doctrine, the more they
distance themselves from society and become estranged from what occurs there.[37]

•

Burnouf's portrait of the Buddha as a man of the real world is
particularly finely drawn in his long and fascinating discussion of
the role of caste in Buddhism. Prior authors had relied for the most
part on Hindu sources for this famous element in the Buddha's biography, especially the appropriation of the Buddha as the ninth avatar
of Vishnu, where, as we saw in chapter 3, the Buddha's opposition to
caste was Vishnu's stratagem for consigning demons to hell. Burnouf,
drawing on Buddhist sources, paints a very different picture, with the
brahmans representing everything that is corrupt in a Hindu society where superiority is a matter of birth rather than character. The
Buddha is the man of the people, opening the path to liberation to all
who would follow, regardless of their place in the social hierarchy. As
Burnouf writes, "As much as brahmans should feel aversion for the
doctrine of Śākya, so much should persons of lower castes welcome
it with eagerness and favor; for if this doctrine abased the first, it up-
lifted the second, and it assured to the poor and the slave in this life
what Brahmanism did even not promise in the next, the advantage
to see oneself, from the religious point of view, as the equal of his
master."[38]

As we read Burnouf's praise of the Buddha as a man who stood
up against the established order of the church in order to champion
the rights of the downtrodden, it is important to remember that he
was a citizen of the French Republic, and that he hated the Jesuits.

Burnouf did not elaborate on the reasons for his antipathy. In 1762, Jean-Jacques Rousseau had published *Émile; or, On Education*, which contained "The Profession of Faith of the Savoyard Vicar," a biting condemnation of Roman Catholic missionaries. The book was publicly burned that same year. However, by the time of Burnouf, *Émile* had come to be regarded as a prescription for modern education.

On the changes that the Buddha brought to Indian society, Burnouf wrote:

·

The priesthood ceased to be hereditary, and the monopoly on religious matters left the hands of a privileged caste. The body charged with teaching the law ceased to be perpetuated by birth; it was replaced by an assembly of monks dedicated to celibacy, who are recruited indiscriminately from all classes. Finally, the Buddhist monk, who receives everything from the teaching and from a kind of investiture, replaced the brahman, who owed it only to birth, that is to say, to the nobility of his origin. This is without question a fundamental change, and it is enough to explain the opposition the brahmans made to the propagation and application of the principles of Buddhism. Indeed, the brahmans disappeared in the new order of things created by Śākya.[39]

·

But after the death of the Buddha, the dharma fell into decline, even before it was exiled from India. This is most clear in Burnouf's chapter on Buddhist tantra, a subject that he takes up with unveiled disdain. "It is not my intention to long dwell on this part of the Nepalese collection, which I am inclined to regard as the most modern of all, and whose importance for the history of human superstitions does not compensate for its mediocrity and vapidity. It is certainly not without interest to see Buddhism, which in its first organization had so little of what makes a religion, end in the most puerile practices and the most exaggerated superstitions."[40] Burnouf seems especially disappointed to see Buddhism, which had for so many centuries distinguished itself from Brahmanism, here make an alliance with "Śivaism." He goes to some lengths to try to understand the origins of this unfortunate alliance.

The final section of the book is entitled "History of the Nepal Collection." When he had delivered his inaugural lecture in 1833, before the arrival of Hodgson's dispatch, Burnouf had noted the lack of a single historical text among all the Sanskrit classics. He lamented, "Among so many riches, one feels regret at not finding the history of the nation that they forever glorify."[41] Here in the *Introduction*, eleven years later, he argues that the history of India only begins to become clear at the time of the Buddha, a development he credits to "the realistic spirit of this doctrine, its materialism and even its ordinariness." And he contrasts Buddhist sutras with the Vedas of the Hindus: "Never descending from heaven and remaining constantly in the vague regions of mythology where the reader grasps only vain forms that are no longer possible for him to fix in time or space, the sacred books of the Buddhists ordinarily present us with a series of entirely human events, a kṣatriya [the warrior caste to which the Buddha belonged] who makes himself an ascetic, who does battle with brahmans, who teaches and converts kings whose names these books have preserved for us."[42]

As we have seen, by the time Burnouf published the *Introduction*, although the African hypothesis for the Buddha's ancestry persisted in some quarters, the leading European scholars understood that the Buddha was a historical figure and that he was of Indian origin. The basic story of his life had been repeated many times in the accounts of travelers and missionaries, but this story was derived largely from oral reports provided by Buddhists outside India in various local vernaculars. The first substantial review of Burnouf's book, by the Indologist Eduard Röer (1805–1866) in the *Journal of the Asiatic Society of Bengal* in 1845, surveyed European knowledge of Buddhism, noting that its initial understanding had come from "secondary sources," that is, works in Chinese, Burmese, and Mongolian. This led Röer to observe, "Our first acquaintance with Buddhism was in fact not a kind to invite research; the mixture of extravagant fables, apparent historical facts, philosophical and religious doctrines was so monstrous, that it seemed to defy every attempt to unravel it."[43] As we have seen, not only had the doctrines of Buddhism been described for centuries as demonic and monstrous, the Buddha himself was sometimes portrayed as a monster. Burnouf would make him into a man.

The Buddha of Burnouf

Eugène Burnouf was the first European to read a large corpus of Indian Buddhist texts in Sanskrit, and it is from these sources that he paints his portrait of the Buddha, a human Buddha. He writes, "I speak here in particular of the Buddhism that appears to me to be the most ancient, the human Buddhism, if I dare call it so, which consists almost entirely in very simple rules of morality, and where it is enough to believe that the Buddha was a man who reached a degree of intelligence and of virtue that each must take as the exemplar for his life."[44] Here is how he describes the Buddha, providing "the purely human character of Buddhism":[45]

•

It is into the milieu of a society so constituted that was born, in a family of kṣatriyas, that of the Śākyas of Kapilavastu, who claimed descent from the ancient solar race of India, a young prince who, renouncing the world at the age of twenty-nine, became a monk under the name of Śākyamuni or also śramaṇa Gautama. His doctrine, which according to the sūtras was more moral than metaphysical, at least in its principle, rested upon an opinion accepted as a fact and upon a hope presented as a certitude. This opinion is that the visible world is in perpetual change; that death succeeds life and life death; that man, like all that surrounds him, revolves in the eternal circle of transmigration; that he successively passes through all forms of life from the most elementary to the most perfect; that the place he occupies on the vast scale of living beings depends on the merit of the actions he performs in this world; and thus the virtuous man must, after this life, be reborn with a divine body, and the guilty with a body of the damned; that the rewards of heaven and the punishments of hell have only a limited duration, like everything in the world; that time exhausts the merit of virtuous actions as it effaces the faults of evil actions; and that the fatal law of change brings the god as well as the damned back to earth, in order to again put both to the test and make them pass through a new series of transformations. The hope that Śākyamuni brought to humanity was the possibility to escape from the law of transmigration, entering what he calls *nirvāṇa*, that is to say, annihilation. The definitive sign of this annihilation was death; but a precursory sign in this life announced the man predestined for this supreme liberation; it was the possession of an unlimited science, which gave him a clear view of the world as it is, that is to say, the knowledge of physical and moral laws; and in short, it was the practice of the six transcendent perfections: that of alms-giving, morality, science, energy, patience, and charity. The authority upon which the monk of the Śākya race supported his teaching was entirely personal; it was formed of two elements, one real and the other ideal. The first was the consistency and the saintliness of his conduct, of which chastity, patience, and charity formed the principal features. The second was the claim he made to be buddha, that is to say, enlightened, and as such to possess superhuman science and power. With his power, he performed miracles; with his science, he perceived, in a form clear and complete, the past and the future. Thereby, he could recount everything that each person had done in their previous existences; and so he asserted that an infinite number of beings had long ago attained like him, through the practice of the same virtues, the dignity of buddha, before entering into complete annihilation. In the end, he presented himself to humanity as its saviour, and he promised that his death would not annihilate his doctrine; but that this doctrine would endure for a great number of centuries after him, and that when his salutary action ceased, there would come into the world a new buddha, whom he announced by name and whom, before descending to earth, the legends say, he himself had crowned in heaven, with the title *future buddha*.[46]

•

Among all the passages about the Buddha in the preceding pages, this one is unusual in its eloquence. At the same time, it seems conventional in its content. This is the Buddha that we know. Yet, as is clear from what has come before, the Buddha had never previously been described in quite these terms by a European or by an Asian, for that matter.

For Burnouf, Buddhism is completely Indian, and much of *Introduction to the History of Indian Buddhism* is devoted to the demonstration of this fact. Yet he also seeks to show the many ways in which Buddhism differed from the dominant Indian religion, Brahmanism. Burnouf portrays Brahmanism in a negative light, as a tradition controlled by complacent clerics obsessed with protecting the privilege of their caste system at all costs, restricting access to an arid sacred knowledge to those who inherit it through the accident of birth. Brahmanism is the persecutor of Buddhism, eventually driving it from Indian soil. This is something that Burnouf clearly regrets, and he distinguishes Buddhism from Brahmanism at almost every turn:

•

Written generally in a form and a language that is quite simple, the sūtras retain the visible trace of their origin. They are dialogues related to morality and philosophy, in which Śākya fulfills the role of master. Far from presenting his thought in this concise form so familiar to the Brahmanical teaching, there is no doubt that he expounds it with tiresome repetitions and diffuseness, but which give his teaching the character of a real preaching. There is an abyss between his method and that of the brahmans. Instead of this mysterious teaching confided almost secretly to a small number of listeners, instead of these formulas whose studied obscurity seems made to discourage the acumen of the disciple as much as to exercise it, the sūtras show us a large audience around Śākya, composed of all those who desire to listen to him and in his language, with this need to make himself understood, having words for all intelligences and, through its perpetual repetitions, leaving no excuse to less attentive minds or more rebellious memories. This profound difference is at the very essence of Buddhism, a doctrine whose characteristic feature is proselytism, but proselytism is itself only an effect of this sentiment of benevolence and universal charity which animates the Buddha, and which is at once the cause and the aim of the mission he gave himself on earth.[47]

•

Like William Erskine before him, Burnouf maintains that this humanity of the Buddha distinguishes him from the Hindu gods: "Śākya does not come, like the Brahmanical incarnations of Vishnu, to show the people an eternal and infinite god, descending to earth and preserving, in the mortal condition, the irresistible power of the divinity. He is the son of a king who becomes a monk and who has only the superiority of his virtue and his science to recommend him to the people."[48]

And yet this human Buddha also performed miracles—to which Burnouf, scientific son of the French Enlightenment, turns a surpris-

ingly blind eye. The selections that he translates contain all manner
of supernatural derring-do; he even includes the story of the most
famous of the Buddha's miracles, the miracle at Śrāvastī, where the
Buddha rose into the air while shooting flames from the upper half
of his body and jets of water from the lower half. Burnouf typically
passes over these wonders in silence, saying at one point that the Buddha performed miracles only because his brahman antagonists chal-
lenged him to do so. Elsewhere, Burnouf says he did so only to favorably dispose his audience to what he has to say: "I often see repeated
this kind of maxim: 'miracles performed by a supernatural power attract ordinary people quickly.' To this means, feelings of benevolence
and faith, awakened in those who come to listen or only to see the
Buddha, always respond through the influence of virtuous actions
they have performed in previous existences."[49] For Burnouf, what
distinguishes the Buddha from his brahmanical opponents (who also
perform miracles) is his teaching, a simple teaching of charity and
morality, which he offers freely to members of all castes, to rich and
poor, to the highborn and the lowly, to women and men.

For Burnouf, that Buddhism is completely Indian. Yet there is
something about the Buddha that distinguishes him from other
teachers who have appeared in India. Throughout the simple sutras,
that is, the sutras that for Burnouf most accurately represent the
teachings of the historical Buddha, the Buddha is above all human,
and the power of his humanity was such that it could overthrow the
great weight of the culture in which he appeared. As Burnouf indi-
cates, "He lived, he taught, and he died as a philosopher; and his humanity remained a fact so incontestably recognized by all that the
compilers of legends to whom miracles cost so little did not even have
the thought of making him a god after his death."[50] The power of the
Buddha's humanity was so great that it protected history from being
overwhelmed by myth. "This respect for human truth in Buddhism,
which prevented the disciples of Śākya from transforming the man
into God, is quite remarkable for a people like the Indians, among
whom mythology has so easily taken the place of history."[51] Burnouf
demonstrates convincingly that the Buddha is a product of a particular place and a particular historical moment. And then he moves him
beyond India and beyond history.

Indeed, one could argue that yet another great achievement of

Burnouf's was to present the Buddha to the West as a universal figure. He was born in India, but he differs from all other Indians, both divine and human. He is an anomaly in a culture devoted to priest craft, hierarchy, metaphysics, and myth. Indians have long had an aversion to corpses, yet the power of the Buddha was so great that his followers worshipped his relics. Like the Buddha descending from the Tuṣita Heaven to enter history, the Buddha arrives as if he is of another time and place, a more modern time, a more Western place. He is the product of a different Enlightenment. For Burnouf, Buddhism is Indian, but the Buddha was not. Buddhism is an Indian religion, yet one that departs from the tradition from which it emerged. It does so through the powerful humanity of the Buddha, a humanity that seems to transcend both the time and the place of his birth.

Yet it seems that this humanity was best preserved by Europeans. In a letter to Hodgson of May 15, 1836, Burnouf wrote, "We learned with vivid satisfaction that you already sent to the Asiatic Society of Great Britain a considerable collection of the Sanskrit originals of Buddhism. We welcomed such news with great pleasure; for at last these precious sources are in Europe, accessible to all, or at least to those who will have the courage to study them; in short, they are removed from the diverse and so numerous causes of destruction to which they would be exposed as long as they remain in the Orient." Since Hodgson agreed with him on this point, or so he thought, Burnouf continued: "It is necessary to remove from the apathy, from the superstition, from the avarice of the Orientals, the literary treasures they have saved from the shipwreck of time; it is necessary to transport them to Europe, where there is less fire, less upheaval, less religious hatred, where there are public repositories open to receive this precious debris as the property, I will not say of the citizens of nations, but belonging to all of humanity."[52]

Burnouf described the Buddha and Buddhism for the first time in ways that would become so ingrained and natural that their origins in an 1844 French tome would eventually be forgotten. These would include that Buddhism is an Indian religion, that the Buddha is a historical figure, and, perhaps of particular consequence, that the Buddha was a human teacher of a religion, or perhaps a philosophy, that preaches ethics and morality without recourse to dogma, ritual, or metaphysics. The consequences of his portrayal of the Buddha and his Buddhism would be profound.

Burnouf's *Introduction to the History of Indian Buddhism* would be studied assiduously by the next generation of European scholars of Buddhism. Yet its influence would extend well beyond France, and beyond the infant discipline of Buddhist studies. It was read in America by Ralph Waldo Emerson and Henry David Thoreau.[53] It was read in Germany by Friedrich Schelling (who praised it for refining his understanding of nirvana and noted how remarkable it was that France, with its political instability, could produce a man like Burnouf), Arthur Schopenhauer, and Friedrich Nietzsche. Richard Wagner wrote, "Burnouf's *Introduction to the History of Indian Buddhism* interested me most among my books, and I found material in it for a dramatic poem, which has stayed in my mind ever since, though only vaguely sketched."[54] The material for this opera came specifically from Burnouf's description of the *Śārdūlakarṇāvadāna*, a story that seems meant for Wagner, in which a beautiful outcaste woman, the daughter of a witch, falls in love with the Buddha's cousin Ānanda. Wagner's Buddhist opera, entitled *Die Sieger*, was listed in the timetable he presented to King Ludwig II, but unfortunately it was never completed.

It is said that Burnouf was in his study each morning at 3:00 a.m. Relying only on his prodigious Sanskrit skills, his dogged analysis, and his imagination of what must have been, he created a historical narrative of Buddhism—from pristine origin, to baroque elaboration, to degenerate decline—based entirely on his reading of a random group of texts that arrived on his desk as if from nowhere. And from those same texts, he painted a portrait of the Buddha that remains pristine.

CONCLUSION. The Aftermath

In the Musée Guimet in Paris stands a famous second-century-CE stone carving from Amaravati in southeast India. It depicts the Bodhi tree, where the Buddha sat on the night of enlightenment. Under the tree is a throne. It has a back, arms, and legs, with a cushion on the seat and a cushion against the back. But the throne has no Buddha. It is not that the carving has no figures; the throne is surrounded by humans and animals. The carving is a famous example of aniconic Buddhist art.

By the nineteenth century, India was like that empty throne. It was the place where Buddhism had been, but its place was vacant. The stupas were overgrown with vegetation, the statues were buried up to their necks like Devadatta sinking into the earth, the rock-cut monasteries housed no monks. Yet, like the figures surrounding the empty throne in the carving, Buddhism flourished all around India—in Nepal, Tibet, and Mongolia to the north, in China to the east, in Sri Lanka, Thailand, Burma, Cambodia, Laos, and Vietnam to the south. Over the course of the nineteenth century, a new Buddha would be carved and placed on the empty throne. Once enthroned, he would come to reign over the world.

In a certain sense, idolatry had come full circle. As we saw in chapter 1, Europeans had condemned Buddhists as idolaters for centuries. In the nineteenth century, European archaeologists and art historians would discover the empty throne, the riderless horse, and other images of early Buddhist art in which the idol is absent. They would argue, like Athanasius Kircher had in the seventeenth century, that Buddhist idolatry had been imported from the West. But their West was not the Egypt of the pharaohs; it was the Greece of Alexander. Greek communities that ruled the eastern reaches of his realm introduced statuary to India; images of the Buddha were modeled after their god

Apollo. The first great European art historian of India, Alfred Foucher (1865–1952), imagined that the first Buddha image had been carved by an artist who was half Greek, half Buddhist.[1] This strange combination of the ethnic and the religious (or perhaps the philosophical), one that Foucher dated to the first century BCE, would recur nineteen centuries later—not in what is now Pakistan but in Paris.

Eugène Burnouf did not live to complete his multivolume project. He died, apparently of kidney failure, on May 28, 1852, at the age of fifty-one and was buried in Père Lachaise cemetery. His father had been interred there just eight years earlier, in 1844, the year that *Introduction to the History of Indian Buddhism* was published. Burnouf's translation of the *Lotus Sutra, Le Lotus de la bonne loi,* appeared in the year of his death. He had left instructions that it be dedicated to Brian Houghton Hodgson, whom he called *fondateur de la véritable étude du Buddhisme par les textes et les monuments,* "founder of the true study of Buddhism through texts and monuments." In the century and a half since Burnouf's death, it has become clear that that phrase more accurately describes Burnouf himself. For in the ensuing years, discourse about Buddhism, what would come to be called Buddhist studies, would reside not in the lands where Buddhism was practiced but in Europe.

Burnouf left France only twice. In 1834, he visited Germany, and in 1835, he visited England. While in Oxford, he met H. H. (Horace Hayman) Wilson (1786–1860). Wilson had returned home after twenty-five years in India to accept an appointment to Britain's first chair of Sanskrit, the Boden Professorship at Oxford University.

Born in London, Wilson was the son of an accountant for the British East India Company. As a young man, he spent school holidays with an uncle who worked as an assayer at the Royal Mint, calculating the quantities of particular metals in coins. At the age of eighteen, he began training as a surgeon, and in 1808 was appointed assistant surgeon to the East India Company. However, upon his arrival in Calcutta the following year, the assay master of the mint there learned of Wilson's metallurgical skills and recruited him. In 1816, Wilson was promoted to assay master and continued in that position until his departure from India in 1833.

Boredom played a significant role in the formation of Britain's knowledge about its colonies; many of the officials of the East India

Company had time on their hands. With little to do in Kathmandu, Brian Hodgson looked into Buddhism. Wilson's duties at the mint did not require his constant attention, and he used the time for a variety of pursuits. In addition to acting in the Calcutta Theatre, he developed a strong interest in Indian languages, especially Sanskrit. His first translation, in 1813, was of the famous lyric poem *The Cloud Messenger* (*Meghadhūta*) by the poet and dramatist Kālidāsa. In 1819, he published his well-regarded *Sanskrit-English Dictionary*. Wilson enjoyed close relations with the Bengali elite of Calcutta (fathering children with an Indian woman) and advocated traditional learning. He famously opposed the 1829 ban on *sati* by Lord Bentinck, Governor-General of India, arguing that it violated the British policy of noninterference in religious practices and that it could lead to insurrection.

In 1833, Wilson returned to Britain to assume the Boden Professorship in Sanskrit, established by Joseph Boden to aid in the transmission of the Gospel to the Indian intelligentsia. His election had been opposed by some because of his close ties to the Hindu literati, his indulgence in "concubinage" during his time in India, and his irregular church attendance. In addition to holding the Boden chair, Wilson also served as librarian of East India House in London, headquarters of the East India Company. After the charges made against him at the time of the Boden appointment, he found London to be a more hospitable environment for his family than Oxford. He was director of the Royal Asiatic Society from 1837 until his death in 1860.[2]

It was as the leading scholar of Sanskrit in Britain and director of the Royal Asiatic Society that on April 8, 1854, Wilson read a long paper, "On Buddha and Buddhism," to the group. The paper begins, "Much has been written, much has been said in various places, and amongst them in this Society, about Buddha, and the religious system which bears his name, yet it may be suspected that the notions which have been entertained and propagated, in many particulars relating to both the history and the doctrines, have been adopted upon insufficient information and somewhat prematurely disseminated."[3] He then goes on to praise Burnouf, who had died two years earlier:

•

Although he has accomplished more than any other scholar, more than it would seem possible for any human ability and industry to have achieved, it is to be deeply and for ever regretted that his life was not spared to have effected all he had intended, and for which he was collecting, and had collected, many valuable and abundant materials. Still, he has left us, in his Introduction à l'Histoire de Bouddhisme [sic], and in his posthumous work Le Lotus de la Bonne Loi, an immense mass of authentic information which was not formerly in our reach, and which must contribute effectually to rationalize the speculations that may be hazarded in future on Buddha and his faith.[4]

•

Next, Wilson reviews the various references to the Buddha in classical sources before turning to "the strange theories which were gravely advanced, by men of the highest repute in Europe for erudition and sagacity, from the middle to the end of the last century, respecting the origin and character of Buddha," theories he attributes primarily to the French: "Deeply interested by the accounts which were transmitted to Europe by the missionaries of the Romish Church, who penetrated to Tibet, Japan, and China, as well as by other travelers to those countries, the members of the French Academy especially, set to work to establish coincidences the most improbable, and identified Buddha with a variety of personages, imaginary or real, with whom no possibility of congruity existed."[5] Wilson neglects to mention that twenty-five years earlier, he himself had espoused the two-Buddha theory, speculating that the first Buddha came from Scythia.[6]

Perhaps the most famous of "the missionaries of the Romish Church" to whom Wilson refers was Saint Francis Xavier, who on January 29, 1552, wrote a letter from Kochi on the southwest coast of India to his companions in Europe: "I tried to learn if these two, Ameda and Xaca, had been men dedicated to philosophy. I asked the Christians to make an accurate translation of their lives. I discovered from what was written in their books that they were not men, since it was written that they had lived for a thousand and two thousand years, and that Xaca will be born eight thousand times, and many other absurdities. They were thus not men, but pure inventions of the demons."[7]

Visiting Siam a little more than a century later, one of the most famous of the "other travelers" to whom Wilson alludes, Simon de la Loubère, envoy of Louis XIV to the court of Siam, would draw a similar conclusion about the historicity of the Buddha: "As therefore they report nothing but Fables of their *Sommona-Codom*, that they respect him not as the Author of their Laws and their Doctrine, but at most as him who has re-established them amongst Men, and that in fine they have no reasonable Memory of him, it may be doubted, in my Opinion, that there ever was such a man. He seems to have been invented to be the Idea of a Man, whom Vertue, as they apprehend it, has rendered happy, in the times of their fables, that is to say beyond what their Histories contain certain."[8]

Wilson provides the names of several eighteenth-century scholars, "no ordinary men," who had taken the missionaries' and travelers' reports and drawn outlandish conclusions about the identity of the Buddha. One of those he mentions is "Paolino"; this is the Carmelite missionary to Malabar in southern India, Paulinus a S. Bartholomaeo (1748–1806), who in 1790 published the first European grammar of Sanskrit, *Dissertatio Historico-Critica in Linguam Samscrdamicam*. Father Paulinus considered the several epithets of the Buddha contained in the *Amarakośa*, a fifth-century Sanskrit thesaurus, and concluded that the Buddha was not a man but a planet. He describes him in his 1796 *Viaggio alle Indie orientali* (*A Voyage to the East Indies*):

•

The next in order among the celestial gods is *Budha*, that is, the intelligent, the vigilant, the crafty, the acute. He is supposed to be a bosom friend of *Shiva*, and supplies the place of his private secretary. This office has been conferred on him by the Indian mythologists; because, according to their ideas, each planet is governed by a particular genius; and because *Budha* represents Mercury, which is nearest the sun. This god is said to have been the author of a great many books, and to have invented arithmetic, the art of writing, geometry, astronomy, and, in short, all those sciences which have been cultivated and improved by the industry of man. The opinion of those who consider him as having been really a writer, a king, a legislator, is ridiculous.[9]

•

Wilson continues, "The influence and example of great names pervaded the inquiry, even after access to more authentic information had been obtained."[10] However, thanks to the work of Jean-Pierre

Abel-Rémusat, Julius Klaproth, and Ernest Augustin Xavier Clerc de Landresse (in addition to Burnouf) in Paris, Alexander Csoma de Kőrös and Brian Hodgson in India, and George Turnour (along with the Wesleyan missionaries Daniel Gogerly and Robert Spence Hardy) in Sri Lanka, "We are not, therefore, in want now of genuine means of forming correct opinions of the outline of Buddhism, as to its doctrines and practices, but there are still questions of vital importance to its history for the solution of which our materials are defective."[11]

Wilson then describes determining "the antiquity and authenticity of the writings in which the Buddhists themselves record the history of their founder and the doctrines which they maintain" by examining the Buddhist scriptures available to scholars of his day, focusing especially on those in Sanskrit and Pāli. He provides a brief summary of the life of the Buddha, drawing especially from the Sanskrit *Lalitavistara* (which had been translated from Tibetan by Burnouf's student Philippe Édouard Foucaux in 1847) and from accounts of the Buddha's death provided by Csoma and Turnour. He concludes, "These accounts of Sákya's birth and proceedings, laying aside the miraculous portions, have nothing very impossible, and it does not seem improbable that an individual of a speculative turn of mind, and not a Brahman by birth, should have set up a school of his own in opposition to the Brahmanical monopoly on religious instruction, about six centuries before Christ."[12] But Wilson is troubled by the discrepancy among the Buddhist traditions regarding when the Buddha lived; in the *Calcutta Quarterly Magazine* he had previously compiled thirteen different dates, ranging from 2420 BCE to 453 BCE. For him, these "throw suspicion upon the narrative and render it very problematical whether any such person as Sákya Sinha, or Sákya Muni, or Sramana Gautama, ever actually existed. . . . It seems not impossible, after all, that Sákya Muni is an unreal being, and that all that is related of him is as much a fiction as is that of his preceding migrations, and the miracles that attended his birth, his life, and his departure."[13]

The importance of the year of the Buddha's death had been recognized by European scholars for some time; Turnour's long translation and summary of the *Great Discourse on the Final Nirvana* (*Mahāparinibbāna Sutta*)—the account of the Buddha's last days, death, and funeral—was motivated largely by his wish to determine the facts surrounding the Buddha's death, including its date, which

Turnour set in 543 BCE. Burnouf was equally convinced of the importance of the Buddha's death date for writing a history of Buddhism in India, and hence *of* India; the various councils in which the Buddhist canon had been compiled and the reign dates of great rulers such as Aśoka were calculated in years following the Buddha's passage into nirvana. Yet Burnouf also knew that the date was variously recorded in the various Buddhist traditions of Asia. Thus, at the end of the first chapter of *Introduction to the History of Indian Buddhism*, where he lays out his multivolume agenda, an agenda that he would not live to complete, he explains that the last volume will be devoted to this topic: "This will be the subject of a memorandum divided into six sections, in which I shall compare the opinions of the principal peoples of Asia on this important point of Oriental history. Taking advantage of the synchronisms that the history of Sinhalese Buddhism and some Tibetan texts of the Kah-gyur indicate, I shall use those that are already recognized by the most capable critics in order to make a choice among the diverse dates assigned to the death of the last buddha."[14]

At the end of the book (volume 1, the only volume to be published), Burnouf explains the vital importance of establishing the date of the Buddha's death:

•

We lack, in short, the fundamental point from which we must proceed to place them [the Sanskrit Buddhist texts sent by Hodgson] in the annals of India and of the world. This initial point is furnished to us by the Buddhists of the North: it is the death of Śākyamuni, the last buddha; here is the major fact that sets the foundation for the entire historical development of Buddhism, notably for this chronology of the councils of which I have spoken above; but the tradition and the texts leave us almost in ignorance on the real date of this fact, on whose positive determination depends that of all those which follow. Instead of a fixed point, the tradition gives us only a collection of dates that differ from one another by several centuries, of which none has obtained the assent of the Buddhists of all schools. It is thus necessary, before placing the series of events related to the sacred collection definitively in history, to have made a choice among the numerous dates assigned to the death of Śākya by the Buddhists of all countries. We are, we see, naturally led to the examination of this difficult question on whose solution

depends the definitive determination of the historical information assembled up to now.[15]

•

For Burnouf, determining this date was essential, not simply to
clarify the history of Buddhism but to demonstrate that India had a
history—a history that emerged from the myths of the Hindu gods in
the person, the human person, of the Buddha. He was convinced that
textual research, augmented by the archaeological discoveries being made by officers of the British East India Company, would arrive
at the correct date of the Buddha's death. Yet H. H. Wilson, a decade
later, would come to a different conclusion. The assayist, skilled in
separating pure metals from base metals, saw only dross in the Buddhist sources. He conceded that Buddhists have their own history, but
he then used that history to question the historicity of the Buddha.
According to the greatest British Sanskritist of the day, the Buddha
never existed. Wilson was not attempting to make one of those fac-
ilely profound points that the Buddha does not exist because according to Buddhism nothing exists. For Wilson, like Saint Francis Xavier
and Simon de la Loubère before him, the Buddha was pure fable, and
a pernicious one; a fable that had corrupted all of Asia. He closes his
long essay with a survey of the work of Christian missionaries in
Asia: "Various agencies are at work, both in the north and the south,
before whose salutary influence civilisation is extending; and the
ignorance and superstition which are the main props of Buddhism,
must be overturned by its advance."[16]

After all the effort to find the Buddha—to determine his name, to
determine whether he was a man or a myth, to determine when and
where he lived, to determine what he taught—Wilson sought to remove him from the throne where he had been so recently invested.

Wilson's view of the Buddha—that the Buddha did not exist, that
the Buddha was not a historical figure, that the Buddha was a myth—
a view that strikes us as eccentric today, was not merely a blind al-
ley to be entered and exited on the road to knowledge. It led from
London across the English Channel to Paris, where it was taken up
in serious ways by serious scholars. The most distinguished of these
was the great French Indologist Émile Senart (1847–1928). His knowledge of Middle Indic languages allowed him to do important work in

Indian epigraphy, most notably the edicts of Aśoka. In his *Essai sur la légende du Buddha*, first published in the *Journal Asiatique* between 1873 and 1875 (with an important revised edition in 1882), he argued that the real events of the life of the historical Buddha had not become encrusted with legends over time; rather, the mythological elements of the life of the Buddha were a coherent whole that had been fully formed in India before the Buddha's birth. In this mythological system, the Buddha was a solar deity. Light floods the entire world when he is born, like the sun at dawn; his defeat of Māra beneath the Bodhi tree is the sun god's conquest of the thunder demon; his turning of the wheel of the dharma is the sun god casting the solar orb in its course across the firmament; his passage into nirvana is the setting sun.

Unlike Wilson, Senart did not deny that there had been a historical figure called the Buddha; because there is Buddhism, there must have been a Buddha. It was not a case, however, of a kernel of truth becoming slowly encrusted by layers of myth. The historical Buddha underwent an immediate apotheosis when his followers inserted him into a preexisting mythological system. As a result, nothing in the surviving texts can be regarded as historically accurate. Therefore, the apparently less mythologized Pāli accounts should not be seen as earlier and more faithful; for Senart, the Buddha of the Pāli canon is a demythologized myth, an attempt to make the myth a man. But after the early followers of the Buddha turned him into a myth, nothing of the man can be recovered. A Buddha may have lived; the Buddha that is known to us never existed.[17] It appeared for the moment that the work of Burnouf had been undone.

At the end of the first chapter of his *Introduction*, Burnouf describes what he will do in that volume, and then describes his plans for the other volumes: "I shall make for the Pāli collection of Ceylon an examination similar to the one to which I will have subjected the Sanskrit collection of Nepal. I shall set forth what the tradition teaches us concerning the existence of this collection and notably on that of the ancient councils during which the doctrine of Śākya was fixed in a standard manner."[18] But he did not live to complete the task. It would be taken up in Germany by Hermann Oldenberg (1854-1920). The son of a Protestant clergyman, Oldenberg studied Sanskrit and Indology in Berlin, receiving his doctorate in 1875. Arguably the most influential German scholar of Buddhism of the nineteenth century, his work focused especially on the monastic code as preserved in the Pāli canon. He contributed translations of these as well as Vedic works to Max Müller's Sacred Books of the East series. Oldenberg's *Buddha, Sein Leben, seine Lehre, seine Gemeinde* (*The Buddha, His Life, His Doctrine, His Community*) was published in 1881. It begins:

•

The history of the Buddhist faith begins with a band of mendicant monks who gathered round the person of Gotama, the Buddha, in the country bordering on the Ganges, about five hundred years before the commencement of the Christian era. What bound them together and gave a stamp to their simple and earnest world of thought, was the deeply felt and clearly and sternly expressed consciousness, that all earthly existence is full of sorrow, and that the only deliverance from sorrow is renunciation of the world and eternal rest.

An itinerant teacher and his itinerant followers, not unlike those bands, who in later times bore through Galilee the tidings: "the kingdom of heaven is at hand," went through the realms of India with the burden of sorrow and death, and the announcement, "open ye your ears; the deliverance from death is found."

Vast gaps separate the historical circle, in the middle of which stands the form of the Buddha, from the world on which we are wont next to fix our thoughts, when we speak of the history of the world.[19]

•

This passage shares much with Burnouf. Like him, and unlike so many of the scholars of the day, Oldenberg expresses what appears to be a genuine sympathy for Buddhism, drawing a parallel between the disciples of the Buddha and those of Jesus. Unlike Burnouf, however, Oldenberg grew up in the church. Burnouf did not and, remarkably for a book of the period, describes the Buddha and Buddhism over the course of 647 pages without mentioning Jesus once; as we recall, he considered early Buddhism a philosophy, not a religion.

The allusion to Jesus by Oldenberg is important for another reason. In 1835, David Friedrich Strauss (1808–1874) had scandalized the world of biblical scholarship with the publication of *Das Leben Jesu, kritisch bearbeitet* (*The Life of Jesus, Critically Examined*; the English translation, by George Eliot herself, was published in 1846). By the time that Oldenberg published his life of the Buddha, Strauss's view—that mythological elements in the Gospels could be identified and eliminated to arrive at the historical Jesus—was well established. The challenge for biblical scholars was to determine a chronology of the various strata of the Gospels to find the earliest sources, those closest to the time of Jesus, even to Jesus himself, before the process of mythologizing had begun. Oldenberg faced a similar challenge with the vast and varied Buddhist canons of Asia. Which was the earliest? He answered this question to his own satisfaction, and his answer would be hugely influential, both for Buddhist scholarship and for the Buddhist world:

•

Does the law of criticism, which requires us to trace back tradition to its oldest form, before forming an opinion on it, not deserve to be as closely observed in the case of Buddhism as in that of Christianity?

The most ancient traditions of Buddhism are those preserved in Ceylon and studied by monks of that island up to the present day.

While in India itself the Buddhist texts experienced new fortunes from century to century, and while the ceremonies of the original Church were vanishing continually more and more behind the poetry and fiction of later generations, the Church of Ceylon remained true to the simple, homely, "Word of the Ancients" (Theravâda). The dialect itself in which it was recorded contributed to preserve it from corruptions, the language of the southern Indian territories, whose Churches and missions had naturally taken the largest share, if not the initiative, in the conversion of Ceylon. This language of the texts ("Pâli"), imported from the south of India, is regarded in Ceylon as sacred: and it is there supposed that Buddha himself, and all Buddhas of the preceding ages, had spoken it. Though the legends and speculations of later periods might find their way into the religious literature produced in the island and written in the popular tongue of Ceylon, the sacred Pâli texts remained unaffected by them.

It is to the Pâli traditions we must go in preference to all other sources, if we desire to know whether any information is obtainable regarding Buddha and his life.[20]

•

For Oldenberg, the majority of the texts included in the Pāli canon had been compiled prior to the Second Council, said to have taken place in the city of Vaiśālī in 380 BCE. These texts were taken to Sri Lanka about a century later, and once there, were preserved and protected from the vicissitudes that Buddhism would suffer in India, vicissitudes that included poetry and fiction. They were preserved in Pāli, which the Sinhalese regarded as a sacred language. Buddhism was not immune from legend and speculation in Sri Lanka, Oldenberg explains, but their medium would be the local vernacular, not the sacred Pāli that the Buddha himself had spoken.

Oldenberg was wrong about this. According to traditional accounts, the word of the Buddha was only preserved orally in the first centuries after his passage into nirvana. It was committed to writing not in India but in Sri Lanka around 35 BCE, when, during a time of famine, it was feared that the monks charged with the task of remembering the Buddha's word might perish. But the texts that these monks produced have not survived. The version of the Pāli canon that exists today was edited in Sri Lanka by the great master Buddhaghosa in the fifth century CE. Yet no manuscripts from that period survive either; the oldest Pāli manuscripts date from around 800 CE. The oldest Buddhist manuscripts discovered to date are not in Pāli, or Sanskrit, but the Indic language Gāndhārī, written in a script called Kharoṣṭhī. They were discovered far from Sri Lanka, in a cave in what is today Afghanistan.

But Oldenberg's view that the Pāli canon provides the most historical and least mythological source for the life and teachings of the Buddha would carry the day, promoted also by the leading Buddhist scholar of Victorian Britain, Thomas W. Rhys Davids (1843–1922), yet another former colonial officer. The son of a Welsh Congregational minister, he served as a government agent in Ceylon for a decade before being dismissed for misconduct. After his return to Britain, he founded the Pali Text Society in 1881.

The Buddha of Burnouf as extended by Oldenberg also traveled to Asia, most notably Japan. Nanjō Bunyū (1849–1927), a priest of the Jōdo Shinshū sect, and later Takakusu Junjirō (1866–1945) would travel to Oxford to study with Max Müller, the disciple of Burnouf. Through the work of these and other scholars, the view that the Pāli canon of the Theravāda tradition of Sri Lanka represents the most ancient

form of the Buddha's teachings gained currency in Mahāyāna Japan—
so much so that a number of Japanese priests, including Shaku Sōen,
the teacher of D. T. Suzuki, traveled to Sri Lanka to receive ordination there. It is noteworthy that the form of Buddhism said to best
represent the original teachings of the Buddha was that found in the
British colony of Sri Lanka. Original Buddhism was not to be found,
in the view of European scholars, in such uncolonized lands as China,
Tibet, Korea, and Japan.

In the late twentieth century, biographies of the Buddha were
still being written based on the Pāli canon, and written not only
by Theravāda monks and Sri Lankan scholars but by authors from
Mahāyāna countries such as Japan and Westerners schooled in Tibetan Buddhism.[21] The Buddha they portray is the human Buddha of
Burnouf.

Burnouf's human and humane Buddha has remained largely unchanged in the European and American imagination. He was also the
Buddha who came to be adopted by Buddhist elites—in Sri Lanka, in
Japan, in China—who were desperately seeking to demonstrate, either to Christian missionaries or to their own skeptical governments,
that Buddhism was not a superstition, that Buddhism was a science.

As we have noted, the late eighteenth and early nineteenth centuries saw significant advances in the science of philology, with the
discovery of language families and ancient connections between the
classical Indian language of Sanskrit and the classical European languages of Greek and Latin, as well as modern German, French, and
English. These were called the Indo-European or Aryan languages;
āryan is a Sanskrit term meaning "noble" or "superior." Through a
complicated process over the course of the nineteenth century, theories of language groups gave rise to theories of racial groups, and the
kinship between the people of ancient India and the people of ancient
Greece and modern Europe became a matter not simply of verb roots
but of bloodlines.

And suddenly, the Buddha was not so foreign. No longer an Ethiopian or a Moor from Memphis, he was, racially, an Aryan. But the
nobility of the prince who had renounced his throne was not merely
hereditary. In his teachings, the Buddha had rejected the idea of the
inherited nobility of the brahman caste, declaring that true nobility
derived instead from wisdom. He thus called his first teaching the

four truths for the noble (not "the four noble truths," as the phrase has so often been mistranslated). The Buddha became doubly noble (*āryan*). He was noble by birth, blood, and language, yet he was also noble because he had renounced his royal birth to achieve a spiritual nobility. In a Europe obsessed with questions of race and questions of humanity, the Buddha was both racially superior and a savior for all humanity, an ancient kinsman, a modern hero. This was a Buddha who would become a magnet for all manner of associations over the course of more than a century and to the present day; a Buddha to whom a strange range of scientific insights would be ascribed, from the mechanisms of the cosmos to the structure of the atom, from a natural law of morality to the deepest workings of the mind. Burnouf's Buddha would be remythologized in the West—shorn of his magical powers, but endowed with a supernatural knowledge, able to anticipate scientific discoveries by two thousand years.[22]

In a sense, the Buddha that we know today is the result of a series of historical accidents. What if the Peace of Amiens had not been broken and "Sanscrit" Hamilton had returned from Paris to Scotland without meeting the Count de Volney? What if Hodgson had had a healthy liver and thus had stayed in Calcutta rather than been posted to the hills of Nepal? What if in signing a treaty with the British, the Gurkhas had not permitted a British delegation to reside in Kathmandu? French savants would have eventually mastered Sanskrit, and the Sanskrit sutras preserved by the Newars of the Kathmandu valley would have eventually come under the European gaze. But without Hodgson in Nepal to learn about the Sanskrit texts and Burnouf in Paris to read them, our picture of the Buddha might have been painted with a different palette.

But Burnouf painted his portrait (with details provided by Oldenberg). It is difficult to identify all the factors that made this portrait possible, beyond these historical accidents. Both Burnouf and Oldenberg had access to Buddhist texts, texts that they were able to read and read accurately. Each, perhaps for different reasons, felt a certain sympathy for the Buddha and his teachings, whatever they might have thought of the Buddhism and Buddhists of their own day—Burnouf never met a Buddhist; Oldenberg visited India once late in his life, in

1912. In addition, Burnouf was French and Oldenberg was German. Neither was British, and thus neither was tied to colonial policy, at least in a direct way (France did not gain its territories in Indochina until after Burnouf's death). This may be one reason they lacked the antipathy to Buddhism that we find in such figures as George Turnour, and later Daniel Gogerly and Robert Spence Hardy, in Sri Lanka.[23] At the same time, each profited directly from the British presence in South Asia. We need only remember Hodgson's gift.

Upon closer inspection, the figures that surround the empty throne are not humans but demons. The carving in the Musée Guimet depicts Māra's attack on the Buddha, when the deity of desire and death unleashed his armies against the bodhisattva just before he would achieve buddhahood. The question that we must ask is whether the European creation of the Buddha was in its own way also an attack on the Buddha. For Wilson, the fact that the Chinese and Tibetans and Sri Lankans had different dates for the death of their Buddha meant that the Buddha did not exist: "Sákya Muni is an unreal being." Perhaps the demons attack a vacant space because the idol has been driven from his throne.

And yet we have our Buddha, today regarded as the founder of a global humanist religion of science. This is the Buddha created by Burnouf. His massive tome is largely forgotten, or at least unread, today. Yet its oblivion derives not so much from its obsolescence as from its influence. The idols we have encountered in these pages have suffered their own oblivion. But they are different forms of forgetting. Burnouf has been forgotten because we tend to feel that he was right. The idols have been forgotten because we tend to feel that what Europeans said about the Buddha—from his name, to his life, to the very fact that he was an idol—was wrong. If there is a structure of scientific revolutions, and if philology is a science, then a shift took place in the wake of Burnouf and his contemporaries, a shift so profound that the previous discourse about the Buddha could be displaced, discarded, and forgotten because it was simply wrong.

But what became of Xaca and Sommona-Codom, of Buddu and Fôe? They are forgotten, recalled only as so many mistakes of a bygone age. We know better now. Unlike the intrepid travelers and missionaries to foreign climes, when we walk through the museum of a European capital and see the works of art on display—a wooden Japanese statue from the Muromachi period, a Tibetan thangka from the time of the Seventh Dalai Lama, a bronze image from the reign of King Rama IV of Thailand, a stone carving from Gandhara—we know that they all represent the same person.

We recall that Ippolito Desideri, the Jesuit missionary to Tibet, wrote that the idols worshipped there were endowed with "bright colors and varnishes of fantastic invention . . . capable of captivating and astonishing, if not the healthiest and clearest eyes, at least weakened eyes that see things indistinctly." Unlike intrepid travelers of the past, our eyes are healthy and clear. They have been properly trained to see through the bright colors and varnishes of fantastic invention, to see through the most striking differences—in form, in color, in style, in accoutrements—to see a single figure, just as our minds have been trained to translate Hotoke and Sangs rgyas and Fo and Pul into a single word: *Buddha*.

But are they the same? Was something lost in the march of scholarly progress, did something disappear when weathered stone turned to smooth flesh, when the idol turned into an "image"? Perhaps the collapse of many gods into a single human Buddha effaced a level of detail, of specificity, of locality that can no longer be discerned, yet was glimpsed long ago by the eyes that could still be captivated and astonished, eyes that could not read, eyes that could only see.

Forgetting and remembering hold great power in Buddhism. A new buddha does not appear in the world until the teachings of the previous buddha have been completely forgotten. We have no memory of the Buddha Kāśyapa, because he had to be forgotten before the next buddha, our buddha, the Buddha Śākyamuni, could appear in the world. From one perspective, it matters little that we have forgotten Kāśyapa, because all buddhas teach the same path to enlightenment. Still, Śākyamuni, who remembered everything, reminded the world of Kāśyapa and the other buddhas of the past. Yet as he remembered the past, he also prophesied the future, predicting his own oblivion. It is only when Śākyamuni and his teachings have been forgotten that the future buddha, Maitreya, will appear.

Forgetting and remembering are also at play in this tale of the European encounter with the Buddha. We seek to remember which European was the first to discern that the various idols known by various names was a single historical figure. Does the credit go to the Portuguese Jesuit Queyroz or to the Westphalian physician Kaempfer at the end of the seventeenth century? We forget that four centuries before, Marco Polo had reported that the idolaters spoke of the sepulcher on the peak of that mountain in Ceylon as belonging to Sagamoni Borcan. He understood, it seems, that the idol worshipped in China was the same as the idol worshipped in Ceylon, and that that idol had been a man, indeed, "the first in whose name idols were made." In the nineteenth century, scholars in France and Germany discovered that *Barlaam and Josaphat* was based on the life of the Buddha. We forget that four centuries earlier, a commentator on Marco Polo's text had noted that the life of Sagamoni Borcan resembled the life of Saint Josaphat.

And so we have forgotten Foë. Yet Foë and Xaca and Sommona-Codom and Buddu should be remembered. They should be remembered in order to recall the learned labors of the remarkable figures described in these pages, who doggedly sought knowledge about them under conditions that are difficult for us to imagine, much less endure. They should be remembered in order to recall that that knowledge about them, so doggedly pursued, contained much that was right amid many things that were wrong. They should be remembered because the stories told about these idols, in retrospect, reveal so clearly the predilections and prejudices of those who recounted them; predilections and prejudices also dwell, perhaps less visibly, in the tales we tell of our Buddha. Foë and Xaca and Sommona-Codom and Buddu should be remembered for what they teach us. In this case, the buddhas of the past should not be forgotten. Contrary to what our buddha, Śākyamuni, taught, it is not true that all buddhas teach the same thing. What Foë and Xaca and Sommona-Codom and Buddu have to teach is perhaps a more modest remembering, yet it should be remembered.

And we might remember them for another reason. The Buddha of Burnouf, though alive in our imagination, is long dead, his image a mere aide-mémoire, a material remembrance for the latest form of self-help. He is not worshipped; he is remembered. Still, we make vain attempts to bring him back to life by imagining that he understood quantum mechanics, imagining that he taught mindfulness of the breath in order to reduce our blood pressure. But the idols called Xaca and Fo and Sommona-Codom remain alive, animated by the rituals of the faithful, granting our wishes, speaking to us in our dreams, inspiring our aspirations. It was not a case of mistaken identity. We should restore the idols to their empty thrones.

Coda

Just as we began with Marco Polo, so let us end with him. In describing a mountain in Sri Lanka, Polo explained that the sepulcher of Sagamoni Borcan was at its summit. This was what the idolaters said. But it seems that Marco Polo never climbed to the top of the peak with the aid of those "great and massive iron chains." For there is no tomb on the mountaintop, only footprints.[1] Or perhaps he did make the climb, but mistook the slab with the footprints as a tombstone in yet another case of mistaken identity.[2]

The story of the sepulcher is a story that Marco Polo told upon his return to Venice, recounted, as the account goes, to his cellmate, Rustichello da Pisa, a writer of romances. This was the story that the historical Marco Polo told, a story filled with fable. But the fabulous Marco Polo told his stories not in a prison cell but in the pleasure dome of Xanadu; not to a fellow inmate, but to the Great Khan himself. Just as we began with his tale of a sepulcher he never saw, so let us close our own tale of desire and memory with his description of an invisible city:

•

When a man rides a long time through wild regions he feels the desire for a city. Finally he comes to Isidora, a city where the buildings have spiral staircases encrusted with spiral seashells, where perfect telescopes and violins are made, where the foreigner hesitating between two women always encounters a third, where cockfights degenerate into bloody brawls among the bettors. He was thinking of all those things when he desired a city. Isidora, therefore, is the city of his dreams: with one difference. The dreamed-of city contained him as a young man; he arrives at Isidora in his old age. In the square there is a wall where the old men sit and watch the young go by; he is seated in a row with them. Desires are already memories.[3]

ACKNOWLEDGMENTS

This book was written with the generous support of a fellowship from the John Simon Guggenheim Memorial Foundation, augmented by funding from the College of Literature, Science, and the Arts at the University of Michigan. Initial research on the project was conducted while I was a scholar-in-residence at the Getty Research Institute in Los Angeles. Among the excellent staff at this distinguished institute, I would like especially to thank Sabine Schlosser, Jasmine Lin, and George Weinberg. My research assistant at the Getty, Candace Weddle, provided invaluable and uncomplaining support in accurately transcribing long passages from arcane texts.

In chapter 4, I have drawn some passages and examples from my book *Buddhism and Science: A Guide for the Perplexed* (2008) and from my introduction to Eugène Burnouf's *Introduction to the History of Indian Buddhism* (2010).

APPENDIX ONE: NAMES FOR THE BUDDHA OCCURRING IN EUROPEAN SOURCES BEFORE 1800

Bad
Baoda
Baouda
Baout
Baouth
Bauté
Bedda
Bedde
Beddhou
Beddou
Bedou
Bhooddha
Bod
Bodda
Boddh
Boodh
Booddhŭ
Boodhoo
Bot
Bota
Bouda dina
Boudan
Boudasf
Boudasp
Boudd
Boudda
Bouddha
Bouddha-Mouni
Bouddou

Bouden-Kirúmei
Boudh
Boudha
Boudhan
Boudhé
Boudhou
Boudsdo
Boudso
Bout
Boutta
Boutta-varam
Bubdam
Buda
Budam
Budas
Budd
Budda
Buddam
Buddh
Budd'ha
Buddho
Buddhoo
Buddhu
Buddhum
Buddo
Buddou
Buddu
Buddûm
Budha

Budha'
Budhu
Budhum
Buds
Budsa
Budsd
Budsde
Budsdo
Budso
Budu
Budz
But
Butta
Buttà
Cadam
Cakya
Çakya
Çakya-Mouni
Cardam
Cardama
Cechian
Chaca
Chacabout
Chaca-bout
Chaka-Chimouna
Chaka-Mouni
Chakémonia
Chakia-mouni
Chechian

Che-Kia

Chekia

Chékia

Chekia-meouni

Che-kia-méou-ni

Chescamoni

Chiaga

Chigemouni-Bourkhan

Codam

Daybot

d'Herna-Raja

Dibote

Dschakdschimmuni

Dschakdshimmuni

Dschakshimuni

Fae

Fe

Fo

Fò

Fô

Foë

Foe

Foé

Fohi

Fot

Fôt

Fotéo

Fotéou

Fotique

Foto

Fotoge

Fotoke

Fotoque

Gauda

Gaudama

Gaudma

Gauteme Boudhou

Gautemeh Bhooddha

Gautemen

Gautimo

Gautuma

Godam

Godama

Godeman

Godoma

Godomem

Godomen

Goodam

Gooutama Boudhou

Gotamas

Gotma

Goutama

Gouton

Goutum

Goutŭmŭ

Gowtama

Guadama

Guadma

Guntuma Buddhoo

Jaca

Kodama

Kotamo

Mahamony

Mahamoonie

Mahamounie

Nacodon

Paouta

Phât

Phoe

Phoë

Photo

Phta

Phutha'

Phutta

Poden

Pood

Pooden

Pooth

Pot

Pota

Poti

Pott

Pout

Pouta

Pouti

Pouti Sat

Prah

Prah-poudi-tchaou

Prah Pudi Dsai

Prahpuditsau

Putha

Putti

Putza

Saca

Saca-Menu

Sacka

Sackia Tubà

Sácya

Sagamoni Borcan

Sa-Kia

Sakiamouni

Sakji-Mouni

Šakmonia

Sakya

Sakya-Mouni

Saman

Samana

Samana-Codom

Samana-Gautama

Sammana-Coudom

Sammana-Kantama

Sammana Khodum

Sammana Khutama

Sammano Codom

Samonocodum	Shākamūnī	Somono
Sang-gyé	Shakiamuny	Sotoqui
Sang-khje	Shakmun	Sougot
Sangol-Muni	Shakmuny	Suman-Nath
Scaka	Shaks	Taut
Schaka	Shakya	Tcháou cà
Schakscha-Tuba	Sharmana Cardama	Tche-kia
Scheke-mouni	Si Tsun	Thicca
Schekia	Siaca	Thích Ca
Schekmouni	Siaka	Van Pout
Schekmouniberkan	Sichia	Xaca
Schiaca	Sidditure Coemarea	Xacabout
Schigemuni	Siga-Mouni	Xaca-Muni
Schigemunich	Sijamony	Xacca
Sciacca	Siquag	Xaka
Sciacchiá Thubbà	Sjaka	Xaqua
Sciachia Muni	Somma Cuddom	Xaque
Sciachiamuny	Sommocodom	Xasa
Sciachia Thupbà	Sommona-Codom	Xechia
Sciachiathupba	Sommonacodon	Xekia
Sciakka	Sommonacodum	Xékia
Sciequia	Sommona Kodom	Xe-Kia
Schji-Mouni	Sommonocodam	Xe Kian
Seaka	Sommonocodom	Xe-quia
Sejatoba	Sommono Gautemeh	Xequia
Sekia	Sommonokhodom	Xequiam
Shaca	Sommonokodom	Xokia
Shaka	Somon	Zeuximgim
Shakamuna	Somona Codom	Ziddatare Cumanca

APPENDIX TWO: THE BUDDHA IN DIDEROT AND D'ALEMBERT'S *ENCYCLOPÉDIE*

In the fifteenth volume of Denis Diderot and Jean le Rond d'Alembert's *Encyclopédie, ou dictionnaire raisonné des sciences, des arts et des métiers* (*Encyclopedia, or Systematic Dictionary of the Sciences, Arts, and Trades*), we find an entry on *Siaka* (that is, Śākya). It was probably written by Diderot's friend and patron, Baron d'Holbach (1723-1789). Much of it is drawn from the tenth volume of the Abbé Prévost's *Histoire générale des voyages*.[1] However, Prévost, and many others of the day, drew in turn from the account of Japan by Engelbert Kaempfer (1651-1716), the remarkable Westphalian physician and employee of the Dutch East India Company discussed in chapter 3. Here is the full entry on the Buddha from Diderot and d'Alembert's *Encyclopédie*. The Buddha (represented by various names) and Buddhism also figure prominently in other entries in the *Encyclopédie*, written by Diderot himself, where a somewhat different view is presented.[2]

•

SIAKA, religion of, (Hist. mod. Superstition) this religion, which is established in Japan, has as its founder *Siaka* or *Xaca*, who is also called *Budsdo* ["Buddha" in Japanese is *Butsu*] & his religion *Budsdoism* ["Buddhism" in Japanese is *Butsudo*]. It is believed that the *buds* or the *siaka* of the Japanese is the same as the *foë* of the Chinese, & the *visnou* [Viṣṇu] the *buda* or *putza* [bodhisattva in Chinese is *pusa*] of the Indians, the *sommonacodum* of the Siamese; for it seems certain that this religion came originally from the Indies to Japan, where previously only the religion of the *sintos* [Shinto] was professed. The Budsdoists say that *Siaka* was born around twelve hundred years before the Christian era; that his father was a king; that his son left his father's palace, abandoned his wife and son, in order to embrace a penitent and solitary life, and in order to devote himself to the contemplation of celestial things. The fruit of these meditations was to penetrate the depths of the most sublime mysteries, those of the nature of heaven and hell; the state of souls after death; their transmigration; the path to eternal felicity, and many other things well beyond ordinary men. *Siaka* had a great number of disciples; feeling that he was near the end, he declared to them that throughout his life, he had wrapped the truth in a veil of metaphors and that it was finally time to reveal an important mystery to them. *There is*, he said, *nothing real in the world, but nothingness and the void: this is the first principle of all things; do not seek anything beyond, and do not place your confidence in anything else.* After this impious plea, Siaka died at the age of seventy-nine years; his disciples accordingly divided his law into two parts; one exterior, which is taught to the people; the other interior, which is only communicated to a small number of proselytes. This latter consisted in establishing the void and nothingness, as the principle and end of all things. They claim that the elements, men, and generally all creatures are formed of this void, and reenter it after a certain time through a dissolution of parts; such that there is only a single substance in the universe, which diversifies itself into particular beings, and for a time receives different modifications, although at bottom it is always the same: almost like water is always essentially water, though it takes the form of snow, rain, hail, or ice.

As for the exterior religion of *budsdoism*, the principal points of its doctrine are, (1) that the souls of men and of animals are immortal; that they are originally of the same substance, and that they differ only according to the different bodies they animate. (2) That the souls of men that have separated from the body are rewarded or punished in another life. (3) That the abode of the blessed is called *gokurakf* [*gokuraku*, the Japanese name for Sukhāvatī, the pure land of Amitābha and more generally a term for "heaven"]; men enjoy a happiness there proportionate to their merit. Amida [Amitābha] is the chief of the celestial domains; it is only through his mediation that one can obtain remission of one's sins, and a place in heaven, this is what makes Amida the object of worship by the followers of *Siaka*. (4) This religion accepts that there is a place called *dsigokf* [*jigoku*, or hell]; where the wicked are tormented according to the number and quality of their crimes. Jemma [Yama] is the sovereign judge of these places; he has a great mirror before him, in which he sees all the crimes of the damned. Their torments only last a certain time, at the end of which the unfortunate souls are returned to the world to animate the bodies of impure animals, whose vices accord with that which soils their souls; from these bodies, they pass successively into those of more noble animals, until they are able to reenter a human body, where they can gain or lose anew. (5) The law of *Siaka* forbids killing any living creature, stealing, committing adultery, lying, and using strong drink. This law prescribes, in addition to that, very bothersome duties, and the continual mortification of the body and spirit. The bonzes or monks of this religion punish the least faults of those under their direction with the utmost severity and in the cruelest manner; these monks are of two kinds, ones called *genguis* and others called *goguis*. They lead an extraordinarily penitent life, and their countenance is something hideous. The people believe them to be saints, and dare not resist their orders, however barbarous they might be, even though their performance must lead to death. These monks make the pilgrims who visit the temple of *Siaka* pass through the cruelest trials, in order to force them to confess their crimes before allowing them to pay homage to this god.

This religion has its martyrs, who give their lives voluntarily in the hope of rendering themselves pleasing to their gods. One sees, along the coasts of the sea, boats filled with fanatics, who after attaching a stone around their neck, throw themselves into the depths of the sea.[3] Others enclose themselves in caves that are walled up, and remain there to die of hunger. Others jump into the abyss of volcanoes. Some crush themselves under the wheels of chariots on which Amida and other gods of their religion are carried in procession;[4] these scenes recur every day, and the so-called martyrs themselves become objects of veneration and worship by the people.

There are several solemn festivals that the followers of the religion of *Siaka* celebrate. The main one is that which is called the *festival of the man*. The statue of the god *Siaka* is carried in procession on a litter. That of his mistress then appears. This latter meets as if by chance the statue of his legitimate wife: then those who carry it begin to run to one side and other, and seek to express by their actions the chagrin that the encounter with a preferred rival caused this unfortunate spouse; this chagrin is communicated to the people, who usually begin to burst into tears. The litters are approached confusedly as if to take sides with the god, his wife, and his mistress, and after some time, each retires peaceably to his own home, after having taken the deities to their temples. These idolaters have another singular festival, which seems made to decide, arms in hand, the precedence that the deities deserve. Horsemen armed from head to foot, inflamed by drunkenness, carry on their back the gods of whom they are the champion; they engage in combat that is nothing less than a game, and the field of battle ends in being covered with the dead; this festival serves as a pretext for those who have personal injuries to avenge, and often the cause of the gods provides the place for the animosity of men.

The religion of *Siaka* has a sovereign pontiff, called *siako*, bishops who are called *tundes* and monks or bonzes called *xenxus* [*zenshu*, or "Zen sect"] and *xodoxins* [*jōdoshin*, or "True Pure Land" sect]. See *these different articles*.

APPENDIX THREE: TABLE OF CONTENTS OF *TRANSACTIONS OF THE LITERARY SOCIETY OF BOMBAY*, 1819

Transactions of the Literary Society of Bombay
Volume 1
1819

Discourse at the Opening of the Society. By Sir James Mackintosh, President

I.   An Account of the Festival of Mamangom, as celebrated on the Coast of Malabar. By Francis Wrede, Esq. (afterwards Baron Wrede.) Communicated by the Honourable Jonathan Duncan

II.   Remarks upon the Temperature of the Island of Bombay during the Years 1803 and 1804. By Major (now Lieutenant Colonel) Jasper Nicholls

III.   Translations from the Chinese of two Edicts: the one relating to the Condemnation of certain Persons convicted of Christianity; and the other concerning the Condemnation of certain Magistrates in the Province of Canton. By Sir George Staunton. With introductory Remarks by the President Sir James Mackintosh

IV.   Account of the Akhlauk-e-Nasiree, or Morals of Nasir, a celebrated Persian System of Ethics. By Lieutenant Edward Frissell of the Bombay Establishment

V.   Account of the Caves in Salsette, illustrated with Drawings of the principal Figures and Caves. By Henry Salt, Esq. (now Consul General in Egypt.)

VI.   On the Similitude between the Gipsy and Hindostanee Languages. By Lieutenant Francis Irvine, of the Bengal Native Infantry

VII.   Translations from the Persian, illustrative of the Opinions of the Sunni and Shia Sects of Mahomedans. By Brigadier General Sir John Malcolm, K.C.B.

VIII.   A Treatise on Sufiism, or Mahomedan Mysticism. By Lieutenant James William Graham, Linguist to the 1st Battalion of the 6th Regiment of Bombay Native Infantry

IX.   Account of the present compared with the ancient State of Babylon. By Captain Edward Frederick of the Bombay Establishment

X.   Account of the Hill-Fort of Chapaneer in Guzerat. By Captain William Miles, of the Bombay Establishment

XI.   The fifth Sermon of Sadi, translated from the Persian. By James Ross, Esq. of the Bengal Medical Establishment

XII.   Account of the Origin, History, and Manners of the Race of Men called Bunjaras. By Captain John Briggs, Persian Interpreter to the Hyderabad Subsidiary Force.

XIII.   An Account of the Parsinath-Gowricha worshipped in the Desert of Parkur; to which are added, a few Remarks upon the present Mode of Worship of that Idol. By Lieutenant James Mackmurdo

XIV.   Observations on two sepulchral Urns found at Bushire in Persia. By William Erskine, Esq.

XV.   Account of the Cave-Temple of Elephanta, with a Plan and Drawings of the principal Figures. By William Erskine, Esq.

XVI.   Remarks on the Substance called Gez, or Manna, found in Persia and Armenia. By Captain Edward Frederick, of the Bombay Establishment

XVII.   Remarks on the Province of Kattiwar; its Inhabitants, their Manners and Customs. By Lieutenant James Mackmurdo of the Bombay Establishment

XVIII.   Account of the Cornelian Mines in the Neighbourhood of Baroach, in a Letter to the Secretary from John Copland, Esq. of the Bombay Medical Establishment

XIX.   Some Account of the Famine in Guzerat in the Years 1812 and 1813, in a Letter to William Erskine, Esq. By Captain James Rivett Carnac, Political Resident at the Court of the Guicawar

XX.   Plan of a Comparative Vocabulary of Indian Languages. By Sir James Mackintosh, President of the Society

NOTES

INTRODUCTION

1. From Henry Clarke Warren, *Buddhism in Translations* (Cambridge, MA: Harvard University Press, 1896), p. 14.

2. Peter Simon Pallas, quoted in John Trusler, *The Habitable World Described* (London: Literary Press, 1788), 2:247. The conjecture that images of the Buddha represented females persisted into the nineteenth century. In a paper read to the Royal Asiatic Society on February 20, 1830, Samuel Davis observed:

Many principles and forms of the religion of the Lamas are evidently borrowed from that of the Hindoos. They have similar ceremonies performed on the banks of rivers, and the Ganges is held in equal veneration. . . . Their supreme deity, called indiscriminately by the name Sijamony, Mahamony, and Sejatoba, is said to have been brought many ages ago by one of the superior Lamas from Benares, and others of them must have been of foreign extraction; for although plainly drawn and carved as females, the priests would not allow them of that sex; and often, as they think, decide the distinction with a pair of whiskers, when the turn of the features and swell of bosom shew whiskers to be misapplied.

See Samuel Davis, "Remarks on the Religious and Social Institutions of the Bouteas, or Inhabitants of Boutan, from the unpublished Journal of the late Samuel Davis, Esq. F.R.S. &c. Communicated by J.F. Davis, Esq. F.R.S. M.R.A.S.," in *Transactions of the Royal Asiatic Society of Great Britain* (1830), 2:491.

3. J. W. de Jong, *A Brief History of Buddhist Studies in Europe and America (Part 1)*, *Eastern Buddhist*, n.s., 7, no. 1 (May 1974): 64.

4. On the later period, see, in addition to the work of de Jong cited above, such works as Philip C. Almond, *The British Discovery of Buddhism* (Cambridge: Cambridge University Press, 1988); Roger-Pol Droit, *The Cult of Nothingness: The Philosophers and the Buddha* (Chapel Hill: University of North Carolina Press, 2003); Elizabeth J. Harris, *Theravāda Buddhism and the British Encounter* (London: Routledge, 2006); Charles Allen, *The Search for the Buddha: The Men Who Discovered India's Lost Religion* (New York: Carroll and Graf, 2003); Thomas A. Tweed, *The American Encounter with Buddhism: 1844–1912* (Bloomington: Indiana University Press, 1992); Eric Reinders, *Borrowed Gods and Foreign Bodies: Christian Missionaries Imagine Chinese Religion* (Berkeley: University of California Press, 2004); and

Judith Snodgrass, *Presenting Japanese Buddhism to the West: Orientalism, Occidentalism, and the Columbian Exposition* (Chapel Hill: University of North Carolina Press, 2003). Among bibliographies, of historical interest is Otto Kistner, ed., *Buddha and His Doctrines: A Bibliographical Essay* (London: Trübner, 1869). The most extensive published bibliography on Buddhism in English is Shinsho Hanayama, *Bibliography on Buddhism* (Tokyo: Hukuseido Press, 1961).

CHAPTER 1

1. John Ferguson, trans., *Clement of Alexandria: Stromateis Books 1–3*, The Fathers of the Church (Washington, DC: Catholic University of America Press, 1992), pp. 76 and 293. It is important to note that Clement describes these holy men as naked, suggesting that he is referring to Jains rather than Buddhists. However, the "pyramids" to which he refers are likely Buddhist stupas.

2. Jerome, *Adversus Jovinianum* 1.42.

3. Philip Schaff and Henry Wace, eds., *A Select Library of Nicene and Post-Nicene Fathers of the Christian Church*, 2nd ser., vol. 2, *Socrates, Sozomenus: Church Histories* (New York: Christian Literature Company, 1890), p. 25. For a study of references to the Buddha in the early church, especially in connection with Manichaeism, see Timothy Pettipiece, "The Buddha in Early Christian Literature," *Millennium: Jahrbuch zu Kultur und Geschichte des ersten Jahrtausends n. Chr., Yearbook on the Culture and History of the First Millennium C. E.* 6 (Berlin: Walter de Gruyter, 2009), pp. 133–43.

4. Bhikkhu Ñāṇamoli, trans., *The Middle Length Discourses of the Buddha* (Boston: Wisdom Publications, 1995), p. 256.

5. J. J. Jones, trans., *Mahāvastu* (London: Luzac and Company, 1952), 2:113.

6. Ibid., p. 114.

7. From *The Travels of Marco Polo: The Complete Yule-Cordier Edition*, trans. and ed. Sir Henry Yule, 3rd ed., revised by Henri Cordier, (New York: Dover, 1993), 2:316–18. See also the extensive notes of Yule and Cordier, pp. 320–30.

8. Alī al-Rūmī, quoted in Carl Ernst, "India as a Sacred Islamic Land," in *Religions of India in Practice*, ed. Donald S. Lopez Jr. (Princeton, NJ: Princeton University Press, 1995), pp. 559–60.

9. Robert Knox, *An Historical Relation of the Island Ceylon in the East-Indies; Together, With an Account of the Detaining in Captivity the Author and divers other Englishmen now Living there, and of the Author's Miraculous Escape* (London, 1681), p. 72.

The footprint remained an object of interest, and some frustration, for the British. In an 1801 essay, "On the Religion and Manners of the People of Ceylon," Joseph Endelin de Joinville, surveyor general for the British Governor General of Ceylon, wrote:

BOUDHOU, in one of his three voyages to *Lankadwipe*, the island of *Ceylon*, left on the top of *Jaman alé Sripade*, Adam's peak, the print of one of his feet; but though

I have been at great pains to find it out, I have not as yet been able to ascertain whether it was his right or his left foot: and I am convinced that it must be, universally, a matter of doubt, for all the feet of BOUDHOU that I have seen in the temples are so awkwardly made, that there is no distinguishing the little toe from the great one.

Mr. [Joseph Endelin de] Joinville, "On the Religion and Manners of the People of Ceylon," *Asiatic Researches* 7 (1801): 416.

10. *The Travels of Marco Polo*, 2:316–17.

11. See Urs App, *The Birth of Orientalism* (Philadelphia: University of Pennsylvania Press, 2010), pp. 223–35. Two years earlier, de Guignes had provided his own description of the life of the Buddha. See his *Histoire générale des Huns, des Turcs, des Mogols, et des autres Tartares occidentaux, &c. avant et depuis Jésus-Christ jusqu'à présent* (Paris: Desaint & Saillant, 1757), 1:223–35.

12. See Robert H. Sharf, "The Scripture on the Production of Buddha Images," in *Religions of China in Practice*, ed. Donald S. Lopez Jr. (Princeton, NJ: Princeton University Press, 1996), pp. 262–63.

13. Louis le Comte, *Memoirs and Observations Topographical, Physical, Mathematical, Mechanical, Natural, Civil, and Ecclesiastical Made in a Late Journey through the Empire of China, and Published in Several Letters. Particularly upon the Chinese Pottery and Varnishing; the Silk and Other Manufactures. Description of Their Cities and Publick Works; Number of People, Their Language, Manners and Commerce; Their Oeconomy, and Government. The Philosophy of Confucius. The State of Christianity, with Many Other Curious and Useful Remarks*, translated from the Paris edition (London, 1697), pp. 323, 325.

14. Quoted in John Andrew Boyle, "The Journey of Het'um I, King of Little Armenia to the Great Khan Möngke," *Central Asiatic Journal* 9 (1964): 188–89.

15. Describing the inhabitants of Thailand ("Siammers"), a Dutch work from the late seventeenth century reports:

The *Siammers*, as also the Neighbouring Nations, are all Idolaters and Heathens, so that they have everywhere great and little Temples and Cloysters for the service of their Gods; and the dwellings of their Priests. These Edifices are builded of Wood and Stone very Artificial and sumptuous, with gilded Towers and Pyramids; each of the Temples and Cloysters being filled with an incredible number of Idols, of divers materials and greatness, gilded adorned and beautified very rich and admirable; some of the Idols are four, six, eight, and ten fathoms long; amongst the rest there is one of an unimaginable greatness, being one hundred and twenty foot high.

In Francois Caron and Joost Schorten, *A True Description of the Mighty Kingdoms of Japan and Siam*, translated from the Dutch by Capt. Robert Manley (London, 1663), p. 140.

16. *The Travels of Marco Polo*, 2:318–19.

For another Italian visitor to Asia several centuries later, the Buddha not only became an idol, but his body became the source of a great many other idols. Adriano di St. Thecla (1667-1765), a missionary to Vietnam from the Discalced (or Barefoot) Augustinian Order, explains:

They add the following: mainly that thirty-six Heavens were made of his head, that his tongue is a column of Heaven made of gold and gems, that his two arms and his two feet are four kings of Heaven, that twenty ribs from both of his sides were turned into twenty idols, and the rest of the bones [were turned] into three hundred sixty idols, two knees [were turned] into eighty-four thousand idols, five internal parts of the body [were turned] into five idols, and in addition major viscera were turned into large rivers, minor [viscera were turned] into small streams; they even worship and have as idols his father, mother, grandfather, and grandmother of the same Thích Ca.

See Father Adriano di St. Thecla, *Opusculum de Sectis apud Sinenses et Tunkinenses: A Small Treatise on the Sects among the Chinese and Tonkinese*, translated and annotated by Olga Dror (Ithaca, NY: Cornell Southeast Asia Program, 2002), p. 202.

17. A. C. Moule and Paul Pelliot, eds. and trans., *The Description of the World*, vol. 1 (London: George Routledge & Sons, 1938), p. 410. The passage occurs in the 1446 Venice edition of *The Book of Ser Marco Polo the Venetian concerning the Kingdoms and Marvels of the East*.

18. Some Europeans believed that the footprints on Adam's Peak were those of Josaphat. For example, the Portuguese author Manuel de Faria e Sousa (or Manoel Faria y Souza) (1590-1649) writes:

25. In the Country of *Dinavaca* which is the Center of this Island rises that vast high Mountain called *Pico de Adam*, because some believed our first Father lived there, and that the print of a foot still seen upon a stone on the top of it, is his; the Natives call it *Amala Saripadi*, that is the Mountain of the footstep. Some Springs running down it, at the bottom form a Rivulet, where Pilgrims wash, and believe it purifies them. The stone on the top is like a Tombstone, the print of the foot seems not artificial, but as if it had been made in the same nature as when one treads in Clay, which makes it be looked upon as miraculous.

26. The Pilgrims of all sorts who come from as far as *Persia* and *China*, being washed, go up to the top, near which hangs a bell which they strike and take the sounding of it as a sign of their being purified, as if any bell being struck, would not sound. The opinion of the Natives is, that *Drama Raja* Son of an ancient King of that Island, doing Pennance in that Mountain with many Disciples, when he was about to depart at their instance, left that print there as a Memorial; therefore they respect it as a relict of a Saint, and generally call him *Budam*, that is *Wiseman*.

27. Some believe this Saint was *Iosaphat*, but it is more likely it was St. *Thomas*, who has left many Memorials in the East, and in the West, in *Brasil* and in *Paraguay*.

Manuel de Faria e Sousa (or Manoel Faria y Souza), *The Portugues Asia; or, The History of the Discovery and Conquest of India by the Portugues Containing All Their Discoveries from the Coast of Africk, to the Farthest Parts of China and Japan, All Their Battels by Sea and Land, Sieges and Other Memorable Actions, A Description of Those Countries, and Many Particulars of the Religion, Government and Customs of the Natives*, trans. Captain John Stevens, vol. 2 (London, 1695), pp. 509–10.

19. Saint John Damascene, *Barlaam and Ioasaph*, trans. G. R. Woodward and H. Mattingly (New York: Macmillan, 1914), p. 31.

20. Ibid., pp. 59–61.

21. See Yule, *The Travels of Marco Polo*, p. 325.

22. For a full-length study and translation, see Daniel Gimaret, *Le livre de Bilawhar et Būdāsf* (Geneva: Librairie Droz, 1971).

23. Saint John Damascene, *Barlaam and Ioasaph*, p. 139. Here is the corresponding passage from the earlier Georgian version:

Equally ridiculous is the faith which men place in idols: for these are things made by human hands, and yet men declare: "These are our creators!" They safeguard these gods of theirs from being stolen by thieves, yet they say: "These are our guardians from evil." They squander their wealth on them, saying, "These are our foster-parents!" They seek to receive from them that which they can never find, and believe them to possess qualities which can never be theirs.

See David Marshall Lang, *The Balavariani (Barlaam and Josaphat): A Tale from the Christian East Translated from the Old Georgian* (Berkeley: University of California Press, 1966), p. 97.

24. Sir Thomas Herbert, *Some years travels into divers parts of Africa, and Asia the great: describing more particularly the empires of Persia and Industan: interwoven with such remarkable occurrences as hapned in those parts during these later times: as also, many other rich and famous kingdoms in the oriental India with the isles adjacent: severally relating their religion, language, customs and habit: as also proper observations concerning them* (London: Printed by R. Everingham for R. Scot, T. Basset, J. Wright, and R. Chiswell, 1677), p. 374.

25. For a study of the Japanese version, see Keiko Ikegami, *Barlaam and Josaphat: A Transcription of MS Egerton 876 with Notes, Glossary, and Comparative Study of the Middle English and Japanese Versions* (New York: AMS Press, 1999).

26. This and subsequent quotations from the Bible are cited from the Revised Standard Version, Catholic Edition.

27. For a study and analysis of the meaning of idolatry, especially as it appears in the Hebrew Bible, see Moshe Halbertal and Avishai Margalit, *Idolatry*, trans. Naomi Goldblum (Cambridge, MA: Harvard University Press, 1992).

28. In addition to being a source for Thomas Aquinas in *Summa Theologica* 2.2.94, the Wisdom of Solomon was central to the critiques of idolatry by such important missionaries as José de Acosta in Peru and Roberto de Nobili in India.

29. See Alain Besançon, *The Forbidden Image: An Intellectual History of Iconoclasm*, trans. Jane Marie Todd (Chicago: University of Chicago Press, 2000), p. 124. In the course of the Byzantine controversy, an image of Christ was reinstated over the Golden Gate, then removed again and once more replaced with a cross. There is some question as to whether this statement, written in the form of an acrostic poem, was written below the first or second cross, that is, by Leo III in 726 or Leo V in 815. See Charles Barber, *Figure and Likeness: On the Limits of Representation in Byzantine Iconoclasm* (Princeton, NJ: Princeton University Press, 2002), pp. 92–93.

30. Gregory the Great, quoted in Besançon, *The Forbidden Image*, p. 149.

31. Quoted in Barber, *Figure and Likeness*, p. 42. See also Hans Belting, *Likeness and Presence: A History of the Image before the Era of Art*, trans. Edmund Jephcott (Chicago: University of Chicago Press, 1994), p. 155.

32. John of Damascus, quoted in Barber, *Figure and Likeness*, pp. 70–71. See also Besançon, *The Forbidden Image*, pp. 126–27.

33. See Origen, *Homilies on Genesis and Exodus*, trans. Ronald E. Heine; Fathers of the Church, vol. 71 (Washington, DC: Catholic University of America Press, 1982), pp. 318–22.

34. See Besançon, *The Forbidden Image*, pp. 65–66.

35. Thomas Aquinas, *Summa Theologica*, 2.2.94, article 1. See *The "Summa Theologica" of St. Thomas Aquinas, Literally Translated by Fathers of the English Dominican Province*, part 2 (second part), QQ LLX–C (New York: Benzinger Brothers, 1922), pp. 179–80.

36. Thomas Aquinas, *Summa Theologica*, 3.25, article 3. See *The "Summa Theologica" of St. Thomas Aquinas, Literally Translated by Fathers of the English Dominican Province*, part 3, first number (QQ I–XXVI), p. 335.

37. Antoine Marcourt, *Conclusion de la messe: Ite, Missa est* (Lyon: Jean Saugrain, 1563), p. 10. I am grateful to George Hoffmann for providing this passage. See his "Anatomy of the Mass: Montaigne's 'Of cannibals,'" *Publications of the Modern Language Association* 117, no. 2 (2002): 207–21.

38. Carlos M. N. Eire, *War against the Idols: The Reformation of Worship from Erasmus to Calvin* (Cambridge: Cambridge University Press, 1986), p. 80.

39. Ibid., p. 58.

40. Ibid., pp. 84–85.

41. Pierre Viret, *Traittez divers pour l'instruction des fidèles qui résident et conversent ès liens et pais esquels il ne leur est permis de vivre en la pureté et liberté de l'Évangile* (Geneva: J. Rivery, 1559), p. 60. I am grateful to George Hoffmann for providing this passage.

42. Quoted in George Roerich, trans., *Biography of Dharmasvāmin (Chag lo-tsa-ba Chos-rje-dpal), A Tibetan Monk Pilgrim* (Patna, India: K. P. Jayaswal Research Institute, 1959), p. 17. This is my translation from the Tibetan text; Roerich's translation on page 71 is inaccurate.

43. See Gwendolyn Bays, trans., *The Lalitavistara Sūtra: The Voice of the Buddha*, vol. 1 (Berkeley, CA: Dharma, 1993), pp. 175–76.

44. On the aniconism question, see Klemens Karlsson, *Face to Face with the Absent Buddha: The Formation of Buddhist Aniconic Art* (Uppsala, Sweden: Uppsala University Library, 1999), and Dietrich Seckel, *Before and Beyond the Image: Aniconic Symbolism in Buddhist Art* (Zurich: Artibus Asiae Publishers, 2004).

45. Martha L. Carter, *The Mystery of the Udayana Buddha* (Naples: Istituto Universitario Orientale, 1990), p. 7.

46. See G. W. F. Leibniz, "On Philosophical Synthesis," selected by Philip P. Wiener, *Philosophy East and West* 12, no. 3 (October 1962): 198.

47. Xuanzang, *The Great Tang Dynasty Record of the Western Regions*, trans. Li Ronxi (Berkeley, CA: Numata Center for Buddhist Translation and Research, 1996), p. 160.

48. Donald K. Swearer, *Becoming the Buddha: The Ritual of Image Consecration in Thailand* (Princeton, NJ: Princeton University Press, 2004), pp. 206–7.

49. Quoted in ibid., p. 62.

50. See Juhyung Rhi, "Images, Relics, and Jewels: The Assimilation of Images in the Buddhist Relic Cult of Gandhāra—or Vice Versa," *Artibus Asiae* 65, no. 2 (2005): 169–211. On relics in Buddhism more generally, see John S. Strong, *Relics of the Buddha* (Princeton, NJ: Princeton University Press, 2004), and David Germano and Kevin Trainor, eds., *Embodying the Buddha: Buddhist Relic Veneration in Asia* (Albany: State University of New York Press, 2007).

51. See Swearer, *Becoming the Buddha*, pp. 213–14.

52. Quoted in ibid., p. 56.

53. For a detailed description of these rituals, see ibid., pp. 77–172.

54. Translated from the Tibetan text in Yael Bentor, *Consecration of Images and Stūpas in Indo-Tibetan Tantric Buddhism* (Leiden: E. J. Brill, 1996), folios 441–42. For Yael Bentor's translation, see p. 320. On the desecration ritual for a Tibetan image, see Tsering Tashi Thingo Rinpoche, "Discovery and Consecration of the Tara," in *World Cultural Heritage: A Global Challenge*, ed. Annamaria Geiger and Arne Eggebrecht (Hildesheim, Germany: City of Hildesheim, 1997), pp. 211–14.

55. Athanasius Kircher, *China Illustrata*, trans. Charles D. Van Tuyl (Bloomington: Indiana University Research Institute, 1987), pp. 142–43.

56. See Lynn Hunt, Margaret C. Jacob, and Wijnand Mijnhardt, *The Book That Changed Europe: Picart and Bernard's "Religious Ceremonies of the World"* (Cambridge, MA: Harvard University Press, 2010).

57. Bernard Picart, *The Ceremonies and Religious Customs of the Various Nations of the Known World: Together with Historical Annotations, and Several Curious Discourses Equally Instructive and Entertaining*, vol. 4 (London, 1733), pp. 101–2.

58. See Tomoko Masuzawa, *The Invention of World Religions; or, How European Universalism Was Preserved in the Language of Pluralism* (Chicago: University of Chicago Press, 2005), pp. 48–49.

59. Edward Brerewood, *Enquiries Touching the Diversity of Languages, and Religions, Through the Chiefe Parts of the World* (first published 1614; London, 1622), pp. 88, 90.

60. Father Fernão de Queyroz, *The Temporal and Spiritual Conquest of Ceylon*, trans. Father S. G. Perera (first published 1688; Colombo, Sri Lanka: A. C. Richards, 1930), p. 120.

61. David Benedict, A. M., *History of All Religions, as Divided into Paganism, Mahometanism, Judaism, and Christianity with an Account of Their Literary and Theological Institutions and Missionary, Bible, Tract, and Sunday School Societies with a General List of Religious Publications Accompanied by a Frontispiece of Six Heads* (Providence, RI: n.p., 1824), p. 277.

62. Ibid., p. 28.

63. Knox, *An Historical Relation of the Island Ceylon in the East-Indies*, p. 82.

64. See J. Gerson da Cunha, *Memoir on the History of the Tooth-Relic of Ceylon* (London: W. Thacker, 1875), pp. 40–46. On the 1560 Portuguese attack on Jaffna, see O. M. da Silva Cosme, *Fidalgos in the Kingdom of Jafanapatam (Sri Lanka: 1543–1658)* (Colombo, Sri Lanka: Harwoods, 1994), pp. 5–10. For an English-language account of the tooth relic incident from 1598, see Iohn Huighen van Linschoten, *His discours of voyages into ye Easte and West Indies* (London: John Wolfe, 1598), p. 81.

65. Guillaume Joseph le Gentil de la Galaisière, *Voyage dans les mers de l'Inde, fait par ordre du roi, à l'occasion du passage de Vénus sur le disque du Soleil, le 6 juin 1761, et le 3 du même mois 1769*, vol. 1 (Switzerland: Libraires Associés, 1780), pp. 224–25. The passage here is my translation from the French. However, the passage had appeared in English shortly after its publication. See William Chambers, "Some Account of the Sculptures and Ruins at Mavalipuram," *Asiatick Researches* 1 (1788): 168–70.

66. M. H. Shakir translation.

67. Mahmud of Ghazni, quoted in Sir Henry Miers Eliot, *The History of India as Told by Its Own Historians*, vol. 18 (1869; reprint, Calcutta: Susil Gupta, 1953), pp. 30–31. All citations are to the reprint edition.

68. Quoted in Bruce B. Lawrence, *Shahrastānī on Indian Religions* (The Hague: Mouton, 1976), pp. 42–43. For a discussion of this passage and other Islamic references to the Buddha, see pp. 110–14 of the same volume.

One of the most detailed biographies of the Buddha in Muslim sources is found in the famous *Compendium of Chronicles (Jāmi' al-tavārīkh)* by Rashīd al-Dīn, the Persian scholar of Jewish descent. In 1300, he was commissioned by the Mongol prince Ghazan to compose a history of the Turkish and Mongol tribes from Genghis Khan down to Ghazan himself. After Ghazan's death, his brother and new khan, Uljaytu, instructed Rashīd al-Dīn to write a second volume, a history of the world or "a detailed history of every nation of the inhabited quarter of the earth," which for the author meant the Persians, Arabs, Greeks, Chinese, Indians, and Franks. This later work is the *Compendium of Chronicles*. It is in the chapter on India that we find a lengthy life of the Buddha, composed in 1305. See Karl Jahn,

Rashīd al-Dīn's "History of India": Collected Essays with Facsimiles and Indices, Central Asiatic Studies (The Hague: Mouton, 1965), pp. xxxi–lxxvii.

For an extensive survey of references to the Buddha in Islamic sources, see Daniel Gimaret, "Bouddha et les Bouddhistes dans la tradition Musulmane," *Journal Asiatique* (1969): 273–316.

69. Eliot, *The History of India as Told by Its Own Historians*, 18:54–55.

70. The story is recounted by the Tibetan scholar Gendun Chopel (1903–1951). See Dge 'dun chos 'phel, *Rgyal khams rig pas bskor ba'i gtam rgyud gser gyi thang ma* (*smad cha*), in *Dge 'dun chos 'phel gyi gsung rtsom*, ed. Hor khang bsod nams dpal 'bar, vol. 1 (Gang can rig mdzod 10) (Lhasa: Bod ljongs bod yig dpe rnying dpe skrun khang, 1990), p. 389.

71. See Roerich, *Biography of Dharmasvāmin*, p. 64.

72. *Ayeen Akbery; or, The Institutes of the Emperor Akber*, trans. Francis Gladwin, vol. 3 (Calcutta: William Mackay, 1786), p. 157. For a more recent translation, see *'Ain-i-Ākbari of Abul Fazl-i-'Allami*, trans. Colonel H. S. Jarrett, corrected and further annotated by Sir Jadu-nath Sarkar, 2 vols. (Calcutta: Royal Asiatic Society of Bengal, 1949).

73. Michael J. Sweet, trans., *Mission to Tibet: The Extraordinary Eighteenth-Century Account of Ippolito Desideri, S. J.* (Boston: Wisdom Publications, 2010), pp. 428–29.

74. Ibid., pp. 374–75. Earlier Jesuit missionaries to Tibet saw evidence of Christianity there and held that the Tibetans were not idolaters. Francisco Godinho, a missionary to western Tibet, wrote in a letter of August 16, 1626, "The peoples of this great Thibeth are not idolaters: for we have found that they acknowledge the adorable Unity and Trinity of the true God; they know there are three Hierarchies of Angelic Spirits, divided into nine Choirs, according to the differences of their excellencies and dignities; that there is a Hell which awaits the wicked, and a Paradise for the reward of the good." See H. Holsten, SJ, "A Letter of Father Francisco Godinho, S. J., from Western Tibet," *Journal of the Asiatic Society of Bengal*, n.s., 21 (1925): 66. The "trinity" likely derives from what he may have learned of the Three Jewels: the Buddha, the dharma, and the sangha; the "hierarchies" and "choirs" are likely the three realms and nine levels (*khams gsum sa dgu*) of the Buddhist cosmos.

CHAPTER 2

1. Joannes Boemus, *The Manners, Lavves, and Customes of All Nations. Collected out of the best VVriters by Joannes Boemus Aubanus, a Dutch-man* (London, 1611), book I, chapter 1, "The true opinion of Divines, concerning mans originall," p. 3.

2. Cited in Colonel Sir Henry Yule, trans. and ed., *Cathay and the Way Hither: Being a Collection of Medieval Notices of China*, vol. 1 (London: Hakluyt Society, 1915), p. 101, note 2. See also Athanasius Kircher, *China Illustrata*, trans. Charles D. Van Tuyl (Bloomington: Indiana University Research Institute, 1987), p. 52.

3. In the seventeenth century, the Portuguese captain João Ribeiro would specu-

late that the Buddha was in fact Saint Thomas. Describing the gods of Sri Lanka, he writes:

Some are monsters with many arms holding bows and arrows—but one takes pre-eminence of all these, who is called Budu, and for whom they profess the greatest reverence. He is represented in the form of a man, of gigantic size, being about 32 feet high. They have a tradition that this Budu lived for a long time in Ceylon, and led there a most penitent and holy life. They reckon their years from his residence among them, and by this calculation it appears that he lived about the 40th year of the Christian era, and it is probable that he was St. Thomas the Apostle, for it is a general tradition in the east that he preached the gospel to all these nations. The Singhalese say that he was not born among them, and that he left their country and died on the continent of India; this is perfectly in accord with the common opinion received among the Christians of India, and especially among those who live on the Coromandel Coast who are called St. Thomas's Christians.

See João Ribeiro, *History of Ceylon Presented by Captain John Ribeyro to the King of Portugal, in 1685, translated from the Portuguese, by the Abbé le Grand. Re-translated from the French edition: with an appendix, containing chapters illustrative of the past and present condition of the island, by George Lee, Postmaster-General of Ceylon; Fellow of the Universal Statistical Society of France* (Colombo, Ceylon: Government Press, 1847), p. 55.

4. Quoted in James Legge, *Christianity in China: Nestorianism, Roman Catholicism, Protestantism* (London: Trübner, 1888), p. 7.

5. Yoshirō Saeki, *The Nestorian Documents and Records in China*, 2nd ed. (Tokyo: Tokyo Institute, 1951), pp. 133–34. See also David Scott, "Christian Responses to Buddhism in Pre-Medieval Times," *Numen*, vol. 32, fasc. 1 (1985): 88–100.

6. Kircher, *China Illustrata*, p. 46.

7. William W. Rockhill, *The Journey of Friar William of Rubruck to the Eastern Parts of the World, 1253–55, as Narrated by Himself* (London: Hakluyt Society, 1900), p. 158.

8. Georg Schurhammer, SJ, *Francis Xavier: His Life, His Times*, vol. 3, *Indonesia and India, 1545–1549*, trans. M. Joseph Costelloe, SJ (Rome: Jesuit Historical Institute, 1980), pp. 484–85, 574.

9. This biographical sketch of Postel is drawn from Marion L. Kuntz, *Guillaume Postel: Prophet of the Restitution of All Things, His Life and Thought* (The Hague: Martinus Nijhoff, 1981).

10. Guillaume Postel, *Des merveilles du monde, et principalemét* [sic] *des admirables choses des Indes, & du nouveau monde: Histoire extraicte des escriptz tresdignes de foy, tant de ceulx qui encores sont a present audict pays, come de ceulx qui encores vivantz peu paravat en sont retournez. Et y est aussi monstré le lieu du Paradis terrestre* (Paris, 1553), pp. 20–23. Translation by Peggy McCracken.

11. Francis Xavier, *The Letters and Instructions of Francis Xavier*, trans. and in-

troduced by M. Joseph Costelloe, SJ (St. Louis: Institute of Jesuit Sources, 1992), pp. 336-37.

12. See Schurhammer, *Francis Xavier*, 3:225-29. For Japanese condemnations of Christianity, see George Elison, *Deus Destroyed: The Image of Christianity in Early Modern Japan* (Cambridge, MA: Harvard University Press, 1973).

13. On the Jesuits' choice of dress, see Willard J. Peterson, "What to Wear? Observation and Participation by Jesuit Missionaries in Late Ming Society," in *Implicit Understandings: Observing, Reporting, and Reflecting on the Encounters between Europeans and Other Peoples in the Early Modern Era*, ed. Stuart B. Schwartz (Cambridge: Cambridge University Press, 1994), pp. 403-21. See also R. Po-chia Hsia, "From Buddhist Garb to Literati Silk: Costume and Identity of the Jesuit Missionary," in *Religious Ceremonials and Images: Power and Social Meaning (1400-1750)*, ed. José Pedro Paiva (Coimbra, Portugal: Palimage Editores, 2002), pp. 143-53.

14. Matteo Ricci, SJ, *The True Meaning of the Lord of Heaven (T'ien-chu Shih-i)*, trans. Douglas Lancashire and Peter Hu Kuo-chen, SJ (St. Louis: Institute of Jesuit Sources, 1985), pp. 453, 455.

This version of the emperor's dream and its aftermath would be repeated by other missionaries. An Italian missionary to Vietnam, Adriano di St. Thecla (1667-1765), provided a more elaborate account, explaining that when the emperor's delegation reached India, "they still had not covered half of the way to the remote West, but, terrified by the incommodities and difficulties of [going] the rest of the way, they took an image of an idol and the books that were kept there [in India] and brought them to the emperor, pretending that they brought the image and the books of the holy man of the West." Father Adriano notes that "this fact became known from the Christian books," and then goes on to provide the traditional Chinese account, concluding, "From this it has been discovered that the aforementioned emperor sent [ambassadors] to India with the intention to bring to China the book and the image of Thích Ca [Śākya] called Phât [Buddha], but [the emperor] did not send them to the remotest West or Europe or even to Palestine to bring from there the image as well as the doctrine of the saintly people who lived there." See Father Adriano di St. Thecla, *Opusculum de Sectis apud Sinenses et Tunkinenses: A Small Treatise on the Sects among the Chinese and Tonkinese*, translated and annotated by Olga Dror (Ithaca, NY: Cornell Southeast Asia Program, 2002), pp. 186-89.

Nevertheless, this idea of China's almost having become Christian persisted into the nineteenth century. In his 1835 translation of Friedrich von Schlegel's *The Philosophy of History* (delivered as a series of lectures in Vienna in 1828), James Burton Robertson (1800-1877) adds this note about the introduction of Buddhism into China:

There is historical evidence that, up to two centuries before the Christian era, idolatry had made little progress among this people. So great was the expectation of the Messiah—"the Great Saint who, as Confucius says, was to appear in the West"—so fully sensible were they not only of the place of his birth, but of the time of his coming, that about sixty years after the birth of our Saviour they sent their envoys to hail the expected Redeemer. These envoys encountered on their way the Missionaries of Buddhism coming from India—the latter, announcing an incarnate God, were taken to be the disciples of the true Christ, and were presented as such to their countrymen by the deluded ambassadors. Thus was this religion introduced into China, and thus did the phantasmagoria of Hell intercept the light of the gospel. So, not in the internal spirit only, but in the outward history of Buddhism, a demonical intent is very visible.

Friedrich von Schlegel, *The Philosophy of History*, trans. James Burton Robertson (London: Henry G. Bohn, 1984), p. 136.

15. Ricci, *The True Meaning of the Lord of Heaven*, p. 143.

16. Ibid., p. 261.

17. Nicholas Trigault, SJ, *The China That Was: China As Discovered by the Jesuits at the Close of the Sixteenth Century*, trans. L. J. Gallagher, SJ (Milwaukee: Bruce, 1942), pp. 164–65.

18. Samuel Purchas (1577?–1626), *Purchas his Pilgrimage; or, Relations of the World and the Religions Observed in All Ages and places discovered, from the Creation unto this Present* (London: William Stansby, 1613), p. 459.

19. Simon de la Loubère, *A New Historical Relation of the Kingdom of Siam* (London, 1693; reprint, Oxford: Oxford University Press, 1986), p. 136. All citations are to the reprint edition.

20. Ibid.

21. Adapted from Bhikkhu Ñāṇamoli, *The Life of the Buddha according to the Pali Canon* (Seattle: BPS Pariyatti Editions, 1992), p. 258.

22. Eugene Burlingame, *Buddhist Legends: Translated from the Original Pali Text of the Dhammapada Commentary*, part 1, Harvard Oriental Series 28 (Cambridge, MA: Harvard University Press, 1921), pp. 240–41.

23. De la Loubère, *A New Historical Relation of the Kingdom of Siam*, p. 156.

24. Alexandre, chevalier de Chaumont, *A relation of the late embassy of Monsr. de Chaumont, Knt. to the court of the King of Siam with an account of the government, state, manners, religion and commerce of that kingdom* (London, 1687), pp. 88–90.

25. The French delegation to the court of Siam visited one of the most famous Buddhist temples in Southeast Asia, Wat Phra Sri Sanphet (today in ruins), known for its magnificent statue of the Buddha. But the abbé showed little interest in the figure depicted. In his diary entry of October 30, 1685, all he can talk about is the gold:

Then, after having walked a lot, we arrived at the King's pagoda. When I went in I thought I was in a church. The nave is supported by tall thick columns, without architectural decoration. . . . The choir is small and very dark; there are at least fifty lamps continually lit there. But what will surprise you is that at the end of the choir is an image in solid gold, that is to say gold poured into a mould. It may be forty-two feet high by thirteen or fourteen feet wide, and three inches in thickness. It is said there is 12,400,000 *livres* of gold here. We also saw in other parts of the pagoda seventeen or eighteen figures in solid gold, as high as a man, most having diamonds on their fingers, emeralds and some rubies on their foreheads and their navels. These images are without doubt of gold; we touched and handled them, and although we only got to within five or six feet of the big statue, without touching it, I think it is made of gold like the others; to the eye it seemed the same metal. In addition to these there were more than thirty idols with golden vestments.

Abbé de Choisy, *Journal of a Voyage to Siam, 1685–1686,* trans. and introduced by Michael Smithies (Kuala Lumpur, Malaysia: Oxford University Press, 1993), pp. 175–76.

26. Guy Tachard, *A relation of the voyage to Siam: Performed by six Jesuits, sent by the French King, to the Indies and China, in the year, 1685; With their astrological observations, and their remarks of natural philosophy, geography, hydrography, and history; published in the original, by the express orders of His Most Christian Majesty; and now made English, and illustrated with sculptures* (London, 1688), pp. 296–97.

27. Francis Buchanan, MD, "On the Religion and Literature of the Burmas," *Asiatick Researches* 6 (1801): 268, note *.

28. Bénigne Vachet, quoted in Michael Smithies, *Mission Made Impossible: The Second French Embassy to Siam 1687* (Chiang Mai, Thailand: Silkworm Books, 2002), p. 6.

29. Tachard, *A relation of the voyage to Siam,* pp. 275–78.

30. Smithies, *Mission Made Impossible,* p. 6.

31. Tachard, *A relation of the voyage to Siam,* pp. 289–92.

32. Nicolas Gervaise, *The Natural and Political History of the Kingdom of Siam* [1688], trans. Herbert Stanley O'Neill (Bangkok: Siam Observer Press, 1928), pp. 74–77.

33. Di St. Thecla, *Opusculum de Sectis apud Sinenses et Tunkinenses,* pp. 184–85.

34. Father Fernão de Queyroz, *The Temporal and Spiritual Conquest of Ceylon,* trans. Father S. G. Perera (Colombo: A. C. Richards, 1930), p. 122. Rui Magone speculates that the text is the four-volume *Shishi yuanliu yinghua shiji* (*The Origins, Transformations and Deeds of Buddha*), published in 1486, itself a version of the *Shijia rulai yinghua lu* (*Record of the Teachings of the Tathāgata Śākyamuni Buddha*) by Baocheng, a Buddhist of the Ming dynasty (1368–1643). See Rui Magone, "The Fô and the Xekiâ: Tomás Pereira's Critical Description of Chinese Buddhism," in *In the Light and Shadow of an Emperor: Tomás Pereira, SJ (1645–1708), the Kangxi Emperor and the Jesuit Mission in China,* ed. Artur K. Wardega, SJ, and António

Vasconcelos de Saldanha (Newcastle upon Tyne: Cambridge Scholars Publishing 2012), pp. 252–74. On the life of Father Pereira, see Luis Filipe Barreto, ed., *Tomás Pereira, S.J. (1646–1708): Life, Work and World* (Lisbon: Centro Cultural e Científico de Macau, 2010).

35. De Queyroz, *The Temporal and Spiritual Conquest of Ceylon*, p. 122.

36. Ibid., p. 135.

37. Ibid., p. 139.

38. Louis le Comte, *Memoirs and Observations Topographical, Physical, Mathematical, Mechanical, Natural, Civil, and Ecclesiastical Made in a Late Journey through the Empire of China, and Published in Several Letters. Particularly upon the Chinese Pottery and Varnishing; the Silk and Other Manufactures. Description of their Cities and Publick Works; Number of People, their Language, Manners and Commerce; their Oeconomy, and Government. The Philosophy of Confucius. The State of Christianity, with Many Other Curious and Useful Remarks*, translated from the Paris edition (London, 1697), pp. 323–25. For a very similar description, see Jean-Baptiste du Halde (1647–1743), *The General History of China: Containing a Geographical, Historical, Chronological, Political, and Physical Description of the Empire of China*, vol. 3 (France, 1735; 3rd ed., London, 1741), pp. 34–37, and Abbé Grosier, *A General Description of China: Containing the Topography of the Fifteen Provinces which Compose This Vast Empire; That of Tartary, the Isles, and Other Tributary Countries; The Number and Situation of the Cities, the State of its Population, the Natural History of its Animals, Vegetables and Minerals; Together with the Latest Accounts that Have Reached Europe, of the Government, Religion, Manners, Customs, Arts and Sciences of the Chinese; Illustrated by a New and Correct Map of China, and other Cooper Plates*, vol. 1 (London, 1788), pp. 215–23.

39. See Roger-Pol Droit, *The Cult of Nothingness: The Philosophers and the Buddha* (Chapel Hill: University of North Carolina Press, 2003).

40. See Urs App, *The Cult of Emptiness: The Western Discovery of Buddhist Thought and the Invention of Oriental Philosophy* (Rorschach, Switzerland: University Media, 2012), especially chapter 2.

41. Christopher (Cristoforo) Borri, "An Account of Cochin-China in Two Parts: The First Treats of the Temporal State of that Kingdom; The Second, of What Concerns the Spiritual," in *A General Collection of the Best and Most Interesting Voyages and Travels in All Parts of the World; Many of Which Are Now First Translated into English; Digested on a New Plan*, ed. John Pinkerton, vol. 9 (London, 1811), pp. 820–22.

42. In a brilliant piece of detective work, Urs App has traced the doctrine of nothingness back further, to the Jesuit mission to Japan, and the Spaniard Juan Fernández (1526–1576), later elaborated by the Italian Alessandro Valignano (1539–1606) and his interpreter, the Portuguese João Rodrigues (1561–1633). The idea that the Buddha had both an exoteric and an esoteric teaching, something that he revealed on his deathbed, would evolve and gain wide currency in Europe, strongly influencing the representation of Indian religions in general and Buddhism in

particular, into the nineteenth century. Both "nothingness" and the Buddha's supposed deathbed confession are treated at length by Urs App in *The Birth of Orientalism* (Philadelphia: University of Pennsylvania Press, 2010) and in his *The Cult of Emptiness*.

43. Alexandre de Rhodes, *Histoire du royaume du Tonkin* (Paris: Kimé, 1999), p. 64.

44. On the Rites Controversy, see, for example, Joan-Pau Rubiés, "The Concept of Cultural Dialogue and the Jesuit Method of Accommodation: Between Idolatry and Civilization," *Archivium Historicum Societatis Iesu* 74, no. 147 (2005): 237–80.

45. Ippolito Desideri, *Mgo skar gyi bla ma i po li do zhes bya ba yis phul ba'i bod kyi mkhas pa rnams la skye ba snga ma dang stong pa nyid kyi lta ba'i sgo nas zhu*, Archivum Romanum Societatis Iesu (ARSI), Goa MS 75, p. 1 recto.

46. Cited in Tsong kha pa, *Mnyam med tsong kha pa chen pos mdzad pa'i byang chub lam rim che ba* (Dharamsala, India: Tibetan Cultural Printing Press, 1991), p. 137. For an English translation, see Tsong kha pa, *The Great Treatise on the Stages of the Path to Enlightenment (Lam Rim Chen Mo)*, vol. 1, ed. Joshua W. C. Cutler (Ithaca, NY: Snow Lion Publications, 2000), p. 184.

47. Desideri, *Mgo skar gyi bla ma . . .* , p. 1 recto.

48. Ibid., p. 3 recto.

49. Michael J. Sweet, trans., *Mission to Tibet: The Extraordinary Eighteenth-Century Account of Ippolito Desideri, S. J.* (Boston: Wisdom Publications, 2010), pp. 394–95. I have restored Desideri's original spelling of Ganden and *lha*.

A similar point had been made in the previous century by his fellow Jesuit Tomas Pereira, Portuguese missionary to China, although he leaves open the possibility of human rather than demonic corruption with his suggestion that the Chinese may have perverted the Gospel they received from Nestorian Christians centuries before: "But the common enemy could not better pervert what we believe of our Redeemer, many centuries before the Incarnation of Christ, as will be seen later, unless it is a false addition due to the malice of the Chinese, after they came to know of our Holy Faith, which was brought thither some 900 years ago." See de Queyroz, *The Temporal and Spiritual Conquest of Ceylon*, p. 123.

50. See, for example, Justin Martyr, *First Apology*, chapters 54, 62, and 66. I am grateful to Elizabeth Clark for providing these references. It is noteworthy that the view of Buddhism as a demonic mimicry of Christianity persisted for several centuries. In *The Philosophy of History*, a series of lectures delivered in Vienna in 1828, the great champion of Oriental wisdom, Friedrich von Schlegel, described the Chinese adoption of Buddhism: "Descending from one degree of political idolatry to a grade still lower, they have at last openly embraced a foreign superstition—a diabolic mimicry of Christianity, which emanated from India, has made Thibet its principal seat, prevails in China, and, widely diffused over the whole middle of Asia, reckons a greater number of followers than any other religion on the earth." Schlegel, *The Philosophy of History*, p. 137.

51. Kircher, *China Illustrata*, p. 66. Kircher goes on to describe the process of discovering the Grand Lama after the death of the preceding. He also explains that the Tanguts pay great bribes to the priests to receive food that has been mixed with the urine of the Grand Lama ("what abominable filth!"). For numerous cases of the comparison of elements of Tibetan Buddhism with Roman Catholicism, see Sven Hedin, *Trans-Himalaya: Discoveries and Adventures in Tibet* (London: Macmillan, 1913), pp. 310–29. A useful survey of the early missions to Tibet may be found in John MacGregor, *Tibet: A Chronicle of Exploration* (New York: Praeger, 1970), pp. 1–111. In an extended passage, Desideri describes the ability of the newly identified Dalai Lama, a young child, to recall events from the life of his predecessor, to comport himself with great dignity, and to "speak prophetically." Rather than dismiss this is as invention and hearsay, Desideri concedes that it "really does happen," but ascribes it to the work of the devil. See Sweet, *Mission to Tibet*, pp. 297–317. For a discussion of Desideri's views on the question, see Michael J. Sweet, "The Devil's Stratagem or Human Fraud: Ippolito Desideri on the Reincarnate Succession of the Dalai Lama," *Buddhist-Christian Studies* 29 (2009): 131–40.

52. Sweet, *Mission to Tibet*, pp. 442–43. This contradicts a statement earlier in this work, when Desideri states, "The salvific gospel appeared many times in Tibet to illuminate these people, as their very hodgepodge of teachings demonstrates; some of these teachings appear to be a sketchy and leftover version of some Christian teaching that was at one time sown among them" (p. 316).

53. Jean Crasset, *The History of the Church of Japan: Written originally in French by Monsieur L'Abbe de T. and now translated into English; By N. N.*, vol. 1 (London, 1705), p. 27.

54. Tsong kha pa, *Mnyam med tsong kha pa . . .* , pp. 133–34. For an English translation, see Tsong kha pa, *The Great Treatise on the Stages of the Path to Enlightenment*, 1:180. In Desideri's writings, the passage appears at Archivum Romanum Societatis Iesu, Rome, Goa 74, p. 7 recto.

55. Matteo Ricci, *China in the Sixteenth Century: The Journal of Matthew Ricci, 1583–1610* (New York: Random House, 1953), pp. 98–99.

56. De Queyroz, *The Temporal and Spiritual Conquest of Ceylon*, p. 141.

57. The same conclusion was also being drawn by non-Jesuits and even non-Catholics around the same time. See, for example, Mathurin Veyssière de la Croze (1661-1739), a Benedictine who converted to Protestantism, in his *Histoire du Christianisme des Indes* (The Hague: Vaillant, & N. Prevost, 1724), pp. 500–502.

58. Kircher, *China Illustrata*, pp. 141–42.

59. Urs App has traced the story as far back as a Jesuit text written in Spanish in 1556, *Sumario de los errores*. See his *The Cult of Emptiness*, p. 38.

60. See App, *The Birth of Orientalism*, p. 125.

61. Arnoldus Montanus, *Atlas Chinensis: Being a second part of a relation of remarkable passages in two embassies from the East-India Company of the United*

Provinces to the vice-roy Singlamong, General Taising Lipovi, and Konchi, Emperor (London: Thomas Johnson, 1671), p. 574.

62. Bernard Picart, *The Ceremonies and Religious Customs of the Various Nations of the Known World: Together with Historical Annotations, and Several Curious Discourses Equally Instructive and Entertaining*, vol. 4 (London, 1733), p. 292.

63. Ibid., p. 196.

CHAPTER 3

1. Engelbert Kaempfer, *The History of Japan, giving an Account of the ancient and present State and Government of that Empire; of Its Temples, Palaces, Castles and other Buildings; of its Metals, Minerals, Trees, Plants, Animals, Birds and Fishes; of The Chronology and Succession of the Emperors, Ecclesiastical and Secular; of The Original Descent, Religions, Customs, and Manufactures of the Natives, and of their Trade and Commerce with the Dutch and Chinese. Together with a Description of the Kingdom of Siam.* Written in High-Dutch by Engelbertus Kaempfer, M. D. Physician to the Dutch Embassy to the Emperor's Court; and translated from his Original Manuscript, never before printed, by J. G. Scheuchzer, F. R. S. and a member of the College of Physicians, London, 1727. Reprinted in Engelbert Kaempfer, *The History of Japan: Together with a Description of the Kingdom of Siam, 1690–1692*, vol. 1 (London: J. MacLehose and Sons, 1906), p. xxix. All citations are to the reprint edition. For a more recent and more accurate translation of Kaempfer's account of Japan, see Beatrice M. Bodart-Bailey, *Kaempfer's Japan: Tokugawa Culture Observed* (Honolulu: University of Hawai'i Press, 1999). Bodart-Bailey's translation, which focuses on Japan, omits most of Kaempfer's account of Siam, which will be cited and discussed below.

2. Kaempfer, *The History of Japan: Together with a Description of the Kingdom of Siam, 1690–1692*, 1:xxi.

3. Ibid., 1:xxxi–xxxii.

4. The preceding account of Kaempfer's life is drawn from "The Author's Preface" and "The Life of the Author by the Translator" in ibid., 1:xxiv–xlvi.

5. Ibid., 1:62–68.

6. Another European scholar of the early eighteenth century to identify the various names of the Buddha as referring to the same person was Mathurin Veyssière de la Croze (1661–1739), who served as librarian to the king of Prussia. In his 1724 *Histoire du Christianisme des Indes*, he calls Buddhism "une Secte infame & miserable," and states that Boudda, Sommona-Codom, and Xaca are the same person. See Mathurin Veyssière de la Croze, *Histoire du Christianisme des Indes* (La Haye [The Hague]: Vaillant and N. Prevost, 1724), p. 502.

7. Sir William Jones, "On the Hindus," *Asiatick Researches, or Transactions of the Society, Instituted in Bengal, for Inquiring into the History and Antiquities, the Arts,*

Sciences, and Literature of Asia 1 (1801): 428. This is the London reprint of the original Calcutta edition of the discourse Jones delivered February 2, 1786. This essay is
also cited as "Third Anniversary Discourse."

8. Edward Moor (1771–1848), *The Hindu Pantheon*, facsimile of original 1810 London edition (New York: Garland, 1984), pp. 231–32.

9. Quoted in Captain Colin McKenzie, "Remarks on Some Antiquities on the
West and South Coasts of Ceylon Written in the Year 1796," *Asiatick Researches* 6
(1799): 451.

10. Henry Clarke Warren, *Buddhism in Translations* (Cambridge, MA: Harvard
University Press, 1896), p. 66.

11. Athanasius Kircher, *China Illustrata*, trans. Charles D. Van Tuyl (Bloomington: Indiana University Research Institute, 1987), p. 214. Kircher was not the first
to trace the religion of China back to Egypt. Some decades before, João Rodrigues
(1561–1633), a Jesuit missionary to Japan and China, had made a similar argument.
See Urs App, *The Birth of Orientalism* (Philadelphia: University of Pennsylvania
Press, 2010), pp. 22–28. Nor was Kircher the last. The Egyptian connection was
developed further by the brilliant French scholar Joseph de Guignes (1721–1800).
Again, see App, pp. 207–23.

12. Kircher, *China Illustrata*, p. 141.

13. Ibid., p. 121. According to Urs App, Kircher may have derived his theory of the
Egyptian origins of Asian idolatry from Lorenzo Pignoria (1571–1631). See Urs App,
*The Cult of Emptiness: The Western Discovery of Buddhist Thought and the Invention of
Oriental Philosophy* (Rorschach, Switzerland: University Media, 2012), p. 113–15.

14. Kircher, *China Illustrata*, pp. 122, 123.

15. Alexander Csoma de Kőrös, "Translation of a Tibetan Fragment with Remarks by H. H. Wilson, Secy.," *Journal of the Asiatic Society of Bengal* 1 (1832): 272.
Reprinted in Alexander Csoma de Kőrös, *Tibetan Studies: Being a Reprint of the Articles Contributed to the Journal of the Asiatic Society of Bengal and Asiatic Researches*
(Budapest: Akadémiai Kiado, 1984), p. 12.

16. Antonio Agostino Giorgi, *Alphabetum Tibetanum: Missionum Apostolicarum
Commodo Editum* (Köln: Editiones Una Voce, 1987), pp. 547–48. My thanks to Isrun
Engelhardt for identifying the passage and translating it from the Latin.

17. Jones, "On the Hindus," 422–23.

18. See François Bernier, *Travels in the Mogul Empire AD 1656–1668*, trans. Archi-
bald Constable (London: Oxford University Press, 1934), p. 336.

19. Moor, *The Hindu Pantheon*, pp. 220–21.

20. Jones, "On the Hindus," 425.

21. Sir William Jones, "On the Chronology of the Hindus," *Asiatick Researches* 2
(1801): 124. This is the London reprint of the original Calcutta edition. Jones wrote
the essay in January 1788.

22. Jones, "On the Hindus," 425.

23. Sir William Jones, "A Supplement to the Essay on Indian Chronology," *Asiatick Researches* 2 (1801): 401. This is the London reprint of the original Calcutta edition.

24. Jones, "On the Hindus," 427–28.

25. See Abbé Mignot, "Premier Mémoire sur les Anciens Philosophes de l'Inde; Sur la Vie, les moeurs, les usages & les pratiques de ces Philosophes," *Histoire de l'Académie Royale des Inscriptions et Belle-Lettres, avec Les Mémoires de Littérature tirés des Registres de cette Académie, depuis l'année M. DCCLXI, jusques & compris l'année M. DCCLXIII* 31 (1768), p. 88 of Mémoires section.

26. Francis Buchanan, MD, "On the Religion and Literature of the Burmas," *Asiatick Researches* 6 (1801): pp. 258–59.

27. John Davy, *An Account of the Interior of Ceylon, and of Its Inhabitants: With Travels in That Island* (London: Longman, Hurst, Rees, Orme, and Brown, 1821), pp. 230–32.

28. George Finlayson, *The Mission to Siam, and Hue, the Capital of Cochin China, in the Years 1821-2: From the Journal of the Late George Finlayson, Esq., Assistant Surgeon of His Majesty's Eighth Light Dragoons, Surgeon and Naturalist to the Mission; With a Memoir of the Author, by Sir Thomas Stamford Raffles, F.R.S.* (London: John Murray. 1826), p. 221. This is a note by Thomas Raffles.

29. James Cowles Prichard, *Researches into the Physical History of Mankind*, 3rd ed., vol. 4 (London: Sherwood, Gilbert, and Piper, 1844), p. 233.

30. Eugène Burnouf, *Le Lotus de la bonne loi* (Paris: L'Imprimerie Nationale, 1852), p. 560. Despite all this, the African hypothesis persists into the twenty-first century. See, for example, Reginald Muata Abhaya Ashby, *The Ancient Egyptian Buddha: The Ancient Egyptian Origins of Buddhism* (Miami: Cruzian Mystic Books / Sema Institute of Yoga, 2006).

31. Louis-Mathieu Langlès, ed. and trans., *Voyages de C.P. Thunberg, au Japon, par le cap de Bonne-Espérance, les îles de la Sonde, &c.: Traduits, rédigés et augmentés de notes considérables sur la religion, le gouvernement, le commerce, l'industrie et les langues de ces différentes contrées, particulièrement sur le Javan et le Malai* (Paris: Chez Benoît Dandré [et al.], an IV [1796]), 3:257–65. Cited by J. Reuilly in his notes to his translation of the German botanist Peter Simon Pallas, entitled *Description du Tibet d'après la relation des Lamas Tangoutes, établis parmi les Mongols* (Paris: Chez Bossange, 1808), pp. 48–49, note.

32. George Stanley Faber, *The Origin of Pagan Idolatry Ascertained from Historical Testimony and Circumstantial Evidence*, vol. 1 (London: F. and C. Rivingtons, 1816), pp. vii–viii.

33. Ibid., 2:355.

34. Ibid., p. 42.

35. Ibid., pp. 441–42. A similar, although somewhat less ambitious, work from the same period, one in which the author acknowledges his debt to "the enlight-

ened Faber," is by Lieutenant Colonel William Francklin of the East India Company, *Researches on the Tenets and Doctrines of the Jeynes and Boodhists: Conjectured to Be the Brachmanes of Ancient India; In Which Is Introduced a Discussion on the Worship of the Serpent in Various Countries of the World* (London, 1817). Here we read, "Whether Bood'h was a sage, a hero, or leader of a colony, cannot be ascertained. It is, however, certain that he was not an Indian. It might be conjectured that Bood'h, in his capacity of Guadma, or Samono Codom of the Brahmins, may be classed with the Cadmus of Greece, who was the leader of a colony, and built Thebes, and many other cities of Greece" (p. 141, note).

Buddhism remained implicated in theories of diffusionism a century later. For example, the Honorable Mrs. E. A. Gordon, in her *Symbols of the Way — Far East and West*, published in Tokyo in 1916, argued that Mahāyāna Buddhism was in fact a form of Christianity, based largely on the existence in the New Testament of the First Epistle of Saint John, which carries the designation *ad Parthos*, "to the Parthians," who inhabited what is today northeastern Iran. She argues that Saint John preached among the Parthians, with the Gospel spreading from there to the East. Biblical scholars had determined, even at the time of Mrs. Gordon, that *parthos* refers not to the Parthians but probably to *parthenoy*, "the virgin," a designation of Saint John himself; it is the Epistle of Saint John the Virgin. This does not prevent Mrs. Gordon from seeing Christianity everywhere in the Buddhism of East Asia. There is a gauze veil on the altar of Korean temples, just as in the churches of Constantinople; Bodhidharma is Saint Thomas; fire and wind are symbols of both Jehovah and the bodhisattva Kannon; Maitreya, the name of the future Buddha, is the Sanskrit form of *messiah*; the fish is associated both with Christ and Kannon; triads and trinities occur in both Christianity and Buddhism, and so on. See E. A. Gordon, *Symbols of the Way — Far East and West* (Tokyo: Maruzen, 1916).

36. Father Sangermano, *A Description of the Burmese Empire, Compiled Chiefly from Native Documents by the Rev. Father Sangermano* (Rome, 1833), pp. 84–85.

37. [Simon de la] Loubère. Notes 37 through 41 in the extract are original to Michael Symes, *An Account of an Embassy to the Kingdom of Ava, Sent by the Governor-General of India, in the Year 1795. By Michael Symes, Esq., Major in His Majesty's 76th Regiment* (London, 1800), pp. 300–302.

38. M. Gentil asserts that the Chinese admit, by their own accounts, that Foe, their object of worship, was originally brought from India.

39. See the account of the Ninth Avatar, by the Rev. Mr. Maurice, in his *History of Hindostan*, Vol. II. Part 3.

40. I need hardly observe that I mean Sir William Jones.

41. General Vallancey, so justly celebrated for his knowledge of the antiquities of his country, has expressed his perfect conviction that the Hindoos have been in Britain and in Ireland. See Major Ouzeley's *Oriental Collection*, Vol. II. Much attention is certainly due to such respectable authority.

42. Michael Symes, *An Account of an Embassy to the Kingdom of Ava, Sent by the Governor-General of India, in the Year 1795. By Michael Symes, Esq., Major in His Majesty's 76th Regiment* (London, 1800), pp. 300–302.

43. William Erskine, "Account of the Cave-Temple of Elephanta, with a Plan of the Drawings of the Principal Figures," *Transactions of the Literary Society of Bombay* 1 (1819): 201–2.

44. William Erskine, "Observations of the Remains of the Bouddhists in India," *Transactions of the Literary Society of Bombay* 3 (1823): 516.

45. Robert Tytler, *Inquiry into the Origin, and Principles of Budaic Sabism* (1817); cited in Philip C. Almond, *The British Discovery of Buddhism* (Cambridge: Cambridge University Press, 1988), p. 31. The page number of the original citation is not provided by Almond, but the passage is also quoted in the fascinating review article, "Indian Buddhism, Its Origin and Diffusion," *Calcutta Review* 4 (July–December 1845): 250.

46. Michel Jean François Ozeray, *Recherches sur Budduo ou Bouddou* (Paris, 1817), p. 111.

47. Charles Friedrich Neumann, *The Catechism of the Shamans; or, The Laws and Regulations of the Priesthood of Buddha, in China* (London: Oriental Translation Fund, 1831), pp. xxiii–xxiv and xxv.

48. Charles Coleman, *The Mythology of the Hindus, with Notices of Various Mountain and Island Tribes, Inhabiting the Two Peninsulas of India and the Neighbouring Islands; and an Appendix, Comprising the Minor Avatars, and the Mythological and Religious Terms, &c. &c. of the Hindus* (London: 1832), p. 184. In the *Ceylon Alamanac* of 1835, we find similar sentiments expressed by Major Jonathan Forbes of the Seventy-Eighth Highlanders, who wrote, "Two great contending parties, the Buddhist and Brahmin, professing irreconcileable principles, appear from the earliest ages to have influenced eastern society. The Buddhists, whose system is essentially contemplative, humane, peaceful, and regulated by plain moral laws, have nevertheless unsuccessfully opposed the arbitrary classification and trammels of caste, bloody sacrifices, and the monopoly of superior rank and special sanctity, claimed by the Brahmins." See J. Forbes, "The Dangistra Dalada, or the Right Canine Tooth of Gautama Buddha," *Ceylon Almanac, and Compendium of Useful Information for the Year 1835* (Colombo, Sri Lanka: n.p.), p. 230.

49. John Crawfurd, *History of the Indian Archipelago: Containing an Account of the Manners, Arts, Languages, Religions, Institutions, and Commerce of Its Inhabitants*, vol. 2 (Edinburgh, 1820), p. 222.

50. Edward Upham, M.R.A.S. & F.S.A., ed., *The Mahávansi, the Rájá-Ratnácari, and the Rájá-Vali, Forming the Sacred and Historical Books of Ceylon: Also, a Collection of Tracts Illustrative of the Doctrines and Literature of Buddhism; Translated from the Singhalese* (London, 1833), 1:xviii–xix. The translations contained in these three volumes were almost immediately condemned by the leading Pāli scholar of the

day, George Turnour, as "one of the most extraordinary delusions, perhaps, ever practised on the literary world." See his *The First Twenty Chapters of the Mahawanso and a Preparatory Essay on Pali Buddhistical Literature* (Ceylon: Cotta Church Mission Press, 1836), pp. v–vi. Turnour's careful evisceration of this translation continues to p. xxi.

CHAPTER 4

1. Eugène Burnouf to Brian Hodgson, July 7, 1834; in *Papiers d'Eugène Burnouf conservés à la Bibliothèque Nationale*, ed. Léon Feer (Paris: H. Champion, 1899), p. 149. For the French text of this passage from Burnouf's letter, see also Akira Yuyama, *Eugène Burnouf: The Background of His Research into the Lotus Sutra* (Tokyo: International Research Institute for Advanced Buddhology, Soka University, 2000), pp. 59–60.

2. Brian H. Hodgson, "Sketch of Buddhism, Derived from Bauddha Scriptures of Nipál," *Transactions of the Royal Asiatic Society of Great Britain and Ireland*, 2 (1830): 222–23. For a more detailed examination of Hodgson's contributions to Buddhist Studies, see, as the title suggests, Donald S. Lopez Jr., "The Ambivalent Exegete: Hodgson's Contributions to Buddhist Studies," in *The Origins of Himalayan Studies: Brian Houghton Hodgson in Kathmandu and Darjeeling, 1820 to 1858*, ed. David Waterhouse (London: Routledge Curzon, 2004), pp. 49–76.

3. On the life of Klaproth, see Harmut Walravens, "Julius Klaproth: His Life and Works with Special Emphasis on Japan," *Japonica Humboldtiana* 10 (2006): 178–91.

4. The same biography had appeared in German in 1823 in Klaproth's *Asia Polyglotta*. The piece, entitled "Leben des Budd'a, nach Mongolischen Nachrichten," appears after page 384, but the pages are numbered 122–44. The French version is an abridged version of the German.

5. Julius Klaproth, "Vie de Bouddha d'après les livres Mongols (I)," *Journal Asiatique* 4 (1824): 9–10.

6. Quoted in József Terjék, "Alexander Csoma de Kőrös: A Short Biography," in Alexander Csoma de Kőrös, *Tibetan-English Dictionary: Collected Works of Alexander Csoma de Kőrös*, vol. 1 (Budapest: Akadémiai Kiadó, 1984), xxix.

7. Alexander Csoma de Kőrös, "Notices on the Life of Shakya, Extracted from the Tibetan Authorities," *Asiatic Researches* 20, part 2 (1839): 294.

8. Ibid., p. 295.

9. Ibid., p. 296.

10. George Turnour, "An Examination of the Pali Buddhistical Annals, No. 2," *Journal of the Asiatic Society of Bengal* 6 (September 1837): 717.

11. Turnour divided his study into four parts, but it occurred in six separate sections of the journal: July 1837 (pp. 501–28), September 1837 (pp. 713–37), August

1838 (686–701), September 1838 (pp. 789–817), November 1838 (pp. 919–33), and December 1838 (pp. 991–1014).

12. George Turnour, "An Examination of the Pali Buddhistical Annals, No. 3," *Journal of the Asiatic Society of Bengal* 8 (August 1838): 686. It is important to note that throughout his work, Turnour displays great respect for the learned Sinhalese monks with whom he worked closely in making his translations, absolving them of any charge of deception. He also notes, "Their attention, therefore, is principally devoted to the examination of the doctrinal and religious questions contained in their sacred books; and that study is moreover conducted in a spirit of implicit faith and religious reverence, which effectually excludes searching scrutiny, and is almost equally unfavorable to impartial criticism." See George Turnour, "An Examination of the Pali Buddhistical Annals, No. 4," *Journal of the Asiatic Society of Bengal* 8 (November 1838): 920.

13. Turnour, "An Examination of the Pali Buddhistical Annals, No. 4," pp. 991–92.

14. Max Müller, *Chips from a German Workshop*, vol. 1, *Essays on the Science of Religion* (reprint, Chico, CA: Scholars Press, 1985), pp. 190–91.

15. Cited in Rosane Rocher, *Alexander Hamilton (1762–1824): A Chapter in the Early History of Sanskrit Philology* (New Haven, CT: American Oriental Society, 1968), p. 7. The other information about Hamilton provided here is drawn from this biography.

16. On Volney, see Urs App, *The Birth of Orientalism* (Philadelphia: University of Pennsylvania Press, 2010), pp. 440ff.

17. Cited in Raymond Schwab, *The Oriental Renaissance: Europe's Rediscovery of India and the East, 1680–1880*, trans. Gene Patterson-Black and Victor Reinking (New York: Columbia University Press, 1984), p. 13.

18. The full title of the work is *Essai sur le pali, ou langue sacrée de la presqu'île au-delà du Gange: Avec six planches lithographiées, et la notice des manuscrits palis de la bibliothèque du Roi* (*Essay on Pāli, or the Sacred Language of the Peninsula beyond the Ganges, with Six Plates and a Note on the Pāli Manuscripts in the Bibliothèque du Roi*).

19. Eugène Burnouf, "De la langue et de la littérature sanscrite: Discours d'Ouverture, prononcé au Collège de France," *Revue des deux mondes*, 2nd ser., 1 (February 1833): 273.

20. Ibid., 275.

21. Friedrich Max Müller, *The Life and Letters of the Right Honourable Friedrich Max Müller, Edited by His Wife* (London: Longmans, Green, and Co., 1902), 1:34.

22. Quoted in Feer, *Papiers d'Eugène Burnouf*, p. 149.

23. Ibid., pp. 157–58.

24. Ibid., pp. 158–59.

25. Ibid., p. 174.

26. My discussion here draws from the fuller description of Burnouf's *Introduction* in my translation of his text. See Eugène Burnouf, *Introduction to the History of Indian Buddhism*, trans. Katia Buffetrille and Donald S. Lopez Jr. (Chicago: University of Chicago Press, 2009), pp. 1–27.

27. For a detailed description of Burnouf's papers, see Feer, *Papiers d'Eugène Burnouf*.

28. Burnouf, *Introduction to the History of Indian Buddhism*, p. 63.

29. As Eduard Röer noted in his 1845 review, "It is certainly not an easy task to go through eighty large manuscript works, written in a barbarous language, made often unintelligible by the ignorance of the copyist, to analyse the contents of all, to bring them in their true chronological order, to compare them with the documents of other nations, written in a different language, and lastly use them as sources for the history, religion, and philosophy of the Buddhists." Eduard Röer, "Review of *Introduction à l'histoire du Buddhisme indien*," *Journal of the Asiatic Society of Bengal* 14, no. 2 (1845): 784–85.

30. Eugène Burnouf to Max Müller, October 7, 1848; in Müller, *The Life and Letters of the Right Honourable Friedrich Max Müller*, p. 81.

31. Burnouf, *Introduction to the History of Indian Buddhism*, pp. 112–13.

32. See George Elison, *Deus Destroyed: The Image of Christianity in Early Modern Japan* (Cambridge, MA: Harvard University Press, 1973), p. 339.

33. Burnouf, *Introduction to the History of Indian Buddhism*, p. 533.

34. Ibid., p. 64.

35. Ibid., pp. 142–43.

36. Ibid., p. 159.

37. Ibid., p. 160.

38. Ibid., pp. 228–29.

39. Ibid., p. 228.

40. Ibid., p. 483.

41. Burnouf, "De la langue et de la littérature sanscrite," 271.

42. Burnouf, *Introduction to the History of Indian Buddhism*, p. 524.

43. Röer, Review of *Introduction à l'histoire du Buddhisme indien*, 783.

44. Burnouf, *Introduction to the History of Indian Buddhism*, p. 328.

45. Ibid., p. 285, note 90.

46. Ibid., pp. 180–81.

47. Ibid., p. 86.

48. Ibid., p. 165.

49. Ibid., p. 214.

50. Ibid., p. 329.

51. Ibid., p. 337.

52. Feer, *Papiers d'Eugène Burnouf*, pp. 155–56.

53. In 1844, Thoreau published "The Preaching of the Buddha" in Emerson's

Transcendentalist journal *The Dial*. It included a translation from the French by Elizabeth Palmer Peabody of the fifth chapter ("Herb") of the *Lotus Sutra*, drawn from two articles published by Burnouf in the *Revue Indépendante* in April and May 1843. The translation itself is often mistakenly attributed to Thoreau. See Roger C. Mueller, "A Significant Buddhist Translation by Thoreau," *Thoreau Society Bulletin* (Winter 1977): 1–2.

54. Richard Wagner, quoted in Schwab, *The Oriental Renaissance*, p. 439. For a study of his interest in Buddhism, see Urs App, *Richard Wagner and Buddhism* (Rorschach, Switzerland: University Media, 2011).

CONCLUSION

1. Alfred Foucher, *La vieille route de l'Inde de Bactres à Taxila* (Paris: Les Éditions d'art et d'histoire, 1942–47), 2:320.

2. On the controversy surrounding Wilson's election to the Boden Professorship, see Thomas R. Trautmann, *The Clash of Chronologies: Ancient India in the Modern World* (New Delhi: Yoda Press, 2009), pp. 201–5.

3. Professor [H. H.] Wilson, "On Buddha and Buddhism," *Journal of the Royal Asiatic Society* 16 (1856): 229.

4. Ibid.

5. Ibid., p. 232.

6. See John Crawfurd, *Journal of an Embassy from the Governor-General of India to the Courts of Siam and Cochin China; Exhibiting a View of the Actual State of Those Kingdoms*, vol. 2 (London: Henry Colburn and Richard Bentley, 1830), pp. 80–85.

7. Francis Xavier, *The Letters and Instructions of Francis Xavier*, trans. and introduced by M. Joseph Costelloe, SJ (St. Louis: Institute of Jesuit Sources, 1992), p. 337.

8. Simon de la Loubère, *A New Historical Relation of the Kingdom of Siam* (London, 1693; reprint, Oxford: Oxford University Press, 1986), p. 138; citation is to the reprint edition.

9. Paulinus Bartholomaeo, *Viaggio alle Indie orientali*, published in English as *A Voyage to the East Indies, Containing an Account of the Manners, Customs, &C. of the Natives, with a Geographical Description of the Country. Collected from Observations Made during a Residence of Thirteen Years, between 1776 and 1789, in Districts Little Frequented by the Europeans* (London: J. Davis, 1800), p. 332. Elsewhere, he writes:

However, that first and original Budha is nothing other than a spirit and the planet Mercurius, apparently the residue of a cult of the ancient celestial army, viz. the sun, moon, and planets, which once existed among all peoples. In fact, it is not possible that one and the same Budha alone taught so many great peoples and refined the Chinese, Indians, the kingdom of Pegu, Tibet, Egypt and finally the entire North in cult, religion, sciences, and law. Thus, he can only be an allegorical and astronomical numen, somehow the fictitious and common tree of basic human institutions.

See his *Systema Brahmanicum liturgicum mythologicum civile ex monumentis indicis Musei Borgiani Velitris dissertationibus historico-criticis* (Rome: Fulgoni, 1791), p. 161. I am grateful to Isrun Engelhardt for locating this passage and translating it from the Latin.

10. Wilson, "On Buddha and Buddhism," 232.

11. Ibid., p. 235.

12. Ibid., p. 247.

13. Ibid., p. 248.

14. Eugène Burnouf, *Introduction to the History of Indian Buddhism*, trans. Katia Buffetrille and Donald S. Lopez Jr. (Chicago: University of Chicago Press, 2009), p. 79.

15. Ibid., p. 533.

16. Wilson, "On Buddha and Buddhism," 265.

17. In 1882 and 1884, the Dutch scholar Hendrik Kern (1883–1917) published his two-volume *Geschiedenis van het Buddhisme in Indië* (*History of Buddhism in India*), in which he also put forward the view that the Buddha was a solar god, with the twelve links of the dependent origination representing the twelve months, the six heretical teachers representing the six planets, and so on.

18. Burnouf, *Introduction to the History of Indian Buddhism*, p. 78.

19. Hermann Oldenberg, *Buddha: His Life, His Doctrine, His Order*, trans. William Hoey (London: Williams and Norgate, 1882), pp. 1–2.

20. Ibid., pp. 74–75.

21. One might mention in this regard such works as Bhikkhu Ñāṇamoli, *The Life of the Buddha According to the Pali Canon* (1972); Hajime Nakamura, *Gotama Buddha* (1977); Narada Maha Thera, *The Buddha and His Teachings* (1980); Michael Carrithers, *The Buddha* (1983); David J. Kalupahana, *The Way of Siddhartha: A Life of the Buddha* (1987); Thich Nhat Hanh, *Old Path, White Clouds: Walking in the Footsteps of the Buddha* (1990); and Stephen Batchelor, *Confession of a Buddhist Atheist* (2010).

22. See Donald S. Lopez Jr., *Buddhism and Science: A Guide for the Perplexed* (Chicago: University of Chicago Press, 2008). This paragraph is drawn from pp. 7–8.

23. We can note that despite the efforts of various scholars, the Buddha seems to have remained an idol in the popular imagination of empire. In Rudyard Kipling's famous poem "Mandalay" from 1892, a British soldier describes a Burmese woman:

> 'Er petticoat was yaller an' 'er little cap was green,
> An' 'er name was Supi-yaw-lat—jes' the same as Theebaw's Queen,
> An' I seed her first a-smokin' of a whackin' white cheroot,
> An' a-wastin' Christian kisses on an 'eathen idol's foot:

Bloomin' idol made o'mud—
Wot they called the Great Gawd Budd—
Plucky lot she cared for idols when I kissed 'er where she stud!

CODA

1. However, see the report of John Marignolli, who spent 1342–46 as papal legate at the court of Beijing. He describes "the Mountain Seyllan":

That exceeding high mountain hath a pinnacle of surpassing height, which, on account of the clouds, can rarely be seen. But god, pitying our tears, lighted it up one morning just before the sun rose, so that we beheld it glowing with the brightest flame. In the way down from this same mountain there is a fine level spot, still at a great height, and there you find in order, first the mark of Adam's foot; secondly, a certain statue of a sitting figure with the left hand resting on the knee, and the right hand raised and extended towards the west; lastly, there is the house (of Adam) which he made with his own hands. It is of an oblong quadrangular shape like a sepulchre, with a door in the middle, and is formed of great tabular slabs of marble, not cemented, but merely laid one upon another.

It is said by the natives, especially their monks who stay at the foot of the mountain, men of very holy life though without the faith, that the deluge never mounted to that point, and thus the house has never been disturbed.

In Colonel Sir Henry Yule, trans. and ed., *Cathay and the Way Thither: Being a Collection of Medieval Notices of China* (London: Hakluyt Society, 1914), 3:232–33.

2. In a Portuguese account from 1666, we read:

25. In the Country of *Dinavaca* which is the Center of this Island rises that vast high Mountain called *Pico de Adam*, because some believed our first Father lived there, and that the print of a foot still seen upon a stone on the top of it, is his; the Natives call it *Amala Saripadi*, that is the Mountain of the footstep. Some Springs running down it, at the bottom form a Rivulet, where Pilgrims wash, and believe it purifies them. The stone on the top is like a Tombstone, the print of the foot seems not artificial, but as if it had been made in the same nature as when one treads in Clay, which makes it be looked upon as miraculous.

26. The Pilgrims of all sorts who come from as far as *Persia* and *China*, being washed, go up to the top, near which hangs a bell which they strike and take the sounding of it as a sign of their being purified, as if any bell being struck, would not sound. The opinion of the Natives is, that *Drama Raja* Son of an ancient King of that Island, doing Pennance in that Mountain with many Disciples, when he was about to depart at their instance, left that print there as a Memorial; therefore they respect it as a relict of a Saint, and generally call him *Budam*, that is *Wiseman*.

27. Some believe this Saint was *Iosaphat*, but it is more likely it was St. *Thomas*, who has left many Memorials in the East, and in the West, in *Brasil* and in *Paraguay*.

In Manuel de Faria e Sousa (or Manoel Faria y Souza), *The Portugues Asia; or, The History of the Discovery and Conquest of India by the Portugues Containing All Their Discoveries from the Coast of Africk, to the Farthest Parts of China and Japan, All Their Battels by Sea and Land, Sieges and Other Memorable Actions, A Description of Those Countries, and Many Particulars of the Religion, Government and Customs of the Natives*, trans. Captain John Stevens, vol. 2 (London, 1695), pp. 509–10.

3. Italo Calvino, *Invisible Cities* (Orlando, FL: Harcourt Books, 1974), p. 8.

APPENDIX 2

1. See John Lough, *Essays on the Encyclopédie of Diderot and D'Alembert* (Oxford: Oxford University Press, 1968), p. 180.

2. These include "Asiatiques, philosophie des asiatiques en general," "Indiens, philosophie des," and "Japonois, philosophie des." (The first two, although unsigned, can be attributed with certainty to Diderot; the last is signed by him.) For a discussion of Diderot's views on Buddhism, see Urs App, *The Birth of Orientalism* (Philadelphia: University of Pennsylvania Press, 2010), pp. 133–87.

3. This practice of drowning oneself in order to be reborn in the pure land of Amitābha—called *Fudaraku tokai*, or "crossing the sea to Potalaka," the abode of the bodhisattva Avalokiteśvara or Kannon—is well documented in Japanese literature and was described by Jesuit missionaries to Japan in the mid-sixteenth century. It is depicted both in Japanese scrolls and in European engravings, including those by Bernard Picart in *Cérémonies et coutumes religieuses de tous les peuples du monde* (*The Ceremonies and Religious Customs of the Various Nations of the Known World*). For a study of the practice, see D. Max Moerman, "Passage to Fudaraku: Suicide and Salvation in Premodern Japanese Buddhism," *The Buddhist Dead: Practices, Discourses, Representations*, ed. Bryan J. Cuevas and Jacqueline I. Stone (Honolulu: University of Hawai'i Press, 2007), pp. 266–96. One of the earliest accounts of the practice in English appeared in 1613:

They beleeve divers Paradises, into each of which their peculiar Gods carrie their owne worshippers: And some make over-hastie journeyes thither on this sort. He watcheth certained daies, and then out of a Pulpit preacheth of the contempt of the world. Otheres betake them to bee his companions, while some give their almes. On the last day hee maketh an Oration to his fellows, who all drinking Wine goe into their Ship, carrying a sithe to cut up all the brambles in their way; and putting on their clothes, stuffe their sleeves with stones, and hanging a great stone about their neckes to helpe them the sooner to their Paradise, hurle themselves into the Sea. And great honour is done to them being thus dead. I saw one (saith *Vilela* [Gaspar Vilela]) that had seven of these companions, which with their great alacratie, and my great amazement, did this. But they which worship *Amida*, observe another rite. Being weary of living, they put themselves in a strait hole of the earth receiving breath only by a Reede, and so continue fasting and praying till death. Some of them in honour of a certaine Idoll doe cast themselves downe from a high Tower, where this Idoll is placed, and after their death are reputed Saints.

In Samuel Purchas (1577?-1626), *Purchas his Pilgrimage. Or Relations of the World and the Religions Observed in All Ages and places discovered, from the Creation unto this Present* (London: William Stansby, 1613), p. 442.

4. This is apparently a confused reference to the Hindu practice, described with horror in European accounts, of devotees throwing themselves under the chariot carrying the image of Jagannātha, a form of the god Vishnu, from which the English word *juggernaut* is derived.

INDEX